TUT...
M... ...S
of
KOREA, CHINA & JAPAN

compiled by
Sun-Jin Kim, Daniel Kogan,
Nikolaos Kontogiannis, and Hali Wong

CHARLES E. TUTTLE COMPANY
Rutland, Vermont & Tokyo, Japan

To Lee Yong-Bok,
whose research for
the Korea Traditional Tae Kyon Research Association
has paved the way for me and so many others.
—SUN-JIN KIM

To my *sensei,* Onaga (Ryoko) Yoshimitsu
Shihan and President of the Zen Okinawa Karate-do Renmei,
who has shown me the way.
—DANIEL E. KOGAN

In memory of Gwaan Fei Gong *Sifu*
my teacher and mentor
who taught me the skills and traditions of Huhng Ga.
—NIKOLAOS KONTOGIANNIS

To my *si gung,* Wong Ha
—HALI WONG

Published by the Charles E. Tuttle Company, Inc. of Rutland, Vermont &
Tokyo, Japan, with editorial offices at 2-6 Suido 1-chome, Bunkyo-ku,
Tokyo 112. © 1995 Charles E. Tuttle Publishing Company. All rights
reserved. LCC Card No. 94-61453, ISBN 0-8048-2016-3
First edition, 1996   Printed in Singapore

TABLE OF CONTENTS

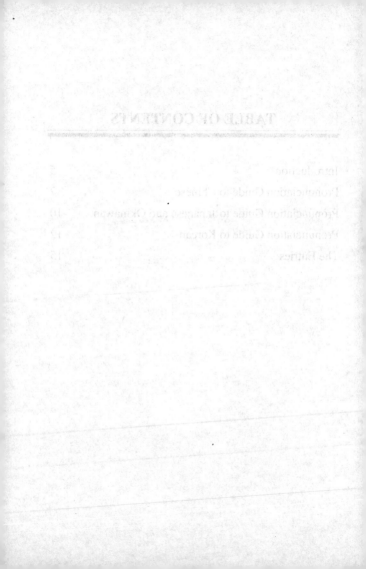

INTRODUCTION

This book was inspired by the genuine desire of its compilers to someday learn the true essence of the traditions of the Asian martial arts. As the martial arts are an expression of Asian values and a cultural heirloom that for most of its history, with the exception of a few notable classic works, has been transmitted as an oral tradition from master to student, today most serious students of the martial arts find it necessary at some point to learn, to some degree, the native language of their respective arts.

To this end, we have compiled this work, a list of relevant names of masters, styles, locations, schools, basic vocabulary of the major religions and philosophies, technical martial arts jargon, as well as common everyday vocabulary that one might encounter while learning, researching, or teaching the martial arts.

Having expressed our intent, we humbly submit this work as a first step in what is a never-ending endeavor. Due to the secret nature of many martial arts, the vast geographic areas they have touched, the countless dialects, and centuries of human history they have spanned, it would be unrealistic to believe that we have by any means compiled an exhaustive list. Although great pains were taken to ensure the accuracy of all materials in this book, some readers with firsthand experience in some of the more obscure arts might find faults or omissions in this work. For that we offer our sincerest apologies and ask for the reader's understanding. Although perfection was our aim, we quickly learned that like the martial arts themselves, our final objective is not a stationary point but rather a moving target. The more the details were checked and verified, the more unrealistic it became to include every relevant entry. Considering the volume of information used and cross-referenced when compiling this work we are confident in its ability to stand on its own merits.

This work concentrates on the major languages of the most commonly practiced martial arts (Cantonese, Japanese, Korean, Mandarin, and Okinawan). This is by no means to say that other dialects or national languages have not added relevant vocabulary, but simply that in the interest of brevity and accuracy, we chose to concentrate on those languages that were the basis of our own studies of the martial arts.

We would like to thank Antonio Flores, Alexander Kask, Scott Shaw, and Meik Skoss for their assistance with the proofing and editing of this text. We would also like to acknowledge the following people without whom this book could not have been completed: Naz Bhayani, Carmen Choy, Rick Dove, Martin Drastil, Robert Gough, Robert Kacpura, Vicki Koh, Rodney Lee, Vincent Liew, Ali Novin, Catherine Walters, and Annette Yang.

Pronunciation Guide to Chinese

In this dictionary, we will be presenting entries from China's two major dialects, Mandarin and Cantonese. In both cases we have tried to make the entries as easy to pronounce as possible while still attempting to use standardized systems of romanization. The fact that Chinese is a tonal monosyllabic language with many sounds that are not used in English presents challenges to attempts at writing it using the roman alphabet. Though there are several different systems available, each of which has its own distinct merits, we have chosen to use the pinyin system for Mandarin entries as it is the standard in the People's Republic of China and the Yale system for Cantonese entries as it is the one most commonly used for that dialect. As the existing literature on the Chinese martial arts is filled with spellings from many of the other systems, we have included them and cross-referenced them to the standardized spellings.

For simplicity and brevity, we have not marked the accents for specific tones. Though Chinese can have anywhere between four (in the case of Mandarin) and nine (in Cantonese) tones, which are ways of inflecting a particular syllable, omitting the markings for them will not impair your ability to look up such a word in this book. The equivalent sounds in English for Mandarin consonants are as follows:

b as in boy
c like the "s" in its
ch as in chew
d as in do
f as in food
g as in go
h as in how
j as in jump
k as in kick
l as in lunch

m as in mother
n as in no
p as in put
q like the "ch" in chew
r as in room
s as in so
sh as in show
t as in to
w as in work
x like the "sh" in shy

yh like the "y" in you

z is a sound between the "d" in do and the "z" in zoo

zh like the "j" in jump

Mandarin vowel-sound equivalents are as follows:

a as in armor

ai like the "i" in size

an like on

ang like the "ong" in song

ao like the "ow" in how

e like the "ea" in treasure

ei like the "ay" in hay

en like the "un" in run

eng like "ung" in hunger

er as in mother

i like the "ea" in eat

ia is a sound between the "ea" in eat and the "a" in armor

ian is a sound between the "ea" in eat and the "e" in pen

iang is a sound between the "ea" in eat and the "ong" in song

iao is between "ea" in eat and the "o" in how

ie like the "ea" in treasure

in like the "ee" in keen

ing as in ring

iong is a sound between the "ea" in eat and the "ow" in how and "n" and "g"

iu is a sound between the "ea" in eat and "you"

o as in office

ong is a combination the "ow" in how and "ng"

u like the "oo" in fool

ua is a sound between the "oo" in fool and "a"

uai is a sound between the "oo" in fool and the "i" in size

uan is a combination of you and "en" in end

uang is a sound between the "oo" in fool and the "ong" in song

ue is a sound between the "oo" in fool and the "ea" in each

ui is a sound between the "oo" in fool and the "ay" in say

un is a sound between the "oo" in fool and the "oon" in soon

uo is a sound between the "oo" in fool and the "o" in office

Cantonese consonants are as follows:

b as in boy
ch as in chew
d as in do
f as in food
g as in go
h as in how
j as in jump
k as in kick
l as in lunch
m as in moon

n as in no
p as in put
s as in so
t as in to
w as in why
y as in you
gw like the "gu" in guava
kw like the "qu" in quick
ng as in ring

Cantonese vowel-sound equivalents are as follows:

a as in armor
ai like eye
ak like the "ock" in sock
am like the "om" in mom
an like "on" in onward
ang like the "ong" in song
ap like the "op" opponent
at like the "ot" in dot
au like the "ow" in now
e like the "ea" in treasure
ei like the "ay" in say
ek like the "eck" in check
eng as in Bengal
eu like the "ork" in cork
eui between the "o" in cork
    and "ee" in seen
euk like the "o" in cork
eun like the "o" in cork with
    an "n" sound

eung like the "o" in cork
    with an "ng" sound
eut like the "o" in cork with
    a "t" sound
i like the "ee" in seen
ik like the "ick" in sick
im like the "eem" in seem
in like the "een" in been
ing like the "ing" in sing
ip like the "eep" in keep
it like the "eat" in meat
iu like the "ew" in pew
o like the "aw" in brawl
oi like the "oy" in toy
ok like the "ock" in mock
on like the "awn" in pawn
ong as in song
ot like the "ought" in bought
ou like the "o" in two

u like the "oo" in too

ui like the "ooey" in gooey

uk like the "uke" in fluke

un like the "oon" in baboon

ung like the "oon" in Loon
with a "g" sound

ut like the "oot" in soot

yu as in you

yun like the "oon" in Loon
with an "y" sound

yut like you with an "it"
sound

In Cantonese, some vowels can be pronounced in a more drawn-out way. In the next section we will show how these sounds are pronounced.

aai like eye

aak like the "ock" in sock

aam like the "om" in mom

aan like the "on" in onward

aang like the "ong" in song

aap like the "op" in opponent

at like the "ot" in dot

au like the "ow" in now

Pronunciation Guide to Japanese and Okinawan

Japanese syllables are from the point of view of a native English speaker easier to pronounce (excluding perhaps the consonant "r" that is rolled) than many other Asian languages, but efforts to write them using roman letters are somewhat hampered by the large number of homonyms that appear. Though these words appear identical when written in roman letters, their meanings, which are often very different, are readily apparent when using Chinese characters. Nonetheless using roman letters one can easily approximate the Japanese pronunciation of any word.

The following table explains how to pronounce the letters used for the Japanese and Okinawan entries in this book.

a as in the "a" in father

e as in echo

i as in it

o as in open

u as in the "ew" in dew

ba as in ball

be like bay
bi like bee
bo as in boat
bu as in Buddhist
bya is a sound between *bi* and *a*
byo is a sound between *bi* and *o*
byu as in the "bu" in bureau
cha as in cha-cha
che as in check
chi as in the "chee" in cheek
cho as in choke
chu as in choose
da as in dock
de like desk
do as in dough
fu as in food
ga as in gasoline
ge like gay
gi as in geek
go as in going
gu like goo
gya is a sound between *gi* and *a*
gyo is a sound between *gi* and *o*
gyu as in the "gu" in argument
ha like haw
he like hay
hi like he
ho like hoe
hya is a sound between *hi* and *a*
hyo is a sound between *hi* and *o*

hyu is a sound between *hi* and *u*
ja as in Japan
je as in the "ge" in gentlemen
ji as in the "gy" gymnasium
jo like Joe
ju as in June
ka like caw
ke like Kay
ki like key
ko as in the "co" in loco
ku like coo
kya is a sound between *ki* and *a*
kyo is a sound between *ki* and *o*
kyu like cue
m as in mother
ma as in mama
me like May
mi as in the "mea" in meat
mo like Moe
mu like moo
mya is a sound between *mi* and *a*
myo is a sound between *mi* and *o*
myu as in the "mu" in music
n as in never
na as in natural
ne like nay
ni like knee
no as in nose
nu as in noon

nya as in "nia" in ammonia

nyo is a sound between *ni* and *o*

nyu as in news

pa as in Papa

pe like pay

pi as in pee-wee

po like Poe

pu like Pooh

pya is a sound between *pi* and *a*

pyo is a sound between *pi* and *o*

pyu as in pew

ra as in rattle

re as in ray

ri as in read

ro as in row

ru as in root

rya is a sound between *ri* and *a*

ryo is a sound between *ri* and *o*

ryu is a sound between *ri* and *u*

sa as in sock

se like say

so as in soak

su as in soon

shi as in sheep

sho as in show

shu as in shoot

ta as in the "to" in toffee

te as in take

to like toe

tsu is the "ts" sound in pants combined with a "u"

wa as in war

wu like woo

ya as in Yankee

yo as in yolk

yu like you

za as in zap

ze as in zany

zo as in zone

zu like zoo

Pronunciation Guide to Korean

Two major transliteration systems are used in Korea: the Ministry of Education system and the McCune-Reischauer system. Because of its frequent use of apostrophes to indicate aspirated consonants and accent marks to change vowel sounds, the McCune-Reischauer system has been avoided here. Instead, we have used the Ministry of Education system, which represents the various sounds of the Korean language as follows:

a as in the "a" in father

ae as in the "a" in fat

b as in boy

ch as in child

d as in door

e as in the "e" in pet

eo as in the "u" in but

eu as in the "oo" in foot

g as in golf

h as in hello

i as in the "ee" in feet

j as in jar

k as in key

l as in light

m as in moon

n as in not

o as in the "o" in go

oi as in the "way" in way

p as in pen

r as in the "r" in red when used to start a word, but rolled as a Spanish "r" when preceded by a vowel within a word

s as in say

t as in toy

u as in the "oo" in soon

w as in was

y as in yellow

You will no doubt notice double consonants such as "bb" in some Korean words. Such pairs receive more aspiration than the corresponding single consonants. For example, *b* sounds like the ordinary "b" in boy, and *p* sounds like the "p" in pen, but "bb" falls in between—much like the *p* in the normal pronunciation of the word "open." Even if you have trouble differentiating single and double consonants, keep in mind that most Koreans will be able to understand you no matter how imprecisely you enunciate. The language's absence of tones—such as those in Chinese—further facilitates pronunciation and understanding.

Please note that the "si" combination is usually pronounced as "she"; therefore, "sip" (the number 10) sounds like "sheep" and not "sip" or "ship." When the letters "ssi" are used together, however, they are pronounced "see" with emphasis on the "s" sound. Thus, Ssi Rum is pronounced "see reum" and not "shee reum."

You will also notice that several letters and sounds—*f, v, th, z,* etc.—are conspicuously absent. This is because they do not exist in Korean.

Note on the labels used within each entry:

The first label indicates which language the term is from. Therefore all terms marked (C) are from Cantonese, (J) are Japanese, (K) are Korean, (M) are Mandarin, and (O) are from the Okinawan dialect. The second label is the category of the word. It indicates what general subject the word concerns, be it a specific style, a religion, a type or part of a weapon, etc. The "common usage" category is for words that are used in a wide variety of categories or are not specific to the martial arts.

Although most non-English terms have been italized when they appear in the text, when entries are cross-referenced, they have been written in roman letters.

TUTTLE DICTIONARY
of the
MARTIAL ARTS
of
KOREA, CHINA & JAPAN

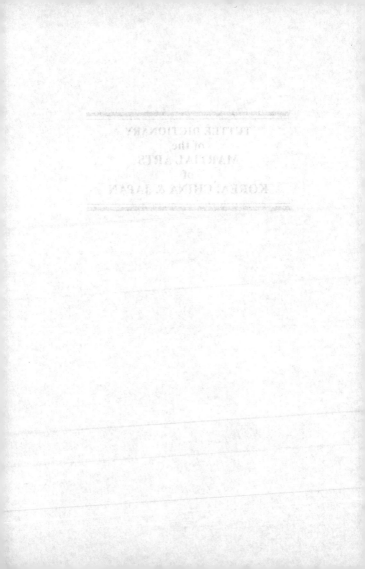

— **A** —

aah gwan (C) [Common Usage] second-place winner

abara (J) [Common Usage] ribs

Abe Gorodaiyu (J) [Master] a master of Taisha-ryu in the eighteenth century, said to have been the first to use the term kendo or *ken no michi*

Abe-ryu (J) [Style] a school of ken-jutsu founded by Abe Gorodaiyu

ae mok japchaegi (K) [Ssi Rum] neck-turning technique

agari zashiki (J) [Sumo] an elevated tatami area overlooking the practice ring in a sumo stable

ageru (J) [Common Usage] to raise

age tsuki (J) [Karate] rising punch

age uchi (J) [Karate] rising strike

age uke (J) [Karate] rising block, usually with the forearm

a geum son (K) [Taekwondo] arc hand

ago (J) [Common Usage] jaw

ago oshi (J) [Judo] jaw squeeze; a technique in the Kodokan Ju no Kata

ago uchi (J) [Karate] a strike to the jaw

ahop (K) [Common Usage] nine

ai (M) [Common Usage] **1** to be short in height **2** to be sad

ai chudan (J) [Kendo, Naginata] both practitioners are holding their weapons in *chudan no kamae*

ai gedan (J) [Kendo, Naginata] both practitioners are holding their weapons in *gedan no kamae*

ai hanmi (J) [Aikido] a stance where both exponents have the same foot forward

ai hanmi katatedori (J) [Aikido] a cross grip on the opponent's wrist when both exponents have the same foot forward; also known as *kosadori*

ai jodan (J) [Kendo, Naginata] both practitioners are holding their weapons in *jodan no kamae*

aiki (J) [Aikido] a state of harmonization of one's mind and body; the basic principle of aikido

aikido (J) [Style] (*lit.* The Way of Harmony) a modern interpretation of the classical art of aiki-jutsu, founded in the 1920s by Ueshiba Morihei

aikidoka (J) [Common Usage] a person who does aikido

Aikigata (O) [Karate] a *kata* practiced in Kojo-ryu

aiki inyo-ho (J) [Aikido] a doctrine of harmony based on the concepts of *yin-yang* and Taoist thought

Aiki Jinja (J) [Aikido] (*lit.* Aiki Shrine) a Shinto shrine in Ibaraki Prefecture, Japan, where the spirit of Ueshiba Morihei, the founder of aikido, is enshrined

aiki ju-jutsu (J) [Style] *see* aiki-jutsu

aiki-jutsu (J) [Style] a martial art based on the philosophy of *aiki,* traditionally passed down in the Takeda family

Aikikai (J) [Aikido] the aikido association currently headed by Ueshiba Kisshomaru, son of Ueshiba Morihei

aiki ken (J) [Aikido] sword techniques practiced and taught in aikido

aiki taiso (J) [Aikido] (*lit.* Exercises for Harmonizing the Spirit) warm-up exercises specific to aikido, concentrating on breathing, stretching, and relaxation

aikuchi (J) [Weapon] a dagger without a *tsuba*

Aioi-ryu (J) [Style] a name used by Ueshiba Morihei to refer to his art for a short time prior to World War II

aite (J) [Common Usage] opponent, training partner

aite no tsukuri (J) [Judo] to set up one's opponent for a predetermined move or position

ai uchi (J) [Competitive Budo] clash, simultaneous attack

Ajigawa (J) [Sumo] a sumo *beya* in Koto Ward, Tokyo

Ajikata no Mainote (O) [Karate] a *kata* practiced in Motobu-ryu

aka (J) [Common Usage] red

akagashi (J) [Common Usage] red oak; used for making wooden training weapons

aka hansoku (J) [Competitive Budo] "red" violation; the red fighter has committed a violation of the rules

aka ippon (J) [Competitive Budo] a full point *(ippon)* awarded to the "red" fighter

aka kiken (J) [Competitive Budo] "red" fighter has conceded the bout

aka no kachi (J) [Competitive Budo] the "red" fighter is the winner of the bout

akeni (J) [Sumo] a trunk made of lacquered bamboo used to hold the personal belongings of *rikishi* in one of the top two divisions

akiresu ken (J) [Common Usage] Achilles' tendon

Amaterasu O Mikami (J) [Shinto] the sun goddess

am hei (C) [Common Usage] secret or hidden weapon

amiuchi (J) [Sumo] *(lit.* Net-Casting Throw) a sumo technique in which the attacker wraps his arms around the inside of his opponent's arm in order to put pressure on his shoulders and throw him

an (M) [Taijiquan, Qin Na] **1** push down; a taijiquan hand technique using both arms to press down **2** to press in Qin Na

ana (J) [Common Usage] hole, opening

Anan (O) [Karate] a *kata* practiced in Ryuei-ryu and Okinawan Kempo

Ananko (O) [Karate] *see* Ananku

Ananku (O) [Karate] a *kata* in Shuri-te, practiced in Shobayashi-ryu, Kobayashi-ryu, Matsubayashi-ryu, Chubu Shorin-ryu, Ryukyu Shorin, Bugeikan, and Shorinji-ryu

Anazawa-ryu (J) [Style] a school of naginata-jutsu

an bal mok (K) [Common Usage] inner ankle

an chagi (K) [Common Usage] inward kick

an dari chagi (K) [Hapkido] inside-leg kick

an dari cha neoki (K) [Hapkido] inside-leg penetrating kick

an dari dollyeo chagi (K) [Kuk Sool] outside-to-inside crescent kick

an dari geolgi (K) [Ssi Rum] inside leg-hooking technique

aneseo (K) [Common Usage] from the inside

aneseo bakkeuro chagi (K) [Taekwondo] inside-outside crescent kick

aneseo bakkeuro makgi (K) [Taekwondo, Tang Soo Do] inside-outside block

aneuro (K) [Common Usage] inward, to the inside

aneuro bada neomgigi (K) [Common Usage] inside parry

aneuro chagi (K) [Taekwondo] inward kick

aneuro ddaerigi (K) [Taekwondo] inward strike

an gyeong sseui u gi (K) [Tae Kyon] eye strike using the fingertips

an heobeokji (K) [Common Usage] inner thigh

anjeon (K) [Common Usage] safety

anjeon ha da (K) [Common Usage] to be safe

an jireugi (K) [Taekwondo] inward strike

anjjang geori (K) [Tae Kyon] ankle-level inside hooking kick

an jjireugi (K) [Taekwondo] inward thrust, inward stab

an jjok bal (K) [Common Usage] inside edge of foot, arch of the foot

Ankoh Itosu (O) [Master] *see* Itosu Yasutsune

anma (J) [Acupressure] a type of massage incorporating pressure points, vibrations, and friction; *an mo* in Mandarin Chinese

an makgi (K) [Taekwondo] inside block

an mo (M) [Common Usage] massage

Ann Shenn Pao (M) [Xingyiquan] *see* An Shen Pao

an palja seogi (K) [Taekwondo] inward open posture

an palmok (K) [Common Usage] inner wrist

an palmok momtong bakkat makgi (K) [Taekwondo] inner-wrist middle outward block

an palmok yeop makgi (K) [Taekwondo] inner-wrist side block

an qi (M) [Common Usage] *see* am hei

an quan (M) [Gou Quan] pressing fist

An Shen Pao (M) [Xingyiquan] (*lit.* Securing the Body Strikes) a two-man form

an sonmok su (K) [Kuk Sool] inside wrist technique

ansudo (K) [Hapkido] ridgehand

antei (J) [Common Usage] balance, equilibrium, stability

an u geori (K) [Tae Kyon] upper-body grasping technique followed by a trapping of the leg

anza (J) [Common Usage] to sit cross-legged; usually used in a casual, informal setting

aoi (J) [Common Usage] blue

Aoyagi (O) [Karate] a *kata* in Shuri-te karate

ap (K) [Common Usage] front

apbal (K) [Common Usage] front foot

apbalggumchi (K) [Common Usage] front sole, ball of the foot

apcha busugi (K) [Taekwondo] front breaking kick

ap chagi (K) [Common Usage] front kick

apcha olligi (K) [Taekwondo] front rising kick

ap chigi (K) [Taekwondo] front strike

apchuk (K) [Common Usage] ball of foot, front sole

apchuk seonhoi ha da (K) [Common Usage] to pivot on the ball of the foot

ap dari (K) [Common Usage] front leg

ap dari chagi (K) [Ssi Rum] technique in which the opponent's front leg is kicked

ap dari deulgi (K) [Ssi Rum] front-leg lifting technique

ap ddaerigi (K) [Taekwondo] front strike

ap dollyeo chagi (K) [Taekwondo] front turning kick, roundhouse kick

apeuro (K) [Common Usage] forward, to the front

apeuro giul da (K) [Common Usage] to lean forward

apeuro ilbo (K) [Common Usage] one step forward

apeuro nureugi (K) [Ssi Rum] front-pressing technique

ap ggoa seogi (K) [Taekwondo] forward cross stance

apggumchi (K) [Common Usage] front sole, ball of the foot

apggumchi chagi (K) [Hapkido] kick with the ball of the foot

ap gubi seogi (K) [Taekwondo] extended forward stance, deep forward stance

ap juchum seogi (K) [Taekwondo] forward riding stance

ap makgi (K) [Taekwondo] front block

ap mireo chagi (K) [Common Usage] front thrust kick, front push kick

ap mureup chagi (K) [Common Usage] forward knee thrust

ap mureup chigi (K) [Ssi Rum] front-knee striking technique

ap mureup dwi jipgi (K) [Ssi Rum] front-knee flipping technique

ap mureup jipgi (K) [Ssi Rum] front-knee grasping technique

ap mureup jip go milgi (K) [Ssi Rum] front-knee grabbing and pushing technique

appalggumchi chigi (K) [Taekwondo] forward elbow strike

appalgup (K) [Taekwondo] forward elbow

ap seogi (K) [Taekwondo] forward stance, walking stance

arae (K) [Common Usage] down, downward

arae jireugi (K) [Taekwondo] downward punch

arae makgi (K) [Taekwondo] downward block

Arakaki Ankichi (O) [Master] a master of Shorin-ryu who studied under Kyan Chotoku

Araki (J) [Sumo] a sumo *beya* located in Kunitachi City in Tokyo

Araki-ryu (J) [Style] a *sogo bu-jutsu* (comprehensive school or style of martial arts) sometimes called Moro Budo Araki-ryu Kempo; it is noted for its unarmed *kogusoku* or ju-jutsu, bo-jutsu, chigiriki-jutsu, and kusarigama-jutsu

aramitama (J) [Shinto] a universal force that is responsible for the constructive energies in the cosmos

Aran (O) [Karate] a *kata* practiced in Chubu Shorin-ryu

arasoi (J) [Common Usage] a dispute, quarrel

ariake (J) [Kyudo] a technique used for seeing the target from the left side of the bow, allowing the archer to fully see and aim at the target before the arrow is released

arigato (J) [Common Usage] thank you

arukikata (J) [Common Usage] methods of walking

asageiko (J) [Common Usage] morning practice

Asahiyama (J) [Sumo] a sumo *beya* located in Edogawa Ward, Tokyo

Asayama Ichiden-ryu (J) [Style] a school of ken-jutsu, iai-jutsu, bo-jutsu, ju-jutsu, and taiho-jutsu

ase (J) [Common Usage] perspiration, sweat

ashi (J) [Common Usage] leg, foot

ashi ate (J) [Judo] kicking techniques

ashi barai (J) [Karate, Judo] leg sweep

ashibo kake uke (J) [Karate] leg-hooking block

ashi bumi (J) [Kyudo] A position in which the bow is held in the left hand and under the left forearm. The arrow is held in the right hand and under the right arm, with the legs shoulder-width apart.

ashi garami (J) [Judo, Suiei-jutsu] **1** a leg entanglement technique used in grappling **2** technique used in suiei-jutsu for fighting in water in which the opponent's legs are caught, forcing him down

ashigaru (J) [Common Usage] (*lit.* Light Foot) foot soldiers, the lowest-ranking warriors

ashi gatame jime (J) [Judo] a strangulation technique in which the legs are used

ashi guruma (J) [Judo] (*lit.* Leg Wheel) a leg throw in which the opponent is thrown over the attacker's leg, similar to *harai goshi*

ashi harai (J) [Common Usage] *see* ashi barai

ashiko (J) [Nin-jutsu] spiked bands worn on the feet, used for climbing as well as for fighting

ashikubi (J) [Common Usage] ankle

ashikubi kake uke (J) [Karate] ankle-hooking block

ashi no tachi kata (J) [Kendo, Naginata] stance, footwork, posture

ashi no ura (J) [Common Usage] sole of the foot

ashi sabaki (J) [Common Usage] footwork

ashitori (J) [Sumo] two-handed leg grab after which the opponent is pushed back and forced to the ground

ashi ura (J) [Common Usage] *see* ashi no ura

ashi waza (J) [Judo, Ju-jutsu] foot or leg techniques

ashi yubi (J) [Common Usage] toes

atama (J) [Common Usage] head

Atarashii Naginata (J) [Style] a modern competitive martial art using the *naginata;* utilizing the same type of protective armor and competitive rules as kendo, it has been popularized as a martial art for women in Japan

Atarito (J) [Iaido] the fourth *kata* in the Muso Shinden-ryu Omori-ryu Shoden series, which is done from *seiza*

atemi (J) [Common Usage] a strike to a weak or vital point on the body

atemi waza (J) [Common Usage] techniques used for striking an opponent's anatomically weak or vital points

ateru (J) [Common Usage] to hit, strike, touch

ato uchi (J) [Kendo] a valid delayed strike or jab, similar to a riposte in fencing

aun (J) [Common Usage] (*lit.* Om, Alpha, and Omega) the name for techniques in several classical weapons arts

awamori (O) [Common Usage] a potent type of Okinawan liquor made from millet or rice

awase (J) [Common Usage] the act of crossing weapons or coming to grips in a match

awase tsuki (J) [Karate] U-punch

ayumi ashi (J) [Common Usage] regular stepping, one foot after another, used to move over large distances

Azato Anko (O) [Master] an Okinawan master of Shuri-te and one of Funakoshi Gichin's teachers

Azumazeki (J) [Sumo] a sumo *beya* located in Sumida Ward, Tokyo

— B —

ba (M) [Common Usage] eight

Baahk Hok (C) [Style] *see* Bai He

Baahk Hok Seung Dihn Cheung Jiu Kyuhn (C) [Baahk Hok] a hand form

baahk mah hin taih (C) [Huhng Ga] (*lit.* White Horse Presents its Hoof) a transition from an upright posture to a kneeling horse stance with both fists at waist level

baahk mah tek (C) [Baahk Meih] (*lit.* White Horse Kicking) a low-line kick

Baahk Meih (C) [Style] (*lit.* White Eyebrow) A style named after its founder Baahk Meih, who was originally a student of the northern Shaolin Temple but later took refuge in the Wauh Meih mountains where he lived as a hermit and blended Daoist *gung fu* with his version of the teachings of the northern Shaolin Temple. This style incorporates the characteristics of the five animals (snake, crane, dragon, tiger, and leopard) and is designed to penetrate vulnerable pressure points.

Baahk Meih Pah (C) [Baahk Meih] White Eyebrow trident form

Baahk Mouh Kyuhn (C) [Choy Leih Faht] (*lit.* White Hair Fist) a form in the Hon Sihng style

Baahk Yuhn Cheut Duhng (C) [Chat Sing Tohng Lohng] (*lit.* White Ape Exits) a hand form

Baahk Yuhn Saam Cheut Duhng (C) [Pek Gwa Kyuhn] (*lit.* White Ape Three Comes Out of Cave) a hand form

baai (C) [Common Usage] to bow, to worship

baai gwaan gung (C) [Common Usage] to pay respects to the War God

baaih je (C) [Common Usage] the loser of a fight, match, or competition

baaih jeung (C) [Common Usage] to defeat, to conquer, or to be defeated, to be conquered

baai jou sin (C) [Common Usage] *see* bai shen

baai sahn (C) [Common Usage] to pray or pay respects to the gods

baai si (C) [Common Usage] a ceremony involving the pouring and offering of tea to a *sifu;* the traditional way of requesting to be a student and making a permanent, lifetime commitment to the teacher

baai sin (C) [Common Usage] paying respects to the ancestors by bowing

baat (C) [Common Usage] eight

Baat Bo Choi Kyuhn (C) [Ying Jaau] a hand form

Baat Cham Dou (C) [Wihng Cheun] (*lit.* Eight Cutting Broadsword) a 108-move weapon form

Baat Dyun Gam (C) [Hei Gung] *see* Ba Duan Jin

Baat Fong Gim (C) [Chat Sing Tohng Lohng] (*lit.* Eight Direction Sword) a weapons form using a straight sword

Baat Fu Daan Kyuhn (C) [Baat Muhn Kyuhn] (*lit.* Eight Tigers Single Fist) a hand form

Baat Gam Daan Kyuhn (C) [Baat Muhn Kyuhn] (*lit.* Eight Brocade Single Fist) a hand form

Baat Gihk Bin Wahn (C) [Baat Gihk Kyuhn] a hand form

Baat Gihk Gim (C) [Baat Gihk Kyuhn] a weapons form using the straight sword

Baat Gihk Kyuhn (C) [Style] *see* Bajiquan

Baat Gihk Luhk Dai Hoy (C) [Baat Gihk Kyuhn] a hand form

Baat Gong Kyuhn (C) [Baat Muhn Kyuhn] (*lit.* Eight Strong Fist) a hand form

baatgwa (C) [Common Usage] **1** (*lit.* Eight Trigrams) an octagonal symbol of the *Yi Jing (I Ching)* or *Book of Changes,* representing the different transitions of *yin* and *yang* **2** baguazhang

Baatgwa Daan Dou (C) [Choy Leih Faht] Bagua Single Broadsword

Baatgwa Jeung (C) [Style] *see* baguazhang

Baatgwa Sam Kyuhn (C) [Choy Leih Faht] (*lit.* Eight Trigram Heart Form) a hand form

baat gwa touh (C) [Common Usage] eight-sided mirror with *yin-yang* symbol; it is used for protection and situated in a way that will ward off evil

Baatgwa Wuh Dip Seung Dou (C) [Choy Leih Faht] (*lit.* Eight Trigram Twin Butterflies Double Swords) a weapons form

Baat Jaau Kyuhn (C) [Chat Sing Tohng Lohng] (*lit.* Eight Elbow Fist) a hand form

Baat Jeun Gwan (C) [Baat Muhn Kyuhn] (*lit.* Eight Advancing Staff) a weapons form using a staff

Baat Kyuhn (C) [Style] (*lit.* Eight Fist) a northern style of Chinese martial arts

baat muhn (C) [Taai Gihk Kyuhn] (*lit.* Eight Gates) the eight gates are hand methods that also relate to the eight compass directions

Baat Muhn Kyuhn (C) [Style] (*lit.* Eight Gates Fist) a northern style of Chinese martial arts

Baat Sin Kyuhn (C) [Style] (*lit.* Eight Important Fist) a northern style of Chinese martial arts

baau (C) [Common Usage] bag

baau fuhk (C) [Common Usage] an archaic term referring to travelers' clothing

baau waih (C) [Common Usage] to surround, to encompass

badak (K) [Common Usage] floor

bada neomgi da (K) [Common Usage] to deflect, to parry

bada neomgigi (K) [Common Usage] parry

ba duan gin (M) [Style] *see* ba duan jin

ba duan jin (M) [Qigong] (*lit.* Eight Pieces of Brocade) a *wai dan qigong* routine of exercises developed during the Song dynasty

bae (K) [Common Usage] abdomen, stomach

bae ggop (K) [Common Usage] navel

Bae Jeom-man (K) [Master] founder and current head of Joeng Tong Muye Do

baejigi (K) [Ssi Rum] stomach-lifting technique

baek (K) [Common Usage] hundred, white

baek ddi (K) [Common Usage] white belt

Baek Du hyeong (K) [Taekwondo] a form named after Baek Du San

baek du jangsa geup (K) [Ssi Rum] 95.1-kilogram and over weight class of professional competition

Baek Du San (K) [Common Usage] (*lit.* White Head Mountain) a volcanic mountain on the border of China and North Korea, claimed to be the mythological home of Tan Gun

Baekje sidae (K) [Common Usage] *see* Paekche sidae

Baekje wangjo (K) [Common Usage] *see* Paekche wangjo

Baekpalgi hyeong (K) [Kuk Sool] 108-technique form, named after the 108 human sufferings or anxieties taught in Buddhism

baekpalsip do (K) [Common Usage] 180-degree angle

baekpalsip do dolgi (K) [Common Usage] 180-degree turn

bae u da (K) [Common Usage] to learn

Ba Gang Quan (M) [Bamenquan] *see* Baat Gong Kyuhn

baggat dari chagi (K) [Hapkido] outside-leg kick

baguazhang (M) [Style] (*lit.* Eight Trigrams Palm) This style was created by Dong Hai Chuan in the latter part of the nineteenth century. This internal style emphasizes circular step patterns and the application of palm techniques, all of which are based on the *yin-yang bagua* theory.

Ba Hu Dan Quan (M) [Bamenquan] *see* Baat Fu Daan Kyuhn

bai (C) [Common Usage] lame, cripple

bai (M) [Common Usage] *see* baai

bai hai (M) [Acupressure] a point located on the inside of the thigh

Bai He (M) [Style] (*lit.* White Crane) A southern Shaolin style developed in Fujian Province by the female master Fang Qi Niang, it mimicked the fighting movements of a crane. White Crane is also referred to as the Yongchun Bai He, and is divided into the following branches: Fei He (Flying Crane), Ming He (Crying Crane), Shi He (Hungry Crane), Su He (Sleeping Crane), and Zhang He (Ancestor Crane).

bai he liang chi (M) [Taijiquan] (*lit.* White Crane Spreads its Wings) a large circular motion of the arms

bai hu chao wei (M) [Yang Taijiquan] (*lit.* White Tiger Waves Its Tail) a movement in the Taiji Sword routine

bai hui (M) [Acupressure] a point located on the top of the head

bai ma ti (M) [Bai Mei] *see* baahk mah tek

bai ma xian ti (M) [Hong Jia] *see* baak mah hin taih

Bai Mei (M) [Style] *see* Baahk Meih

bai shen (M) [Common Usage] paying respect to ancestors

bai she tu xin (M) [Baguazhang] (*lit.* White Snake Strikes Out With Its Tongue) a technique used to advance and attack

bai shi (M) [Common Usage] *see* baai si

bai xian (M) [Common Usage] *see* baai jou sin

bai yuan jing tao (M) [Luohan Quan] (*lit*. The White Monkey Plucks the Fruit) a hand attack aimed at the groin area of an opponent

Bai Yuan San Chu Dong (M) [Pi Gua Quan] *see* Baahk Yuhn Saam Cheut Duhng

bai yuan xian guo (M) [Yang Taijiquan] (*lit*. White Ape Offers the Fruit up) a movement in the Taiji Sword routine

bai zhang (M) [Common Usage] to defeat, to conquer

bai zhe (M) [Common Usage] the loser of a fight, match, or competition

bai zhi (M) [Medicine] the root of this plant is used in Chinese herbal medicine to reduce swelling and pain

baji (K) [Common Usage] pants

Baji Dan Quan (M) [Bamenquan] *see* Baat Gam Daan Kyuhn

Ba Jin Gun (M) [Bamenquan] *see* Baat Jeun Gwan

Bajiquan (M) [Style] (*lit*. Eight Ultimate [Tactics] Fist) a northern style that is characterized by sudden releases of power and long- and short-arm movements; also referred to as Kai Men Bajiquan (Opening the Gate Eight Ultimate Fist) and Yue Shan Bajiquan (Yue Mountain Eight Ultimate Fist)

Baji San Chui Li (M) [Bajiquan] (*lit*. Baji Three Step Power) The three sources of power for explosive techniques in Bajiquan: one is from the shoulder, another from the turning of the waist, and the last from the stamping of the legs and dropping of the body.

Baji Xiao Jia (M) [Bajiquan] (*lit*. Baji Small Frame) a hand form

ba-jutsu (J) [Style] (*lit*. Horsemanship) The art of riding in combat and using the bow, sword, spear, and glaive while mounted. The first school of this art was the Kamakura-period Otsubo-ryu

bak (C) [Common Usage] north

bakchigi (K) [Common Usage] head butt

bakchigi ha da (K) [Common Usage] to strike with a head butt

bakkat bal mok (K) [Common Usage] outer ankle

bakkat chigi (K) [Taekwondo] outward strike

bakkat dollyeo chagi (K) [Kuk Sool] inside-to-outside crescent kick

bakkat heobeokji (K) [Common Usage] outer thigh

bakkat makgi (K) [Taekwondo] outward block, outside block

bakkat palmok (K) [Common Usage] outer wrist

bakkat palmok momtong bakkat makgi (K) [Taekwondo] outer-wrist mid-level outward block

bakkat palmok yeop makgi (K) [Taekwondo] outer-wrist side block

bakkeseo (K) [Common Usage] from the outside

bakkeseo aneuro chagi (K) [Taekwondo] outside-inside crescent kick

bakkeseo aneuro makgi (K) [Taekwondo, Tang Soo Do] outside-inside block

bakkeuro (K) [Common Usage] to the outside

bakkeuro bada neomgigi (K) [Common Usage] outside parry

bakkeuro chagi (K) [Taekwondo] outward kick

Bak Sihng Choy Leih Faht (C) [Style] (*lit.* Northern Winning Choy Leih Faht) a southern style founded by Tahm Saam that combined the original Choy Leih Faht style (founded by Chahn Heung) and Northern Shaolin

Bak Siu Lahm (C) [Style] (*lit.* Northern Shaolin) a northern style originating in the Shaolin Temple

Ba Kua (C) [Style] *see* baguazhang

Bakufu (J) [Common Usage] (*lit.* Tent Government) A military government run by a *shogun* in the emperor's name. The first shogunate was installed by Minamoto no Yoritomo in 1185.

bal (K) [Common Usage] foot

bal badak (K) [Common Usage] bottom of the foot

bal beolli go moaseo seogi jase (K) [Tang Soo Do] heel-together stance

bal buri (K) [Common Usage] tip of the toes

bal chagi (K) [Common Usage] kick

bal dda gwi (K) [Tae Kyon] outside-to-inside crescent kick

bal deulgi (K) [Common Usage] foot-lifting technique

bal deung (K) [Common Usage] instep of the foot

bal deung geori (K) [Tae Kyon] jamming technique in which the foot strikes the arch of the opponent's kicking foot

bal dwichuk (K) [Common Usage] bottom of the heel

baleul dwiro mulli da (K) [Common Usage] to withdraw the foot

baleul gureu da (K) [Common Usage] to stomp the foot

balgarak (K) [Common Usage] toe

balggeut (K) [Common Usage] end of the foot, tip of the toes

balggeut chagi (K) [Taekwondo] toe kick

balggeut jireugi (K) [Hapkido] toe thrust kick

balggeut jjigeo chagi (K) [Hapkido] toe chopping kick

balggumchi (K) [Common Usage] heel

balggumchi chagi (K) [Common Usage] heel kick

balggumchi seonhoi ha da (K) [Common Usage] to pivot on the heel

bal gureum (K) [Common Usage] footwork

baljil (K) [Tae Kyon] kick

bal jireugi (K) [Taekwondo] thrusting kick

bal moa seogi (K) [Taekwondo, Tang Soo Do] closed foot stance

bal mok (K) [Common Usage] ankle

bal mok biteulgi (K) [Common Usage] ankle twist

bal mok dollyeo chagi (K) [Hapkido] ankle-turning kick

bal mok georeo teulgi (K) [Ssi Rum] ankle-hooking and body-twisting technique

bal moseori (K) [Tae Kyon] blade of the foot

bal nal (K) [Taekwondo] blade of the foot

bal nureugi (K) [Taekwondo] pressing kick

baltop (K) [Common Usage] toenail

bamen (M) [Taijiquan] *see* baat muhn

Bamenquan (M) [Style] *see* Baat Muhn Kyuhn

bam jumeok (K) [Taekwondo] protruding-knuckle fist

banchik (K) [Common Usage] foul, illegal technique in sparring competition

banchik ha da (K) [Common Usage] to violate a rule in sparring competition

bandae (K) [Common Usage] counter, opposite, reverse

bandae banghyang (K) [Common Usage] opposite direction

bandae dollyeo chagi (K) [Taekwondo] reverse turning kick

bandae dollyeo georeo chagi (K) [Taekwondo] reverse turning hook kick

bandae jireugi (K) [Taekwondo] reverse punch

bandal chagi (K) [Taekwondo] half-moon kick, crescent kick

bandal jireugi (K) [Taekwondo] half-moon punch, crescent punch

bandal son (K) [Taekwondo] half-moon hand, crescent hand, arc hand

ban deng (M) [Weapon] a wooden bench that can be used for attacking, trapping, or blocking

bang (M) [Common Usage] arm

Bang Bo (C) [Chat Sing Tohng Lohng] (*lit.* Crushing Step) a hand form

bangeo (K) [Common Usage] defense

bangeo chagi (K) [Common Usage] defensive kick

bangeo gisul (K) [Common Usage] defensive technique

bangeo ha da (K) [Common Usage] to defend, to protect

bangeo ja (K) [Common Usage] defender

bangeo jase (K) [Kuk Sool] defensive posture

bang geom sul (K) [Kuk Sool, Hapkido] sword-defense technique

bang gweon sul (K) [Kuk Sool, Hapkido] punch-defense technique

banghyang baggugi (K) [Common Usage] change of direction

banghyang byeon gyeong (K) [Common Usage] change of direction

bang jok sul (K) [Common Usage] kick-defense technique

bang pae (K) [Common Usage] shield

bang tusul (K) [Hapkido] throw-defense technique

bangyeok (K) [Common Usage] counterattack, counter technique

bangyeok ha da (K) [Common Usage] to counterattack

ban jayu daeryeon (K) [Taekwondo] semi-free sparring

banjeol gwansu (K) [Taekwondo, Tang Soo Do] bent-knuckle spearhand

bankoku choki (J) [Weapon] a concealed weapon consisting of a metal ring with protruding knobs or spikes; taught in the Edo-period Emmei-ryu and Nagao-ryu schools

bantam geup (K) [Taekwondo] bantamweight class in sparring competition

ban xia (M) [Medicine] a plant stem used in Chinese herbal medicine

banzai (J) [Common Usage] (*lit.* Ten Thousand Years) used as a cheer, much like "hooray!" in English

banzuke (J) [Sumo] Ranking list of the *rikishi* for each *basho*. Each *rikishi* is listed in order of rank, the highest ranks written in large characters at the top of the page and the lowest ranks in tiny ones at the bottom.

bao (M) [Common Usage] **1** leopard, panther **2** bag

bao gao (M) [Common Usage] to announce, to tell

bao jian (M) [Weapon] double-edged sword

bao wei (M) [Common Usage] to surround, to encompass

barai (J) [Judo, Karate] *see* harai

baro (K) [Common Usage] **1** a command to "return" **2** straight

baro jireugi (K) [Taekwondo] straight punch, lunge punch

Bart Cham Dao (C) [Wihng Cheun] *see* Baat Cham Dou

Ba Shan Fan (M) [Style] *see* Fan Zi

basho (J) [Sumo] an official sumo tournament held six times a year in different parts of Japan; it lasts for fifteen days

basho teate (J) [Sumo] a monetary reward or allowance given to *rikishi* for appearing at official tournaments

Ba Shyh Chuan (M) [Xingyiquan] *see* Ba Xu Quan

Bassai (J) [Karate] *see* Passai

batang son (K) [Taekwondo] palm heel

batang son teok chigi (K) [Taekwondo] palm strike to the jaw

Bat Cham Dao (C) [Wihng Cheun] *see* Baat Cham Dou

batdari gama dolligi (K) [Ssi Rum] outside leg-wrapping and turning technique

batdari geolgi (K) [Ssi Rum] outside leg-hooking technique

batdari hurigi (K) [Ssi Rum] outside leg-sweeping technique

bat fuhk chuhng (C) [Common Usage] *see* waih bui

bat gung pihng (C) [Common Usage] unfair, unjust, injustice

bat haau (C) [Common Usage] disrespectful

batjang dari (K) [Tae Kyon] ankle-level kick to the outside

batjul (K) [Common Usage] rope

batjul sul (K) [Common Usage] rope technique

bat moon (C) [Taai Gihk Kyuhn] *see* baat muh

batsai jase (K) [Tang Soo Do] cross posture

batto-jutsu (J) [Style] the art of drawing and cutting with a sword; also referred to as iai-jutsu or *bakken*

batto tai (J) [Common Usage] (*lit.* Sword Squadron) a branch of the Japanese police during the Meiji era equivalent to the modern-day riot police

bat yih (C) [Common Usage] not righteous, unjust

ba wang ju ding (M) [Hong Jia] *see* ba wohng queui ding

bawi milgi (K) [Taekwondo] push-boulder movement

ba wohng queui ding (C) [Huhng Ga] (*lit.* King Raising his Talisman) a two-handed block above the head with the hands in the *kiuh sau* position and the elbows slightly bent

ba xian guo hai (M) [Baguazhang] (*lit.* The Eight Immortals Crossing the Seas) A technique used to intercept attacks and to advance. The arms are swung in a small circular motion in front of the body while stepping forward; also known as *xuan feng chang* or "whirlwind palm."

Ba Xu Quan (M) [Xingyiquan] (*lit.* Eight Posture Sequence) a hand form

Bbachaei hyeong (K) [Tang Soo Do] form named after a karate form composed of 104 movements

bbaegi (K) [Hapkido] release technique

bbalgan (K) [Common Usage] red

bbalgan ddi (K) [Common Usage] red belt

bbalgan saek (K) [Common Usage] red color

bballi (K) [Common Usage] fast

bbeot gi (K) [Common Usage] extension of a limb

bbi da (K) [Common Usage] to sprain

bbim (K) [Common Usage] sprain

bbyam (K) [Common Usage] cheek

bbyeo (K) [Common Usage] bone

bbyeo ga bureoji da (K) [Common Usage] to break a bone

bbyeo hwasal chuk (K) [Kung Do] arrowhead made of bone

bei (C) [Common Usage] forearm

bei (M) [Common Usage] north

Bei Chao Dai (M) [Common Usage] Northern Imperial dynasties; consisting of the Northern Wei, Qi, Zhou, and the Western and Eastern Wei, these dynasties ruled China from A.D. 386 to 581

bei choi (C) [Common Usage] competition

bei choi hyun (C) [Common Usage] ring of competition, arena

bei ci (M) [Medicine] a shell that is ground into a powder and used in Chinese herbal medicine

bei hai jiang long (M) [Qigong] (*lit.* Dragon Submerges into the Northern Lake) a Taoist breathing exercise in Shi San Tai Bao Gong

beih go (C) [Common Usage] nose

beih go lung (C) [Common Usage] nostril

bei kap (C) [Common Usage] secretive book of martial arts; lost or hidden martial art forms or books

bei liang (M) [Acupressure] a point located on the spine between the shoulder blades

bei mihn (C) [Common Usage] to avoid

bei min (C) [Common Usage] to give face to someone, or to allow someone to preserve his dignity

bei mouh (C) [Common Usage] competition, to compete

bei pang (M) [Common Usage] to betray, betrayed

Bei Quan (M) [Common Usage] (*lit.* Northern Boxing) a generic term used to describe Chinese martial art styles developed north of the Yangtze river

Bei Shaolin (M) [Style] *see* Bak Siu Lahm

bei xin (M) [Acupressure] a point located on the spine on the lower back

Benkei (J) [Common Usage] a warrior monk famous for his martial prowess and loyalty to his master, Minamoto Yoshitsune

beollyeoseo go jase (K) [Tang Soo Do] walking posture

beom (K) [Common Usage] tiger

beom a gwi (K) [Tae Kyon] area of the open hand between the thumb and index finger

beom seogi (K) [Taekwondo] tiger stance, cat stance

beo seon (K) [Tae Kyon] traditional Korean socks, now worn by students of Tae Kyon as part of their uniform

beya (J) [Sumo] *see* heya

bi (M) [Common Usage] forearm

biao qiang (M) [Weapon] a short spear with a pear-shaped point

bi beop (K) [Common Usage] secret technique, secret method

bie (M) [Qin Na] to separate

bigol (K) [Common Usage] fibula, shinbone

biht (C) [Kahm Na] *see* bie

bik (C) [Common Usage] 1 stubborn 2 to coerce, to force

Bik Bo Saam Tuhng Kyuhn (C) [Luhng Yihng Kyuhn] a hand form

biki da (K) [Common Usage] to move out of the way

bi kong (M) [Common Usage] nostril

bi liang (M) [Acupressure] a point located between the eyes

bi myan (M) [Common Usage] *see* bei mihn

binao (M) [Acupressure] a point located between the deltoids and triceps muscles of the arm

bin cheuih (C) [Common Usage] a horizontal back fist moving in a lateral motion.

bing hei (C) [Common Usage] weapons

Bin Gwai Seung Tauh Gwan (C) [Choy Leih Faht] (*lit.* Bin Gwai Double-Ended Staff Form) a weapons form using the staff

bing xie (M) [Common Usage] weapons

bintsuke (J) [Sumo] a fragrant hair pomade used when dressing the hair of a *rikishi* in their *chonmage* (old-style top knot)

bi sai (M) [Common Usage] competition, to compete

bi sai quan (M) [Common Usage] competition ring

bisento (J) [Weapon] a polearm resembling a glaive, with a long, heavy haft and a heavy, curved blade

Bishamon-ten (J) [Common Usage] God of Treasure

bit chagi (K) [Taekwondo, Tang Soo Do] diagonal kick

bitei (J) [Acupressure] a vital point located at the bottom of the spine

biteul da (K) [Common Usage] to twist

biteureo chagi (K) [Taekwondo] twisting kick

biteureo makgi (K) [Taekwondo] twisting block

bitgyeo seogi (K) [Taekwondo] escaping technique

bitjang geori (K) [Ssi Rum] technique in which one leg is inserted between the opponent's legs before he is thrown

Biu Ji (C) [Wihng Cheun] (*lit.* Thrusting Finger) the third hand form in this style

biu ji sau (C) [Wihng Cheun] thrusting fingers movement

biu johng (C) [Common Usage] horizontal forearm strike usually aimed at the temple or chest

Biu Tze (C) [Wihng Cheun] *see* Biu Ji

biu tze sau (C) [Wihng Cheun] *see* biu ji sau

biu yin (C) [Common Usage] demonstration, performance

biwa (J) [Common Usage] loquat wood; used for making wooden training weapons used in Japanese martial arts

Biyako (O) [Karate] one of five empty-hand *kata* introduced to Meibukan Goju-ryu by Yagi Meitoku

Bi Yue Xia (M) [Master] a prominent master of baguazhang

bi zi (M) [Common Usage] nose

bo (C) [Common Usage] stance or posture

bo (J) [Weapon] a wooden staff, generally made of oak and measuring *rokushaku* (approximately 198 centimeters) in length

bo (M) [Common Usage] **1** shoulder, upper arm **2** neck **3** lame, crippled

bo cao xun she (M) [Hong Jia] *see* buht chou chahm seh

Bo Eun hyeong (K) [Taekwondo] *see* Po Un hyung

bogu (J) [Common Usage] protective armor used in kendo, naginata, and jukendo

Bohk Fu Dou (C) [Sai Chong Baahk Hok Kyuhn] a weapons form using a broadsword

bo jumeok (K) [Taekwondo] covering fist

bo-jutsu (J) [Style] Art of the Staff

bok (C) [Common Usage] shoulder or upper arm

bokbu (K) [Common Usage] abdomen

bokken (J) [Weapon] wooden sword used for weapons training; widely used in martial arts schools of various types today; it is also called a *bokuto*

bok tauh (C) [Common Usage] shoulders

Bokuden-ryu (J) [Style] a school of ken-jutsu founded by Tsukahara Bokuden and now located in Aomori Prefecture

bokuto (J) [Weapon] *see* bokken

bonbu (K) [Common Usage] headquarters of an organization

bonddae (K) [Tae Kyon] form, solo training routine

bong (C) [Common Usage] arm

bong (K) [Common Usage] club, staff

bong sau (C) [Wihng Cheun] (*lit.* Wing Arm) a block using the outer-edge of the arm as the point of contact

bon guk geom beop (K) [Kum Do] (*lit.* Native Country Sword Method) an old sword form

bong yeuhng (C) [Common Usage] example, role model

bonji (J) [Weapon] Sanskrit characters, often written on the blade of a weapon, for the purpose of invoking divine protection in combat

bou gou (C) [Common Usage] *see* bao gao

bouh (C) [Common Usage] stance, posture

bou ngaap chyun lihn (C) [Huhng Ga] (*lit.* Golden Duck Treading the Lotus Lily) a circular blocking technique made with the *kiuh sau* block

bou wuh (C) [Common Usage] to protect

bo zi ren (M) [Medicine] a seed used in Chinese herbal medicine

bu (J) [Common Usage] martial, military

bu (M) [Common Usage] step; stance; footwork

Bubishi (O) [Common Usage] A book whose roots have been traced to Fujian, China, although it is most often associated with Okinawan martial arts. It is a thirty-two article treatise on Bai He and Luohan Quan technique, strategy, philosophy, vital point striking, and herbal medicine.

buchae (K) [Common Usage] fan

buchae sul (K) [Kuk Sool] fan technique

Bucheo Nim (K) [Common Usage] the Buddha (with the honorific suffix "nim" appended)

budo (J) [Common Usage] (*lit.* Martial Ways) martial arts for personal or spiritual cultivation rather than for purely combative purposes; sometimes written as *bu no michi*

budoka (J) [Common Usage] a person studying martial arts or ways

budokan (J) [Common Usage] martial ways hall

budo seishin (J) [Common Usage] martial spirit

bu fu cong (M) [Common Usage] *see* waih bui

bugei (J) [Common Usage] a term used to refer to classical Japanese martial arts

Bugeikan (O) [Style] a school of karate and *kobudo* founded by Higa Seitoku

bugeisha (J) [Common Usage] martial arts exponent

bu gong ping (M) [Common Usage] unjust, unfair

buht chou chahm seh (C) [Huhng Ga] (*lit.* Spreading the Grass to Find the Snake) a redirecting movement that brings an opponent inward before striking

buht ji (C) [Common Usage] heel of the foot

bui buhn (C) [Common Usage] to betray; betrayal

bujin (J) [Common Usage] warrior

bu-jutsu (J) [Common Usage] martial arts; the characters for this word are read *wushu* in Chinese

Bu-jutsu Taihaku Seiden (J) [Common Usage] a sixteenth-century manual containing many of the martial teachings of its time

buk (K) [Common Usage] drum

bukchae (K) [Common Usage] drumstick

bukchae sul (K) [Common Usage] drumstick technique

buke (J) [Common Usage] warrior family; the military caste of Japan

Buke Sho Hatto (J) [Bushido] (*lit.* Rules of the Warrior Families) a list of articles and rules of behavior, compiled in 1615 by Tokugawa Ieyasu, that stresses the importance of a balance between literary and martial pursuits for warriors

Buk Han (K) [Common Usage] South Korean name for North Korea

buki (J) [Common Usage] weapons

Buk Joseon (K) [Common Usage] North Korean name for North Korea

bul anjeong ha da (K) [Common Usage] to be unsteady

bul gul eui euiji (K) [Taekwondo] indomitable will

Bulgyo (K) [Common Usage] Buddhism

Bulgyo Musul (K) [Style] Buddhist Martial Skill

Bulmudo (K) [Style] Buddhist Martial Way

Bunbu Ryodo (J) [Bushido] (*lit.* Literary and Martial, Both Paths [are the same]) a phrase stressing the importance of both the literary and martial arts as part of the education of a *bushi*

bunkai (J) [Karate] analysis, or interpretation, of *kata;* the true meanings behind the moves in karate *kata*

Bun Lihn (C) [Chyu Ga] (*lit.* Half Lotus) the fourth form taught in this southern style

buri gonggyeok (K) [Taekwondo] sudden attack

buri hwal (K) [Kung Do] unstrung bow

buryoku (O) [Common Usage] *see* chii kara

busabeom (K) [Common Usage] assistant instructor

bushi (J) [Common Usage] samurai, warrior

Bushi Matsumura (O) [Master[*see* Matsumura Sokon

bushido (J) [Common Usage] (*lit.* Way of the Warrior) the union of martial traditions and strategy with the moral codes of the warrior class, especially as influenced by Neo-Confucian thought

bushi no nasake (J) [Bushido] (*lit.* Compassion of the Warrior) according to Bushido, the skills, power, and strength acquired from practice of the martial arts should ultimately be used to protect the weak and to enlighten the ignorant

busu da (K) [Common Usage] to break

but fuh jaak yahm (C) [Common Usage] irresponsible

but jaba chagi (K) [Taekwondo] grasping kick

but jaba makgi (K) [Taekwondo] grasping block

Butokuden (J) [Common Usage] (*lit.* Hall of Martial Virtue) established in the 1890s in Kyoto and the site of the Budo Senmon Gakko, this was a government-sponsored training school for martial arts teachers in the pre-WW II period

Butokukai (J) [Common Usage] *see* Dai Nippon Butokukai

butsukari geiko (J) [Sumo] an exercise in which a *rikishi* pushes another wrestler across and out of the ring; it is used as a means to build both stamina and fighting spirit

bu yi (M) [Common Usage] *see* bat yih

bu zhong xin (M) [Common Usage] disloyal

— C —

cai (M) [Common Usage] *see* choi

cai (M) [Common Usage] **1** pull down; a movement used in taijiquan that has the power to shock and disrupt the balance and concentration **2** to guess, to speculate **3** vegetables

cai dao (M) [Weapon] a metal cleaver that is used in some Chinese styles

Cai Jia (M) [Style] *see* Choy Ga

Cai Li Fo (M) [Style] *see* Choy Leih Faht

cai pan yuan (M) [Common Usage] judge

cai se (M) [Common Usage] color

Cai Yu Ming (M) [Master] *see* Choy Yuhk Mihng

can jia (M) [Common Usage] to participate (in a competition, demonstration, etc.)

can sai zhe (M) [Common Usage] contestants, participants

Cao Lian Fang (M) [Master] a prominent master of xingyi-quan

cao yue (M) [Common Usage] protocol

Cao Zhong Sheng (M) [Master] a prominent master of ba-guazhang

cha (M, J) [Common Usage] tea

cha (M) [Weapon] pitchfork, trident

chaai (C) [Common Usage] to tread upon

chaam choi je (C) [Common Usage] contestant, participant

chaam ga (C) [Common Usage] to participate

chaan (C) [Weapon] shovel

chaang geuk (C) [Common Usage] side kick

chaang sau (C) [Wihng Cheun] spade hand

chaap cheuih (C) [Common Usage] straight forward thrust-ing punch using the leopard fist

chaap jeung (C) [Common Usage] insert palm

Chaap Yat Ji Heung (C) [Choy Leih Faht] (*lit.* Insert One Stick Of Incense Form) a hand form

cha balggi (K) [Tae Kyon] stomping kick

cha bapki (K) [Taekwondo] stomping kick

cha busugi (K) [Taekwondo] breaking kick, destroying kick

cha cha (C) [Common Usage] cymbal, used in lion dance performances

cha chi huang (M) [Medicine] a plant used in Chinese herbal medicine to help reduce swelling

cha chui (M) [Common Usage] a double-handed striking tech-nique that uses two fists thrusting forward on a downward angle

cha da (K) [Common Usage] to kick

chado (J) [Common Usage] *see* cha no yu

cha dolligi (K) [Ssi Rum] turning-and-sideways-kicking tech-nique

chaejjik (K) [Common Usage] whip

chaejjik jil ha da (K) [Common Usage] to strike with a whip

chaejjik sul (K) [Common Usage] whip technique

chaek (K) [Common Usage] book

Chah Kyuhn (C) [Style] *see* Cha Quan

chahm fa (C) [Common Usage] (*lit.* Placing the Flower) a paper flower used in a ceremony to decorate a new lion of a traditional southern Chinese martial arts school or on the altars of ancestors

Chahm Kiuh (C) [Wihng Cheun] (*lit.* Searching the Bridge) the second hand form in this southern style

chahm kiuh chyun jeung (C) [Huhng Ga] (*lit.* Sinking Bridge Thrusting Palm) a blocking movement using the base of the hand followed by a strike using the fingers of a flat palm

Chahn Ban Saam (C) [Master] *see* Chen Pin San

Chahn Buk (C) [Master] *see* Chen Bu

Chahn Daaht Fu (C) [Master] a prominent master of Choy Leih Faht

Chahn Dang Fo (C) [Master] *see* Chen Deng Ke

Chahn Gong (C) [Master] *see* Chen Geng

Chahn Gun Paak (C) [Master] a prominent master of Choy Leih Faht and son of the founder Chahn Heung

Chahn Heung (C) [Master] founder of Choy Leih Faht

Chahn Hohng Chuhn (C) [Master] a prominent master of Huhng Ga who was taught by Lahm Sai Wihng

Chahn Ma Daan Dou (C) [Choy Leih Faht] (*lit.* Horse-Cutting Broadsword Form) a weapons form

Chahn Sahn Hing (C) [Master] *see* Chen Chen Xing

Chahn San Yuh (C) [Master] *see* Chen Shen Ru

Chahn Taai Gihk (C) [Style] *see* Chen Taijiquan

Chahn Tihng Nihn (C) [Master] *see* Chen Ting Nian

Chahn Tohng (C) [Master] *see* Chen Tang

Chahn Wah Shuhn (C) [Master] a prominent master of Wihng Cheun

Chahn Yiu Chi (C) [Master] a prominent master of Choy Leih Faht and a third-generation disciple

chai (M) [Bai He] *see* zhai

chai (M) [Common Usage] **1** to rend **2** to tread upon

chaih jing (C) [Common Usage] neat, tidy

chaih toih (C) [Common Usage] a stomping kick using the instep of the foot

cha jireugi (K) [Taekwondo] thrust kick

chakugan (J) [Common Usage] to pay attention to; take aim at

cham da (K) [Common Usage] to endure

cha meom chugi (K) [Taekwondo] checking kick

cham yahp (C) [Common Usage] unlawful entry, trespassing

chan (M) [Qin Na] to bind

chan (M) [Weapon] *see* chaan

chang (K) [Common Usage] spear

chang (M) [Common Usage] **1** long **2** intestines

chang (M) [Common Usage] *see* jeuhng

Chang Chuan (M) [Style] *see* Chang Quan

chang geuk (C) [Common Usage] a heel kick

chang jeung (C) [Common Usage] spread palm

chang jian (M) [Weapon] a straight sword with the hand guard shaped like the petals of a flower

chang ju (M) [Common Usage] long range; the distance between two opponents at which neither can connect with a kick or a punch without first advancing forward

Chang Moo Kwan (K) [Style] a Taekwondo school founded at the Seoul YMCA by In Yun Pyung in 1946

Chang Quan (M) [Style] (*lit.* Long-Range Fist) a northern style developed from the Cha Quan, Hua Quan, and a variety of Shaolin styles specializing in long-range fighting techniques and a variety of kicking techniques; also the name used to refer to taijiquan in International Wushu Competition

chang sau (C) [Wihng Cheun] *see* chaang sau

chang sul (K) [Common Usage] spear technique

chankonabe (J) [Sumo] the staple diet of the *rikishi*, a nutritious stew prepared by the lower-ranking trainees in the sumo stable

cha no yu (J) [Common Usage] tea ceremony

Chan Tat Fu (C) [Master] *see* Chahn Daaht Fu

cha nureugi (K) [Taekwondo] press kick

cha obi (J) [Common Usage] brown belt

chao dai (M) [Common Usage] imperial dynasty

cha olligi (K) [Taekwondo] rising kick

Chao Shen San Jaio Zhan (M) [Bai He] (*lit.* Dynasty Body Three Horn Battles) a hand form in Zong He

Cha Quan (M) [Style] (*lit.* Cha Fist) A northern style established during the Ming dynasty by Cha Shang Yi, commonly practiced among the Muslims of Yunnan. The fighting characteristics of this style are based on the five animals: tiger, dragon, crane, snake, and monkey.

charyeot (K) [Common Usage] a command to "stand at attention with the feet together"

charyeot jase (K) [Taekwondo] attention posture

charyeot seogi (K) [Taekwondo] attention stance

chat (C) [Common Usage] seven

Chatan Yara no Kon (O) [Kobudo] a staff *kata* practiced in Ryukyu Kobudo

Chat Bouh Lihn Fa (C) [Suk Hok Kyuhn] *see* Qi Bu Lian Hua

chat ching luk yuk (C) [Common Usage] (*lit.* Seven Emotions, Six Desires) The seven emotions are happiness, anger, love, joy, sorrow, hate, and desire. The six desires are the six senses, which include: sight, hearing, taste, smell, touch, and the sixth sense of the mind.

Chat Hok Chiu Suhng Kyuhn (C) [Baahk Hok] a hand form

chat jit bin (C) [Weapon] seven-sectional whip

Chat Jit Muih Fa Bin (C) [Chat Sing Tohng Lohng] (*lit.* Seven Section Plum Blossom Whip) a weapons form using a steel whip

Chat Sau Kyuhn (C) [Chat Sing Tohng Lohng] (*lit.* Seven Hand Fist) a hand form

Chat Sing (C) [Gau Kyuhn] *see* Qi Xing

Chat Sing Cheuih Kyuhn (C) [Baat Muhn Kyuhn] (*lit.* Seven Star Beating Fist) a hand form

Chat Sing Muih Fa Seung Dou (C) [Choy Leih Faht] (*lit.* Seven Stars Plum Blossom Double Sword Form) a weapons form

Chat Sing Tohng Lohng (C) [Style] (*lit.* Seven Star Praying Mantis) a northern style founded in the seventeenth century by Wong Lohng, it combines Monkey footwork with Praying Mantis hand movements and is known for its clawing, punching, and fierce grasping techniques

chau tin (C) [Common Usage] fall or autumn season

che geup (K) [Common Usage] weight class

cheh fung baai lauh (C) [Huhng Ga] (*lit.* Tornado Swirling the Willow) a redirecting movement using the back of an open palm to hook an opponent's attack

chei (M) [Bai He] *see* chai

chejo (K) [Common Usage] gymnastics

chek cheuk (C) [Medicine] a root of a plant used in Chinese medicine

Chen Bu (M) [Master] a prominent master of Chen taijiquan and a first-generation disciple

Chen Chen Xing (M) [Master] a prominent master of Chen taijiquan

Chen Deng Ke (M) [Master] a prominent master of Chen taijiquan and a seventeenth-generation disciple

Chen Geng (M) [Master] a prominent master of Chen taijiquan and a second-generation disciple

cheng fa (M) [Common Usage] to punish

cheng gong (M) [Common Usage] to succeed

Cheng Man Ching (M) [Master] a prominent master of Yang taijiquan

Cheng Ngh (C) [Master] a prominent master of Wihng Cheun

chen hua (M) [Common Usage] *see* chahm fa

Chen Pin San (M) [Master] a prominent master of Chen taijiquan and a sixteenth-generation disciple

chen qiao chuan zhang (M) [Hong Jia] *see* chahm kiuh chyun jeung

Chen Shen Ru (M) [Master] a prominent master of Chen taijiquan and an eleventh-generation disciple

Chen taijiquan (M) [Style] An internal style originating in Henan Province in northern China founded by the Chen family in the village of Chenjiagou. Said by some to be the original style of taijiquan, it is characterized by graceful and soft movements as well as forceful movements with bursts of strength.

Chen Tang (M) [Master] a prominent master of Chen taijiquan and a fifth-generation disciple

Chen Ting Nian (M) [Master] a prominent master of Chen taijiquan and a sixteenth-generation disciple

Chen Wei Ming (M) [Master] a prominent master of Yang Taijiquan

Chen Xiang (M) [Master] *see* Chahn Heung

chen xiang (M) [Medicine] a plant used in Chinese herbal medicine to treat asthma

chen xiang guai (M) [Weapons] weapons usually used in pairs resembling the Okinawan *tonfa*

cheokchu (K) [Common Usage] spine

cheokgolbu (K) [Hapkido] area of the arm between the elbow and wrist, which is used as a striking surface

cheolhak (K) [Common Usage] philosophy

cheolhak ja (K) [Common Usage] philosopher

cheon (K) [Common Usage] heavens, sky

cheoncheonhi (K) [Common Usage] slowly

cheoncheonhi ha da (K) [Common Usage] to slow down, to do slowly

cheong (K) [Common Usage] blue

cheong ddi (K) [Common Usage] blue belt

cheon gi (K) [Common Usage] internal energy from the sky or heavens

cheong jang geup (K) [Ssi Rum] 75.1-kilogram to 80-kilogram adult weight class of amateur competition

cheong saek (K) [Common Usage] blue color

cheon gweon pumse (K) [Taekwondo] seventh-degree form

cheonha jangsa (K) [Ssi Rum] championship title meaning "strongest man under heaven"

Cheon Ji hyeong (K) [Taekwondo] *see* Chon Ji hyung

cheuhng (C) [Common Usage] long in length

cheuhng keuih (C) [Common Usage] *see* chang ju

cheuhng kiuh dahng (C) [Weapon] horse bench

Cheuhng Kyuhn (C) [Style] *see* Changquan

cheuih (C) [Common Usage] fist

cheuk bang nakbeop (K) [Hapkido, Kuk Sool] side-falling technique

cheung (C) [Weapon] spear

cheung gon (C) [Common Usage] (*lit.* Spear Pole) a staff that
has a spear head attached to one end

cheung jim (C) [Common Usage] (*lit.* Spear Point) the tip of
a spear head

cheung tauh (C) [Common Usage] spear head

cheun jit (C) [Common Usage] Spring festival

cheun tin (C) [Common Usage] *see* chun tian

cheut ga (C) [Common Usage] to become a monk or nun

cheut lihk (C) [Common Usage] to make an effort

cheut maaih (C) [Common Usage] to betray; betrayed

cheut saih (C) [Common Usage] to be born; birth

cheut sang (C) [Common Usage] *see* cheut saih

cheyuk gwan (K) [Common Usage] gymnasium

chi (M) [Common Usage] to eat

Chibana Choshin (O) [Master] a master of Shuri-te, student
of Itosu Anko, and founding president of the All Okinawa
Karate-Do Federation; he named the "Kobayashi" lineage of
Shorin-ryu

Chiba Shusaku (J) [Master] founder of the Hokushin Itto-ryu

chiburi (J) [Iaido] a movement found in virtually all *iai kata;*
it is a large swinging motion intended to remove the blood of
a fallen opponent from the sword blade

chi daan sau (C) [Wihng Cheun] single-arm clinging

chi dan sau (C) [Wihng Cheun] *see* chi daan sau

Chi Do Kwan (K) [Style] a Taekwondo school founded by
Yon Kue Pyan in 1946

chidori ashi (J) [Bu-jutsu] a type of stepping movement in
which one foot crosses over the other

chigiriki (J) [Weapon] a staff with a weighted chain attached
to one end used in the Araki-ryu and Kiraku-ryu

chigusa (J) [Weapon] hard steel used in Japanese blades

chi gwun (C) [Wihng Cheun] pole clinging

chih (C) [Common Usage] to resemble, to be like

chihn (C) [Common Usage] **1** front, in front of **2** a Chinese
measurement used in weighing herbal medicines

chihng faht (C) [Common Usage] to punish

chihn san (C) [Common Usage] the area of a broadsword that starts from the tip to the middle of the blade

chih pah lahp jing (C) [Baahk Meih] A ready position in the Baahk Meih Pah form. While in a standing position, the trident is held in the right hand behind the back with the point of the weapon facing the ground.

chih shao (M) [Medicine] red peony root; a light red root used to invigorate blood flow

chii kara (Ok) [Common Usage] (*lit.* From the Chii) *Chii* is equivalent to the Japanese *ki* and the Chinese *qi*. *Chii kara* should not be confused with *chikara*. Although they sound similar, they are two completely different ways of understanding the physical ability a *budoka* generates. The Japanese term *chikara,* meaning strength, refers to the physical power of a person whereas the Okinawan *chii kara* refers to the internal energy *(ki)* .

chiisai (J) [Common Usage] small

chijireugi (K) [Taekwondo] uppercut punch

chikai (J) [Common Usage] close, nearby

chika ma (J) [Common Usage] a close-range position in which either opponent can attack without stepping forward

chikara (J) [Common Usage] strength, power

chikara gami (J) [Sumo] (*lit.* Strength Paper) a small piece of white paper used by a *rikishi* to wipe his mouth after rinsing it out with *chikara mizu* before a match

chikara ishi (O) [Karate] a stone with a handle drilled into it used as a weight training device, mainly for the wrists, shoulders, and forearms

chikara mizu (J) [Sumo] (*lit.* Strength Water) water used by *rikishi* to rinse the mouth in symbolic purification prior to a bout

chikayoru (J) [Common Usage] to shorten the distance between yourself and someone else

chikujo-jutsu (J) [Bu-jutsu] the art of fortification, both for permanent and field structures

chi kung (M) [Common Usage] *see* qigong

Chikurin-ha Heiki-ryu (J) [Kyudo] a classical school of kyudo

chikuto (J) [Kendo] *see* shinai

chi kwun (C) [Wihng Cheun] *see* chi gwun

chil (K) [Common Usage] seven

childan (K) [Common Usage] seventh-degree black belt

chil geup (K) [Common Usage] seventh rank under black belt

chilsip (K) [Common Usage] seventy

Chi Lung Feng (M) [Master] *see* Ji Long Feng

chim (K) [Common Usage] acupuncture needle

chimei (J) [Karate] a term for a technique or strike that if executed with force and accuracy would be fatal; lethal

chim gam sau (C) [Wihng Cheun] front pinning hand

chim sul (K) [Common Usage] acupuncture

chimu (O) [Common Usage] liver

chin (C) [Common Usage] money

chin (M) [Common Usage] *see* chi yuhk

Chi Na (M) [Style] *see* Qin Na

chi nah (C) [Common Usage] anchor hand

Chinenshi Kyachu no Kon (O) [Kobudo] a staff *kata* practiced in Ryukyu Kobudo

ching (C) [Common Usage] *see* qing

Chin Gempin (J) [Master] Chen Yuanbin; a Chinese *quan fa* and pottery master who went Nagasaki in the early seventeenth century and taught several samurai who later created styles of ju-jutsu

ching jihng (C) [Common Usage] peaceful

ching jong (C) [Choy Leih Faht] balanced wooden dummy

ching long tan jaw (M) [Yang Taijiquan] *see* qing long dan zhao

ching luhng cheut seui sai (C) [Mouh Taai Gihk Kyuhn] *see* qing long chu shui shi

ching luhng daaih dou (C) [Weapon] long-handled green dragon big knife

ching luhng gaai meih (C) [Baahk Meih] a posture in the Baahk Meih Pah form in which the legs form a triangular stance with the left foot in front, and the base of the trident is swung toward the right front corner

Ching Luhng Yuht Daaih Dou (C) [Huhng Ga] (*lit.* Green Dragon Moon Big Sword) a weapons form using a *gwaan dou*

Ching Tihng Wah (C) [Master] a second-generation disciple of baguazhang

chin gum sau (C) [Wihng Cheun] *see* chim gam sau

Chinkon Kishin (J) [Shinto] a meditation technique practiced by the Omoto-kyo sect of Shinto

Chin Lauh Sik Kyuhn (C) [Ying Jaau] a hand form taught in this northern style

Chin Luhng Daahn Tauh Gwan (C) [Choy Leih Faht] (*lit.* Constricting Dragon Single-Ended Staff Form) a weapons form using a staff

chin ma (M) [Zhu Jia] *see* qin ma

Chi no kata (O) [Karate] a *kata* practiced in Kojo-ryu

Chinpugata (O) [Karate] a *kata* practiced in Kojo-ryu

Chinte (O) [Karate] an advanced *kata* in Shuri-te

Chinto (O) [Karate] a *kata* from the Shuri-te schools of Okinawa, also practiced in some Tomari-te schools; referred to as Gankaku in mainland Japan

chi pa li zheng (M) [Bai Mei] *see* chih pah lahp jing

chipuru (O) [Common Usage] head

chirichozu (J) [Sumo] a series of ritual movements in which *rikishi* vow to the gods to fight fairly and honestly that is made before each bout

chi sau (C) [Wihng Cheun] (*lit.* Sticky hands) a training exercise practiced between two people for developing sensitivity in the hands and arms and to improve trapping skills

Chiseigangata (O) [Karate] a *kata* practiced in Kojo-ryu

chi seung sau (C) [Wihng Cheun] double-arm clinging

chi sheung sau (C) [Wihng Cheun] *see* chi seung sau

chi shih (M) [Common Usage] *see* qi shi

Chisochin (O) [Karate] *see* Shisochin

Chito-ryu (J) [Style] a style of Japanese karate founded by Chitose Tsuyoshi

Chitose Tsuyoshi (O) [Master] a student of Aragaki Seisho and founder of the Chito-ryu

Chiu Kauh (C) [Master] a prominent master of Huhng Ga who was taught by Lahm Sai Wihng

Chiu San Saam Gok Jin (C) [Jung Hok Kyuhn] *see* Chao Shen San Jiao Zhan

chiu sau (C) [Common Usage] push-hand technique

Chiu Sau Daan Tauh Gwan (C) [Choy Leih Faht] (*lit.* Chiu Sau Single-Ended Staff Form) a weapons form

chi yuhk (C) [Common Usage] to disgrace

cho (C) [Kahm Na] *see* cuo

cho banjeon (K) [Taekwondo] elimination round in sparring competition

chobo ja (K) [Common Usage] beginner

chodan (K) [Common Usage] first-degree black belt

chodan ja (K) [Common Usage] person with a first-degree black belt

chogeup ban (K) [Kuk Sool] beginning-level course

chogeup hyeong (K) [Kuk Sool] beginning-level form

Choh (C) [Choy Leih Faht] *see* Choh Tauh

cho ho (J) [Nin-jutsu] the study of espionage and the recruiting of agents

Choh Tauh (C) [Choy Leih Faht] Farmer's Hoe form

choi (C) [Common Usage] vegetables

Choi Hong-Hi (K) [Master] founder of Taekwondo

choih pun yuhn (C) [Common Usage] *see* ping pan yuan

choijong gyeolseung (K) [Taekwondo] final match in sparring competition

Choi Yahp Bo Kyuhn (C) [Sai Chong Baahk Hok Kyuhn] a hand form

Choi Yeong hyeong (K) [Taekwondo] *see* Choi Yong hyung

Choi Yeuhng Daaih Dou (C) [Choy Leih Faht] (*lit.* Choy Yeung's Long-Handled Broadsword Form) a weapons form

Choi Yong hyung (K) [Taekwondo] form named after a Koryo dynasty general

Choi Yong-Sul (K) [Master] the founder of Hapkido; he is said to have learned Daito-Ryu aiki-jutsu from Takeda Sokaku in Japan

chojeom (K) [Common Usage] focus, focal point

chojeom eul matchu da (K) [Common Usage] to focus

chokusen (J) [Common Usage] (in a) straight line

choku to (J) [Weapon] a sword without any curvature

chong (K) [Common Usage] gun

chon gake (J) [Sumo] a sweep and arm pull that results in the opponent's loss of balance and subsequent fall

chong bangeo sul (K) [Kuk Sool] gun-defense technique

chong bonbu (K) [Common Usage] headquarters of an organization

chong geom (K) [Common Usage] bayonet

Chon Ji hyung (K) [Taekwondo] Heaven and Earth form

chonmage (J) [Sumo] topknot

choon pei (M) [Zhu Jia] *see* zhun bei

choshi waza (J) [Common Usage] harmonious technique

Chosun sidae (K) [Common Usage] Chosun dynasty period (1392–1910), also called the Yi dynasty period

Chosun wangjo (K) [Common Usage] Chosun dynasty, a political entity that ruled the entire Korean peninsula (all of modern North and South Korea, but none of modern China), also called the Yi dynasty

choteki (J) [Common Usage] rebel *bushi* of the Tokugawa era; a term used by the regime when referring to the enemies of the *bakufu*

Choun no Kon (O) [Kobudo] a staff *kata* practiced in Ryukyu Kobudo

chou ren (M) [Common Usage] enemy

chou yeuhk (C) [Common Usage] *see* cao yue

chowa (J) [Common Usage] harmony

chowa suru (J) [Common Usage] to attain harmony; in aikido it refers to harmony of movement while training with a partner

Choy Ga (C) [Style] (*lit.* Choy Family) A southern style founded by Choy Gau Yih. It has its origins at the Shaolin Temple and was prevalent in the late Qing dynasty. This fighting style uses a variety of long-range fighting movements and is one of the five family styles of martial arts of Guangdong Province.

Choy Lee Fut (C) [Style] *see* Choy Leih Faht

Choy Leih Faht (C) [Style] A southern Shaolin style founded by Chahn Heung in 1836. The name of this style is derived from the three teachers that had taught him his martial arts skills. Choy Leih Faht is known for its long-range arm techniques and agile foot work, as well as its large variety of weapons forms.

Choy Li Fut (C) [Style] *see* Choy Leih Faht

Choy Yuhk Mihng (C) [Master] the founder of the Ngh Jou Kyuhn style

chu (M) [Coi Li Fo] *see* choh tauh

chuan (M) [Common Usage] boat

chuan (M) [Common Usage] *see* quan

chuan fa (M) [Common Usage] *see* quan fa

Chuan Quan (M) [Hong Quan] (*lit.* Chain Fist) a hand form

chuan sun chiao nan (M) [Luohan Quan] *see* chuan sun jiao nan

chuan sun jiao nan (M) [Luohan Quan] (*lit.* The Emperor Strikes The Gate) a blocking technique using the outside edge of the arm

chudan (J) [Common Usage] mid-level, midsection

chudan geri (J) [Karate] mid-level kick

chudan nidan geri (J) [Karate] double mid-level kicks

chudan no kamae (J) [Common Usage] mid-level *kamae;* perhaps the most commonly used *kamae* (stance; ready position) in the martial arts

chudan shotei uke (J) [Karate] mid-level palm heel block

chudan shuto uke (J) [Karate] mid-level knifehand block

chudan soto uke (J) [Karate] mid-level inner block

chudan tsuki (J) [Karate] mid-level punch

chudan uke (J) [Karate] mid-level block

chudan yoko shuto uke (J) [Karate] mid-level sideward knifehand block; found in the Naihanchi (Tekki) Shodan *kata*

Chuden (J) [Iaido] a series of ten *kata* in Muso Shinden-ryu done from *tatehiza;* also known as Hasegawa Eishin-ryu

chuehn kiuh (C) [Wihng Cheun] piercing arm

chuehn lihn (C) [Medicine] an ingredient in Chinese medicine

chuehn muhk gwa (C) [Medicine] quince fruit, used in Chinese medicine for strengthening bones and tendons

chuen kiu (C) [Wihng Cheun] *see* chuehn kiuh

chuen lin (C) [Medicine] *see* chuehn lihn

chuen mook gua (C) [Medicine] *see* chuehn muhk gwa

chu fa (M) [Common Usage] *see* fa

Chu Gar (C) [Style] *see* Chyu Ga

chugi (J) [Common Usage] loyalty, devotion to the emperor

chu goshi (J) [Judo] a posture in which one is half-sitting

chui (J) [Competitive Budo] warning

chui (M) [Common Usage] *see* cheuih

chujeok ha da (K) [Common Usage] to chase

Chujo Nagahide (J) [Master] founder of Chujo-ryu ken-jutsu in the fifteenth century

Chujo-ryu (J) [Ken-jutsu] an ancient style of ken-jutsu, from which numerous styles of ken-jutsu and iai-jutsu have been derived

chuk douh (C) [Common Usage] *see* su du

chukitsu (J) [Acupressure] a vital point located in the fold of the elbow

chu li (M) [Common Usage] to put in full effort

chu mai (M) [Common Usage] *see* bui buhn

Chum Kiu (C) [Wihng Cheun] *see* Chahm Kiuh

chun (M) [Common Usage] *see* jeui

chung (C) [Common Usage] green onion

Chung Do Kwan (K) [Style] a Taekwondo school founded in 1945 by Won Kook Lee

Chung Gun hyung (K) [Taekwondo] form named after patriot An Chung-Gun

Chung Jang hyung (K) [Taekwondo] form named after General Kim Deok-Ryong

Chung Kyeong-hwa (K) [Master] highest-ranked student of Tae Kyon Master Shin Han-Seung

Chung Laih Chyun (C) [Master] a prominent master of Baahk Meih

chung lo (C) [Wihng Cheun] *see* jung lo

chung mihng (C) [Common Usage] smart, clever

Chung Mu hyung (K) [Taekwondo] form named after Admiral Yi Sun-sin, who was nicknamed Chung Mu Gong

chung sin (C) [Wihng Cheun] *see* jung saam sin

Chung Tihn Kyuhn (C) [Baahk Hok] a hand form

chunin (J) [Nin-jutsu] a rank in the ninja hierarchy between *genin* and *jonin*

chun tian (M) [Common Usage] the spring season

Chuo Jiao (M) [Style] (*lit.* Stabbing Foot) a northern style specializing in leg techniques

chu sheng (M) [Common Usage] *see* cheut saih

chushin (J) [Common Usage] center, heart

chusoku (J) [Common Usage] ball of the foot

Chutan Yara no Jo (O) [Kobudo] a *jo kata* practiced in Ryukyu Kobudo

chyu faht (C) [Common Usage] to punch

Chyu Ga (C) [Style] (*lit.* Royal Family) A Praying Mantis style that originated in the Fujian Shaolin Temple during the late Ming dynasty by Chyu Fuhk Tyuh and taught secretly only to the Haak Ga people. A branch of this style later developed in the Kwaang Sai province that later became known as Kwaang Sai Juhk Lahm. The characteristics of Chyu Ga are the use of the Phoenix Eye Fist, the Bamboo Slicing Hand, the Three Finger Spear Strike, and the Ginger Fist for attacking pressure points. All hand attacks are drawn from the elbow.

Chyun Kyuhn (C) [Huhng Kyuhn] *see* Chuan Quan

chyun sam geuk (C) [Common Usage] (*lit.* Piercing Heart Foot) a kick aimed at the heart

cong (M) [Common Usage] *see* chung

cong ming (M) [Common Usage] *see* chung mihng

cuo (M) [Qin Na] mistake

— D —

da (M) [Common Usage] **1** to hit, to punch, to strike **2** strike; a key movement in Zang He

daa (C) [Baahk Hok] *see* da

daahn (C) [Common Usage] single

daahn chi sau (C) [Wihng Cheun] (*lit.* Single Sticky Hand) a sensitivity exercise practiced between two people using one arm

daahn dou (C) [Common Usage] single broadsword

Daahn Dou Bin (C) [Choy Leih Faht] (*lit.* Sword and Chain Whip Form) a weapons form

Daahn Dou Deui chuk Huhng Ying Cheung (C) [Choy Leih Faht] (*lit.* Broadsword Versus Red Tassel Spear Form) a two-man fighting form

Daahn Dou Tahng Paaih Dip (C) [Choy Leih Faht] (*lit.* Sword and Rattan Shield Form) a weapons form

daahn fu jaau (C) [Common Usage] single tiger claw

daahn geuk (C) [Common Usage] (*lit.* Single Leg) a move in lion dance that requires jumping with one leg onto the partner's horse stance

daahn kiuh sau (C) [Huhng Ga] single bridge hand

daahn wong jong (C) [Choy Leih Faht] (*lit.* Spring Dummy) a training aid that consists of a log balanced on a spring, used for the practicing of various hand and leg techniques

daahn wuhn jeung (C) [Baatgwa Jeung] *see* dan huan zhang

daahp (C) [Common Usage] to step upon

daai (C) [Common Usage] belt, sash

Daaih Baat Gihk Kyuhn (C) [Baat Gihk Kyuhn] (*lit.* Big Eight Ultimate Fist) a hand form

daaih bei (C) [Common Usage] thigh

daaih daam (C) [Common Usage] brave

Daaih Daat Gwa Kyuhn (C) [Choy Leih Faht] (*lit.* Great Eight Trigram Fist Form) a hand form

Daaih Fu Yin Kyuhn (C) [Chat Sing Tohng Lohng] (*lit.* Big Tiger Swallow Fist) a hand form

Daaih Huhng Keih Daahn Tauh Gwan (C) [Choy Leih Faht] (*lit.* Great Flag Single-Ended Staff Form) a weapons form using a staff

Daaih Huhng Keih Gwan (C) [Chat Sing Tohng Lohng] (*lit.* Big Red Flag Staff) a weapons form using a staff

Daaih Huhng Kyuhn (C) [Ying Jaau] a hand form

Daaih Luhn Sau Fa San Kyuhn (C) [Baahk Hok] a hand form

Daaih Sahp Jih Kyuhn (C) [Choy Leih Faht] (*lit.* Great Cross Pattern Form) a hand form

daaih sauh (C) [Common Usage] (*lit.* Big Anniversary) the Chinese usually celebrate their sixtieth or eightieth birthdays with banquets

Daaih Sou Ji Gwan (C) [Chat Sing Tohng Lohng] (*lit.* Big Sweeping Son Staff) a weapons form using a staff

daaih teui (C) [Common Usage] *see* geuk

Daaih Tou Saam Jin Kyuhn (C) [Ngh Jou Kyuhn] (*lit.* Big Set Three Battles Fist) a hand form

daaih wong (C) [Medicine] the root of this plant has germicidal properties and is used in Chinese medicine to balance other herbal ingredients

Daaih Yuhk (C) [Master] a Buddhist monk at the Woh Sou Toi temple who taught the Dragon style to Lahm Yiu Kwaih in the early nineteenth century

daai sau yan (C) [Common Usage] large hand stamp

daam (C) [Common Usage] gallbladder; courage

daam bou (C) [Common Usage] *see* dan bao

daam bou yahn (C) [Common Usage] *see* dan bao ren

daam sam (C) [Common Usage] *see* yau sauh

daam seui (C) [Common Usage] to carry water, to bring water

daam siu (C) [Common Usage] to be cowardly or timid

daan (C) [Common Usage] *see* daahn

daan dou (C) [Weapon] (*lit.* single broadsword) a heavy, slightly curved single-edged sword with a protective hand guard

Daan Dou Bin (C) [Huhng Ga] (*lit.* Single Sword Whip) a weapons form using a broadsword and a whip

daap (C) [Common Usage] to respond, answer

da baaih (C) [Common Usage] *see* da bai

da bai (M) [Common Usage] to defeat, to conquer

dachi (J) [Common Usage] stance

daebi makgi (K) [Taekwondo] guarding block

dae do (K) [Common Usage] halberd

daegakseon chigi (K) [Kum Do] diagonal cut

daegeom (K) [Kum Do] great sword, a sword larger than normal size

daegeup ban (K) [Kuk Sool] high-level course

daegeup hyeong (K) [Kuk Sool] advanced-level form

daegung (K) [Kung Do] great (archer's) bow, a bow larger than normal size

Dae Han Cheyuk Hoi (K) [Common Usage] Korea Amateur Sports Association, which oversees kum do, kung do, boxing, fencing, etc.

Dae Han Guk Sul Hapkido Hyeophoi (K) [Common Usage] Korea Kuk Sool-Hapkido Association

Dae Han Gung Do Hyeophoi (K) [Kung Do] Korea Archery Association

Dae Han Hapkido Hyeophoi (K) [Common Usage] Korea Hapkido Association

Dae Han Min Guk (K) [Common Usage] Republic of Korea

Dae Han Peuro Tae Su Do Hyeophoi (K) [Common Usage] Korea Pro Tae Soo Do Association

Dae Han Ssi Rum Hyeophoi (K) [Ssi Rum] Korea Ssi Rum Association

Dae Han Taekwondo Hyeophoi (K) [Common Usage] Korea Taekwondo Association

Dae Han Ushu Hyeophoi (K) [Common Usage] Korea Wushu Association

Dae Han Yudo Hoi (K) [Common Usage] Korea Yudo (Judo) Association

Dae Kwae Do (K) [Common Usage] painting that shows Tae Kyon sparring and Ssi Rum wrestling, created around 1846

Daeman (K) [Common Usage] Taiwan

daeryeon (K) [Common Usage] sparring

daeryeon guseong (K) [Taekwondo] sparring system

daeryeon ha da (K) [Common Usage] to spar

daetoigol (K) [Common Usage] femur

Da Fu Baatgwa (C) [Choy Leih Faht] (*lit.* Fighting the Tiger Baatgwa Form) a hand form

da gu (M) [Common Usage] to play the drum; usually done to accompany lion dances

Daht Ting Baatgwa (C) [Choy Leih Faht] (*lit.* Daht Ting's Eight Trigram Form) a hand form

Dai (J) [Karate, Kobudo] (*lit.* Large, Big) used in names of karate *kata* to identify the more difficult of two *kata* derived from the same original form; the use of *Sho* indicates the less complex of the two *kata*

dai (M) [Common Usage] *see* daai

dai bian (M) [Common Usage] *see* douh lei

dai biao (M) [Common Usage] *see* doih biu

dai cha (M) [Common Usage] to bring or to serve tea

daih (C) [Common Usage] to offer, to bring to someone, to serve

daih chah (C) [Common Usage] *see* dai cha

daih ji (C) [Wihng Cheun] *see* muhn yan

dai jong ma (C) [Common Usage] low horse stances

dai kong (C) [Common Usage] to resist

dai li (M) [Common Usage] *see* douh leih

daimyo (J) [Common Usage] (*lit.* Great Name) the lords of the feudal domains; the chief employers of samurai

Dai Nippon Butokuden Bu-jutsu Senmon Gakko (J) [Common Usage] a martial arts teacher's training college, established in 1911 at the Butokukai in Kyoto

Dai Nippon Butokukai (J) [Common Usage] (*lit.* Greater Japan Association of Martial Virtue) a nationwide martial arts organization, first established in 1895 in Kyoto, for the preservation and promotion of the modern martial arts

Dai Nippon Kyudo Kyohan (J) [Kyudo] a manual on the principles of kyudo published in 1934

Dai-Ni Seisan (O) [Karate] an Uechi-ryu *kata* that is a combination of Sanchin and Seisan

daisho (J) [Weapon] a set of long and short swords that were worn by all members of the warrior class

Dai Sing (C) [Style] a northern style founded by Kau Sae, based on the fighting movements of the monkey, divided into five forms: Drunken, Lost, Stone, Tall, and Wood Monkey

Dai Sing Pek Gwa (C) [Style] (*lit.* Great Sage Chopping and Raising) a northern style incorporating the fighting movements of the monkey founded by Gan Duk Hoi; it incorporates the Deih Sing style and the Pek Gwa style into one fighting system

daito (J) [Weapon] long sword

Daito-ryu (J) [style] a system of unarmed and armed combat systematized by Takeda Sokaku; it was studied by Ueshiba Morihei before he created modern aikido

dai wong (C) [Medicine] *see* daaih wong

dajio (O) [Weapon] a pair of short wooden rods joined by a long rope

daki age (J) [Judo] a technique in which the opponent is raised from the mat

dak jeuih (C) [Common Usage] to offend, to insult

da kuai hsing (M) [Yang Taijiquan] *see* da kuai xing

da kuai xing (M) [Yang Taijiquan] (*lit.* The Big Chief Star) a movement from the Yang Taiji Sword form

dallyeon baek (K) [Taekwondo] training bag

dallyeon gong (K) [Taekwondo] training ball, striking ball

dallyeon gu (K) [Taekwondo] training aids

dallyeon ha da (K) [Common Usage] to train

dallyeon ju (K) [Taekwondo] training post, *makiwara* post

Dal Ma (K) [Common Usage] *see* Da Mo

Dal Ma Daesa (K) [Common Usage] great priest Bodhidharma (honorific title for Bodhidharma)

Da Mo (M) [Common Usage] Bodhidharma; an Indian prince turned Buddhist monk, who is credited with the introduction of *Chan* (Zen) philosophy to China. It is believed he went to the Shaolin Temple around 520 and introduced a series of exercises known as the *Shiba Luohan Shou* to help the monks stay awake during the marathon meditative sessions required in *Chan*. He is also the reputed founder of the Xi Sui Jing and the Yi Ji Jing styles.

dan (J, K) [Common Usage] degree of black belt rank

dan (M) [Common Usage] *see* daam

dan (M) [Common Usage] single; only one

dan bao (M) [Common Usage] to sponsor an activity or a person

dan bao ren (M) [Common Usage] sponsors of an activity

danbong (K) [Common Usage] short stick

danbong sul (K) [Kuk Sool] short-stick skill

dan chi sau (C) [Wihng Cheun] *see* daahn chi sau

dan dao (M) [Weapon] single broadsword

dando (K) [Common Usage] short sword, dagger

dan dobok (K) [Taekwondo] uniform with black collar for students over fifteen years of age

dando makgi (K) [Kuk Sool] short-sword block

dan du (M) [Weapon] *see* daan dou

dan fan (M) [Medicine] a Chinese herbal medicine to treat open wounds

dang (M) [Common Usage] *see* dong

dangeom (K) [Common Usage] dagger

dangeom ssanggeom hyeong (K) [Kuk Sool] double short-sword form

dan geup jedo (K) [Taekwondo] rank system

Dang Fong (C) [Master] a prominent master of Huhng Ga and founder of the Yih Yuhng Tohng who studied under Wohng Fei Huhng and was a contemporary of Lahm Sai Wihng

danggyeo makgi (K) [Taekwondo] pulling block

dangnang (K) [Common Usage] praying mantis

dang saan sik (C) [Saan Dung Hak Fu Paai] *see* deng shan shi

Dang Su Do (K) [Style] *see* Tang Soo Do

Dan Gun (K) [Common Usage] *see* Tan Gun

Dan Gun hyeong (K) [Taekwondo] *see* Tan Gun hyung

dan huan zhang (M) [Baguazhang] single change palm

danjeon (K) [Common Usage] *see* danjun

danjeon hoheup (K) [Common Usage] abdominal breathing

danjeon hoheup beop (K) [Common Usage] abdominal-breathing method

dan jeung (K) [Common Usage] rank certificate

danjun (K) [Common Usage] energy center in the abdominal region, called the *dan tian* in Chinese

danpatsu shiki (J) [Sumo] a ceremony for the cutting of the topknot of a *rikishi,* signifying his retirement

danryoku (J) [Common Usage] flexibility

dan shui (M) [Common Usage] *see* daam seui

dantai (J) [Common Usage] group

dan tian (M) [Common Usage] An area in which the body can generate and store *qi*. There are three such areas: the upper area is located between the eyebrows; the middle is located at the solar plexus; and the lower is the area a few inches below the navel.

dan xiao (M) [Common Usage] *see* daam siu

dan xin (M) [Common Usage] *see* yau sauh

dan zhong (M) [Acupressure] a point located on the sternum

dao (M) [Common Usage] (*lit.* Way/Path) the way of the universe/nature; the "natural" way to one's end; or the journey down the path to enlightenment

Dao De Jing (M) [Common Usage] (*lit. Classic of the Virtue of the Way*) a book supposedly written by Lao Zi that consists of eighty-one verses that expound the philosophy of the *dao*

dar (M) [Bei He] *see* da

dari (K) [Common Usage] leg

dari beolligi (K) [Common Usage] leg split

dari beollyeo seogi (K) [Taekwondo] stance with the feet shoulder-width apart

dari hurigi (K) [Hapkido] leg-sweeping technique

dari pyeogi (K) [Common Usage] leg-stretching technique

dari reul gotge ha da (K) [Common Usage] to straighten the leg

dari reul pyeo da (K) [Common Usage] to stretch the legs

dari sai (K) [Common Usage] crotch, area between the legs

Daruma (J) [Common Usage] *see* Da Mo

daruma taiso (J) [Karate] a stretching exercise done in lotus position, involving a series of rolling and breathing movements

da seung fei (C) [Common Usage] turning butterfly kick

dasu (J) [Common Usage] to extend, as in an arm or leg; to put (something) out

Da Tao San Zhan Quan (M) [Wu Zu Quan] *see* Daaih Tou Saam Jin Kyuhn

da tri (M) [Common Usage] *see* geuk

da zao (M) [Medicine] a plant used in Chinese herbal medicine

da zhou tian (M) [Qigong] grand circulation; a training method in which the *qi* is circulated throughout the entire body

ddaeri da (K) [Common Usage] to hit, to strike

ddaerigi (K) [Taekwondo] striking technique

ddaeryeo makgi (K) [Tae Kyon] push-downward blocking technique

ddanjuk (K) [Tae Kyon] inside ankle sweep

dde milgi (K) [Tae Kyon] open-handed strike to the chest

ddi (K) [Common Usage] belt

ddimaeneun beop (K) [Common Usage] belt-tying method

Ddi Ssi Rum (K) [Style] type of Ssi Rum practiced in Chungchong Province

ddulgi (K) [Taekwondo] thrusting technique, puncturing technique

ddwi da (K) [Common Usage] to jump

ddwieo an dari cha neoki (K) [Hapkido] jumping inside-leg penetrating kick

ddwieo ap chagi (K) [Taekwondo] jumping front kick

ddwieo ap dollyeo chagi (K) [Taekwondo] jumping roundhouse kick

ddwieo apggumchi chagi (K) [Hapkido] jumping ball-of-the-foot kick

ddwieo bal deung bitgyeo chagi (K) [Hapkido] jumping arch-of-the-foot diagonal kick

ddwieo balggeut jjigeo chagi (K) [Hapkido] jumping toe chopping kick

ddwieo balggumchi chagi (K) [Taekwondo] jumping heel kick

ddwieo bandae dollyeo chagi (K) [Taekwondo] jumping reverse-turning kick

ddwieo bandal chagi (K) [Taekwondo] jumping half-moon kick, jumping crescent kick

ddwieo biteureo chagi (K) [Taekwondo] jump twisting kick

ddwieo chagi (K) [Taekwondo] jumping kick

ddwieo dora yeop chagi (K) [Hapkido] jump turning side kick

ddwieo dora chagi (K) [Taekwondo, Hapkido] jump spinning kick

ddwieo dwi chagi (K) [Taekwondo] jumping back kick

ddwieo dwi dora yeop chagi (K) [Taekwondo] jump back-turning side kick

ddwieo dwiggumchi cha dolligi (K) [Hapkido] jumping heel spin kick

ddwieo dwiggumchi cha naerigi (K) [Hapkido] jumping heel-downward kick

ddwieo gawi chagi (K) [Taekwondo] jumping scissor kick

ddwieo jeonggweon (K) [Taekwondo] jumping straight punch

ddwieo jjikgi (K) [Kuk Sool] jumping axe kick, skipping axe kick

ddwieo jokdo seweo cha milgi (K) [Hapkido] jumping push kick in which the blade of the foot is used as a striking surface

ddwieo modeumbal ap chagi (K) [Taekwondo] jumping double-foot front kick

ddwieo modeumbal yeop chagi (K) [Taekwondo] jumping double-foot side kick

ddwieo mom dollyeo chagi (K) [Taekwondo] jumping body-turning kick

ddwieo neomeo chagi (K) [Taekwondo] jump-across kick

ddwieo yeoksudo (K) [Taekwondo] jumping reverse knife-hand

ddwieo yeop chagi (K) [Taekwondo, Hapkido] jumping side kick

ddwigi (K) [Taekwondo] jump

ddwimyeo ap chagi (K) [Taekwondo] jumping front kick, flying front kick

ddwimyeo chagi (K) [Taekwondo] jumping kick, flying kick

ddwimyeo dollyeo chagi (K) [Taekwondo] jumping roundhouse kick, flying roundhouse kick

ddwimyeo nopi chagi (K) [Taekwondo] jumping high kick, flying high kick

ddwimyeo yeop chagi (K) [Taekwondo] jumping side kick, flying side kick

deai (J) [Common Usage] when opponents clash in combat

deai osae uke (J) [Karate] a smothering block, done as one moves forward

deashi barai (J) [Judo] a forward moving leg sweep, used to sweep one's opponent

debana kote (J) [Kendo, Naginata] a strike to the wrist; an attack that takes advantage of the opponent's attack in order to strike his *kote* with one's own attack

debana men (J) [Kendo] avoiding an opponent's attack by moving and countering with a *men uchi* of one's own

debana tsuki (J) [Kendo] evading the opponent's attack, then countering with a *tsuki*

debana waza (J) [Kendo] techniques that try to take advantage of the openings made by the opponent's attack

degeiko (J) [Sumo] (*lit.* Outside Practice) practice outside of one's own stable, done before a tournament to help one improve technique and to learn something about one's possible opponents

deih (C) [Common Usage] earth

Deih Seuht Kyuhn (C) [Style] *see* Di Shu Quan

deih tauh (C) [Common Usage] (*lit.* Territory) a colloquial term used to refer to one's area of control

deih to (C) [Common Usage] mop

deih tong (C) [Style] *see* Di Tang

Deng Fang (M) [Master] *see* Dang Fong

deng shan shi (M) [Shandong Hei Hu Pai] Climbing mountain stance; an exercise in the Shandong Hei Hu Pai style used to strengthen the arms and legs. The movements resemble those of a tiger climbing a mountain.

deolmi geori (K) [Tae Kyon] hand technique in which the back of the neck is grasped with the palm facing outward, then pulled forward and downward

deolmi jaebi (K) [Tae Kyon] hand technique in which the back of the neck is grasped with the palm facing inward, then jerked forward and downward

deonji da (K) [Common Usage] to throw

deonjigi (K) [Taekwondo, Hapkido] throwing technique

deot geori (K) [Ssi Rum] technique in which the opponent's leg is trapped and his body pushed backward

deru ippon (J) [Judo] a judo match won by a single *ippon* in the opening seconds of the match, before the opponent even starts his attack and has no time to counter

deshi (J) [Common Usage] disciple, pupil; in many martial arts, a distinction is made between regular trainees *(seito)* and live-in disciples engaging in special training *(uchideshi)*. *Uchideshi* dedicate themselves fully to their art, often living at or near the dojo, even in their master's home, in order to spend as much time as possible with their teacher to train and learn everything about their art.

deuhn (C) [Common Usage] to bow the head

Deuht Mihng Sin Seung Tauh Cheung (C) [Chat Sing Tohng Lohng] a weapons form using a double-headed spear

deui sau (C) [Common Usage] opponent

deul ana noki (K) [Ssi Rum] lifting-and-throwing technique

deul baejigi (K) [Ssi Rum] bent-knee stomach-lifting technique

deung (K) [Common Usage] back

deung bbyeo (K) [Common Usage] backbone

deung chaegi (K) [Ssi Rum] back-jerking technique

deungchyeo gama dolligi (K) [Ssi Rum] bent-over leg-sweeping technique

deung chyeo gama jeochigi (K) [Ssi Rum] bent-over body-flipping technique

deungjumeok (K) [Taekwondo] backfist

deungjumeok dollyeo chigi (K) [Taekwondo] spinning backfist

deungjumeok jil ha da (K) [Common Usage] to throw a back-fist

deureo japchaegi (K) [Ssi Rum] technique in which one leg is inserted between the opponent's legs and a *japchaegi* is executed

deureo makgi (K) [Taekwondo] lifting block, scooping block

deureo noki (K) [Ssi Rum] technique in which the opponent is lifted to chest level and dropped

deuryeo masi da (K) [Common Usage] to inhale

Dewanoumi (J) [Sumo] a sumo *beya* located in Sumida Ward, Tokyo

de zui (M) [Common Usage] *see* dak jeuih

dian (M) [Qin Na] to point

dian gang jue (M) [Weapon] short double-edged straight swords usually used in pairs

dian mai (M) [Style] attacking acupuncture points so as to stop or disrupt the flow of *qi*, which can cause death; often referred to as *dim mak*

dian xue (M) [Qin Na] the art of pressing or striking specific acupuncture points to kill or immobilize an opponent

dian xue ding (M) [Weapon] sharp darts with a supporting base that can be placed on the ground or thrown at opponents

diao (M) [Qin Na] to be deceptive

die (M) [Common Usage] *see* dit

dihk yahn (C) [Common Usage] *see* chou ren

dihng jih ma (C) [Common Usage] wedge horse stance

di kang (M) [Common Usage] *see* dai kong

dik sau (C) [Common Usage] *see* deui sau

dim (C) [Common Usage] to point

dim mak (C) [Style] *see* dian mai

ding geuk (C) [Common Usage] inside crescent kick

ding jaan (C) [Wihng Cheun] butting elbow

ding jarn (C) [Wihng Cheun] *see* ding jaan

ding sahn (C) [Common Usage] to stabilize the spirit

di pen bu (M) [Bajiquan] horse stance

dip jeung (C) [Common Usage] butterfly palm

di qi (M) [Common Usage] earth's energy

di ren (M) [Common Usage] *see* chou ren

di shou (M) [Common Usage] *see* deui sau

Di Shu Quan (M) [Style] *see* Gou Quan

dit (C) [Common Usage] to fall

Di Tang (M) [Style] (*lit.* Ground Lying) a ground-fighting art that is divided into northern and southern styles

dit da jow (C) [Medicine] *see* tit da jau

diu (C) [Kahm Na] *see* diao

diu kok ma (C) [Wihng Cheun] *see* doih kok mah

diu lian (M) [Common Usage] *see* mouh min

diu lihm (C) [Common Usage] *see* mouh min

di wo (M) [Common Usage] *see* deih to

do (J, K) [Common Usage] (*lit.* the Way) A term used to denote many Japanese and Korean ascetic disciplines. It is written with the same character as the Chinese term *Dao.*

do (J) [Kendo, Naginata] **1** a blow that strikes the torso of the body **2** chest protector, plastron; the part of the armor that protects the torso of the trainee

do (K) [Common Usage] broadsword

dobok (K) [Common Usage] (*lit.* Way Clothes) uniform

dobok baji (K) [Common Usage] uniform pants

dobok gae neun beop (K) [Common Usage] uniform-folding method

dobok sang eui (K) [Common Usage] uniform top

doburoku (J) [Common Usage] strong, less refined, thick, white sake

Dogen (J) [Zen] a master of Zen and founder of the Soto school of Zen, who lived in the thirteenth century

doggijil (K) [Tae Kyon] strike with the blade of the hand

dogi (J) [Common Usage] training uniform

Dogyo (K) [Common Usage] Taoism

dohimo (J) [Kendo, Naginata] cords or strings at the back of the *do,* used to tie it in place

doh lohk (C) [Common Usage] to lose dignity, to fall

dohyo (J) [Sumo] sumo ring; it is 4.55 meters in diameter and is delineated by half-buried straw bales that have been filled with earth. Women are not allowed to enter practice and competition *dohyo*, in accordance with ancient Shinto beliefs

dohyo iri (J) [Sumo] (*lit.* Ring Entrance) a ceremony in which the *rikishi* enter the *dohyo,* and pledge themselves to fight fairly

doi (C) [Common Usage] big

Doi Choi Fa Daaih Gok Kyuhn (C) [Baahk Hok] a hand form

doih biu (C) [Common Usage] to represent

doih kok mah (C) [Wihng Cheun] diagonal stance

doih tai (C) [Common Usage] to replace

dojang (K) [Common Usage] (*lit.* Way Place) training hall

dojang gyuchik (K) [Common Usage] training-hall rules

do jeh (C) [Common Usage] *see* gam jeh

doji jogai (J) [Competitive Budo] both competitors have moved outside of the competitive area

do jime (J) [Judo] (*lit.* Body Strangle) a technique in which the opponent's torso is squeezed with one's legs; a body scissors hold

dojo (J) [Common Usage] (*lit.* Place of the Way) originally a site for Buddhist meditation or spiritual exercises, in budo it means the martial arts training hall

dojo arashi (J) [Common Usage] (*lit.* Dojo Storming) the practice of visiting a dojo to challenge a teacher or his senior students to extort money or to make a name for oneself; also called *dojo yaburi*

doju (K) [Common Usage] the founder of an art

dojung e seo garo mak da (K) [Common Usage] to intercept

doju nim (K) [Common Usage] the founder of an art (with the honorific suffix "nim" appended)

doka (J) [Common Usage] **1** (*lit.* Songs of the Way) short didactic poems, written by budo teachers that present their views on the principles and technical aspects of the art **2** a type of match (incendiary device) used and made by ninja

dokaeshi men (J) [Kendo] a counter used against an attack to *do,* attacking the opponent's head after parrying his attack

dokko (J) [Acupressure] the pressure point in the hollow behind the jawbone and below the ears

Dokkodo (J) [Common Usage] the name of a text by Miyamoto Musashi, explaining some of the philosophical and spiritual concepts he felt were important in studying the martial arts

Dokogata (O) [Karate] a *kata* practiced in Kojo-ryu

doksuri (K) [Common Usage] eagle

Dokyo (J) [Common Usage] Taoism

dol da (K) [Common Usage] to turn

dolgi (K) [Taekwondo] turn

doljae jil (K) [Tae Kyon] jumping leg block

dolli da (K) [Common Usage] to turn (something), to twist (something)

dollim baejigi (K) [Ssi Rum] balance-turning stomach-lifting technique

dollimyeo makgi (K) [Taekwondo] circular turning block

dollyeo bburi chigi (K) [Ssi Rum] turning-and-throwing technique

dollyeo chagi (K) [Taekwondo, Tang Soo Do] turning kick, spinning kick, round kick

dollyeo jireugi (K) [Taekwondo] turning punch, round punch

dollyeo naeryeo chagi (K) [Taekwondo] turning downward kick, turning axe kick

dolmyeo chagi (K) [Taekwondo] midair kick

domang ga da (K) [Common Usage] to escape (from an attacker), to run away

domo (J) [Common Usage] used in informal settings as both a way to say thank you and as a greeting

Domyogata (O) [Karate] a *kata* practiced in Kojo-ryu

dong (C) [Common Usage] to block, resist, obstruct

dong (K) [Tae Kyon] equivalent of the dan rankings of other Korean and Japanese martial arts

dong (M) [Common Usage] east

dong gae (K) [Kung Do] bow case

dong gwaih maih (C) [Medicine] the tail end of a root commonly used in Chinese medicine to reduce swelling and pain

dong gwai mei (C) [Medicine] *see* dong gwaih maih

Dong Hai Chuan (M) [Master] the founder of baguazhang

Dong Hak (K) [Common Usage] (*lit.* Eastern Learning) a indigenous Korean religion created in the 1860s that combined Buddhism, Taoism, Confucianism, and Shamanism

dongjak (K) [Common Usage] movement, move

dong tian (M) [Common Usage] the winter season

Dong Yang musul (K) [Common Usage] Asian martial art

don hei jo geuk (C) [Common Usage] a crane stance on the left leg

don lon (C) [Common Usage] horizontal palm strike

dora chagi (K) [Kuk Sool] turning kick, spinning kick

dosa (K) [Common Usage] Taoist or Buddhist master, spiritual guide

Dosan hyeong (K) [Taekwondo] *see* To San hyung

doshin (J) [Common Usage] a low-ranking police officer in Japan's feudal police force

Doshu (J) [Aikido] (*lit.* Master of the Way) term for the head of Aikikai aikido; used when referring to Ueshiba Kisshomaru, the son of Ueshiba Morihei

do sul (K) [Common Usage] **1** broadsword technique **2** Taoist magical skill

dotai (J) [Sumo] a term meaning both *rikishi* have fallen or stepped out of the ring simultaneously

dot cheuih (C) [Common Usage] horizontal backfist

doton-jutsu (J) [Nin-jutsu] camouflage and concealment techniques

dou (C) [Weapon] broadsword or knife

dou biu (C) [Common Usage] broadsword back

do uchi otoshi men (J) [Kendo, Naginata] a counter-attack using *men uchi* against an attack to the *do* after striking down the opponent's weapon

douh (C) [Common Usage] *see* dao

dou hau (C) [Weapon] edge of a sword or blade

douh hip (C) [Common Usage] apologies

douh lei (C) [Common Usage] reason, logic

dou jim (C) [Common Usage] broadsword tip

dou pah (C) [Common Usage] broadsword handle

dou san (C) [Common Usage] broadsword body

dou sau (C) [Common Usage] (*lit.* Sword Head) the area at the end of the broadsword handle where the *piu choi* is tied

dou yahn (C) [Common Usage] broadsword edge

dozukuri (J) [Kyudo] the ready or stable position of an archer, sometimes referred to as the second position. The archer holds his right fist at the right hip, legs apart, with both the arrow and bow held in the left hand.

du (M) [Common Usage] belly, abdomen

duan (M) [Common Usage] **1** short in length **2** to be severe

duan ba zhui yun chan (M) [Weapon] weapons usually used in pairs that have a small metal rectangular-shaped blade at the end of a short shaft

duan ding (M) [Common Usage] *see* dyun dihng

duan gu (M) [Common Usage] *see* tyun gwat

duan gun (M) [Weapon] *see* dyun gwan

duan ju (M) [Common Usage] short range; the minimum distance at which two opponents can reach each other with their hands

Duan Quan Liu Lu (M) [Hong Quan] (*lit.* Short Fist Six Ways) a hand form

du bal beollyeo cha olligi (K) [Hapkido] jumping kick in which each foot strikes a target on either side of the body

du bal dangsang chagi (K) [Tae Kyon] jumping twin kick

du bal ddaro nopi chagi (K) [Hapkido] high-jumping kick in which two consecutive front kicks are delivered

du bal moa cha olligi (K) [Hapkido] jumping kick in which both feet strike forward into the same target

du bal moa yeop chagi (K) [Hapkido] side kick in which both feet strike the target together

dubeon chagi (K) [Taekwondo] double kick

dubeon chigi (K) [Taekwondo] double strike

dubeon jireugi (K) [Taekwondo] double punch

dudeurigi (K) [Tae Kyon] hand-patting exercise intended to loosen and warm up the muscles without conventional stretching

duhk laahp (C) [Common Usage] *see* du li

duhk lahp paak pah (C) [Baahk Meih] a movement in the Baahk Meih Pah form in which the base of the trident is swung toward the lower left corner to block an attack to the lower body

Duhng Hoi Chuhn (C) [Master] *see* Dong Hai Chuan

dui kok ma (C) [Wihng Cheun] *see* doih kok mah

duk dou (C) [Common Usage] *see* daan dou

duk laahp ma (C) [Common Usage] crane stance

dul (K) [Common Usage] two

du li (M) [Common Usage] independent

du li pai pa (M) [Bai Mei] *see* duhk lahp paak pah

dun (M) [Bai He, Qin Na] **1** escape; a key movement in Zhang He **2** to pause

dung (C) [Common Usage] east

dung tin (C) [Common Usage] *see* dong tian

dun pai (M) [Weapon] a hand-held shield usually decorated with a lion's face

duo luo (M) [Common Usage] *see* doh lohk

duo xie (M) [Common Usage] *see* gam jeh

du palmok arae hechyeo makgi (K) [Taekwondo] two-wrist low wedge block

durumari (K) [Common Usage] scroll

dutong (K) [Common Usage] headache

du tui tong ren (M) [Weapon] a club shaped like a human figure with raised arms

du zhong (M) [Medicine] the bark of a tree used in Chinese herbal medicine to treat pain in the joints

dwi (K) [Common Usage] rear, back

dwi bbeodeo chagi (K) [Tang Soo Do] back extension kick

dwi chagi (K) [Common Usage] back kick

dwichuk (K) [Common Usage] heel, back sole

dwichuk georeo milgi (K) [Ssi Rum] rear-heel hooking and pushing technique

dwi dora yeop chagi (K) [Taekwondo] back turning side kick

dwi ggoa seogi (K) [Taekwondo] back cross stance

dwiggumchi (K) [Common Usage] heel

dwiggumchi aneuro chagi (K) [Hapkido] heel-inside kick

dwiggumchi cha dolligi (K) [Taekwondo] upward heel kick

dwiggumchi chagi (K) [Taekwondo] heel kick

dwiggumchi cha naerigi (K) [Taekwondo, Hapkido] downward heel kick

dwiggumchi cha olligi (K) [Hapkido] upward heel kick

dwiggumchi dollyeo chagi (K) [Taekwondo] turning heel kick

dwiggumchi natgecha dolligi (K) [Hapkido] low heel spinning kick

dwi huryeo chagi (K) [Taekwondo, Tang Soo Do] rear whip kick, rear slap kick

dwijibeo jireugi (K) [Taekwondo] upset punch

dwi jireugi (K) [Taekwondo] backward punch

dwimakgi (K) [Taekwondo] rear block

dwi nakbeop (K) [Common Usage] rear falling technique

dwi palggumchi chigi (K) [Taekwondo] rear elbow strike

dwiro chigi (K) [Common Usage] rear strike

dwiro dol da (K) [Common Usage] to turn around

dwiro giul da (K) [Common Usage] to lean backward

dwiro ilbo (K) [Common Usage] one step backward

dwiro mil da (K) [Common Usage] to push backward

dwitbalggumchi (K) [Common Usage] back sole of the foot

dwit bal mok geori (K) [Ssi Rum] rear-ankle hooking technique

dwit bal seogi (K) [Taekwondo] rear foot stance, cat stance

dwitcha busugi (K) [Taekwondo] back-breaking kick

dwit chagi (K) [Tang Soo Do] back kick

dwitcha jjireugi (K) [Taekwondo] back thrust kick

dwitgeoreum jil (K) [Tae Kyon] back step

dwit ggoa seogi (K) [Taekwondo] backward cross stance

dwit gubi seogi (K) [Taekwondo] extended back stance, deep back stance

dwit jase (K) [Common Usage] back posture

dwit ogeum jipgi (K) [Ssi Rum] rear back-of-the-knee pulling technique

dwi tong su (K) [Common Usage] back of the head

dwit palgup chigi (K) [Taekwondo, Tang Soo Do] back elbow strike

dyou lyau (M) [Common Usage] *see* sat mihn ji

dyun (C) [Kahm Na] to be severe

dyun dihng (C) [Common Usage] judgment, decision

dyun gwan (C) [Weapon] short staff

dyun keuih (C) [Common Usage] *see* duan ju

Dyun Kyuhn Luhk Louh (C) [Huhng Kyuhn] *see* Duan Quan Liu Lu

— E —

ebisuko (J) [Sumo] sumo slang for a hearty meal

eboshi (J) [Common Usage] a hat made from lacquered horsehair used by Shinto priests and *gyoji* (sumo referees); also worn by senior kyudo exponents on special occasions

Edo (J) [Common Usage] the old name for Tokyo

Edo jidai (J) [Common Usage] historic period between 1603 and 1867, when the country was ruled by the Tokugawa *Bakufu,* the last feudal government of Japan

Edo Yagyu Shinkage-ryu (J) [Ken-jutsu] a branch of the Shinkage-ryu school of ken-jutsu created by Yagyu Munenori

eiku (O) [Kobudo] *see* ekku

Eiza (O) [Common Usage] Okinawan Summer Dance Festival

ekku (O) [Weapon] a fisherman's oar; used in Okinawa as a weapon in the same manner as a staff or spear; *kai* in Japanese

embu (J) [Common Usage] 1 martial arts demonstration 2 a two-person training technique in Shorinji Kempo

embujo (J) [Common Usage] a site or area for a martial arts demonstration

emei ci (M) [Weapon] daggers with a ring in the center and two sharp points on each end, usually used in pairs

Emei Shan (M) [Common Usage] a mountain in China's Sichuan Province where many internal styles of martial arts originated

Emmei-ryu (J) [Ken-jutsu] a school of ken-jutsu created by Miyamoto Musashi; it was noted for its use of *kakushi buki,* or concealed weapons

Empi (J) [Karate] the Japanese name for the Okinawan *kata* Wanshu

empi uchi (J) [Karate] elbow strike

en (M) [Common Usage] benevolence

encho (J) [Competitive Budo] extension; overtime

encho hajime (J) [Competitive Budo] beginning of overtime period

enkei (J) [Aikido] circular movement

en no irimi (J) [Aikido] a circular form of the *irimi* technique; developed by Ueshiba Morihei

ennyo-jutsu (J) [Nin-jutsu] an art of infiltrating enemy lines during combat or sabotage missions

enshin (J) [Common Usage] the center of the circle; a preparatory position used for certain group training exercises

Enzan no Metsuke (J) [Kendo] (*lit.* Looking ((As If)) At A Distant Mountain) a method of looking at an opponent without being trapped by what one sees

eobeo deonjigi (K) [Ssi Rum] lifting hip-throwing technique

eoggae (K) [Common Usage] shoulder

eoggae bbyeo (K) [Common Usage] shoulder blade

eoggae dolligi undong (K) [Ssi Rum] shoulder-circling exercise

eoggae makgi (K) [Taekwondo] shoulder block

eoggae neomeo deonjigi (K) [Ssi Rum] technique in which the opponent is lifted on one's shoulders and thrown over the back

eoggae reul dolli da (K) [Common Usage] to turn the shoulders

eoggae ro mil da (K) [Common Usage] to push with the shoulders

eolgul (K) [Common Usage] face

eolgul makgi (K) [Taekwondo] face block, high-level block

eomji (K) [Common Usage] thumb

eong deong baejigi (K) [Ssi Rum] hip-lifting technique

eonjeun hwal (K) [Kung Do] strung bow

eopeokeot (K) [Common Usage] uppercut punch

eopeun pyeonson ggeut (K) [Taekwondo] palm-downward spear-finger

eorini (K) [Common Usage] child

eot georeo makgi (K) [Taekwondo] cross block

er (M) [Common Usage] two

er dwo (M) [Common Usage] *see* yih jai

er hu cang zong (M) [Hong Jia] *see* yih fu chohng jung

eri (J) [Common Usage] lapel, collar

eri dori (J) [Judo, Karate, Aikido] lapel grab

eri jime (J) [Judo] a strangulation technique that uses the lapels of the *judogi* to choke the opponent

erikubi (J) [Common Usage] the nape or back of the neck

eri seoinage (J) [Judo] a throw done by grabbing the opponent's lapels or collar

eri tori waza (J) [Aikido] a set of techniques used against a lapel grab

ermen (M) [Acupressure] a point located near the front area of the ear

Er Shi Ba Su (M) [Bai He] (*lit.* Twenty-Eight Sleeping) a hand form in Ming He

Er Shi Si Quan (M) [Wu Zu Quan] *see* Yi Sahp Sei Kyuhn

Er Shi Zhao Fa (M) [Bai He] (*lit.* Twenty-four Beckoning Method) a hand form in Zong He

etsunen geiko (J) [Common Usage] (*lit.* Year-Crossing Practice) a practice held from eleven in the evening until one in the morning on New Year's Eve; also called *toshikoshi keiko*

euibok su (K) [Kuk Sool, Hapkido] self-defense technique for use when the clothing is grabbed

eui sik (K) [Common Usage] awareness

eum-yang (K) [Common Usage] *yin-yang*

— F —

fa (C) [Common Usage] *see* hua

fa (M) [Common Usage] to punish

faahn (C) [Common Usage] cooked rice

faahn jeuih (C) [Common Usage] to commit an offense, to break a law

faahn kwai (C) [Common Usage] to disobey rules

faahn nouh (C) [Common Usage] to worry; troubles

faai (C) [Common Usage] **1** quick, fast **2** chopsticks

faai lohk (C) [Common Usage] *see* hoi sam

faai maahn (C) [Common Usage] *see* su du

Faai Tou (C) [Pek Gwa Kyuhn] (*lit.* Rapid Set) a hand form

Faan Ji (C) [Style] *see* Fan Zi

Faan Ji Kyuhn (C) [Style] (*lit.* Reverse Son Fist) Continuous Attacking Fist

faan kong (C) [Common Usage] *see* fan kang

Faan Kyuhn (C) [Style] *see* Fan Zi

faan ying (C) [Common Usage] *see* fan ying

faat (C) [Common Usage] method

Faat (C) [Common Usage] *see* Fo

fahn nowh (C) [Common Usage] *see* fennu

Faht (C) [Common Usage] Buddha

faht (C) [Common Usage] *see* fa

Faht (C) [Common Usage] *see* Fo

Faht faat (C) [Common Usage] *see* Fo fa

Faht Ga Kyuhn (C) [Style] (*lit.* Buddha Family Style) A southern style founded by Leuhng Tien Chyu in the early twentieth century that combined the Huhng Ga system and the Choy Ga system.

Faht ging (C) [Common Usage] Buddhist scripture

Faht hohk (C) [Common Usage] Buddhism, the study

Faht Hon Kyuhn (C) [Style] (*lit.* Buddha Fist) a northern style of Chinese martial arts

Faht Jeuhng Kyuhn (C) [Choy Leih Faht] (*lit.* Buddha Palm) a hand form

Faht muhn (C) [Common Usage] (lit. Buddhist Door) Buddhist sect or school; a temple and the disciples there

fai (C) [Common Usage] lungs

fak sau (C) [Wihng Cheun] *see* fat sau

fa ling (M) [Common Usage] *see* jeung chihng

fan (C) [Common Usage] **1** to seal (off) **2** to sleep **3** (*lit.* to Divide, Cent) a Chinese measurement used in weighing herbal medicines

fan (M) [Common Usage] *see* faahn

fan gaau (C) [Common Usage] sleep, slumber

fang bian chan (M) [Weapon] a staff with a flat bell-shaped blade at one end and a spear point at the other

fang chuan he ye (M) [Yang Taijiquan] (*lit.* Wind Blowing The Lotus Leaf) a movement in the Taiji Sword form

fang feng (M) [Medicine] siler; a yellow root used to expel external harmful influences

fang huang shuang chan chi (M) [Yang Taijiquan] (*lit.* The Phoenix Spreads Its Wings) a movement in the Yang Taiji Sword form

Fang Qi Niang (M) [Master] the founder of Bai He

fang sao mei hua (M) [Yang Taijiquan] (*lit.* The Wind Sways The Plum Blossoms) a movement in the Yang Taiji Sword form

fang song (M) [Common Usage] *see* fong sung

fang tian ji (M) [Weapon] A spear that has a crescent-shaped blade on the side of the point, with tassels decorating the base of the blade. The spear is mounted on a wooden shaft and has a spear head on the opposite end.

fang zi (M) [Common Usage] home

fan kang (M) [Common Usage] to resist; resistance

fan nao (M) [Common Usage] *see* faahn nouh

Fan Quan (M) [Style] *see* Fan Zi

fan ying (M) [Common Usage] reaction

Fan Zhi Quan (M) [Style] *see* Faan Ji Kyuhn

Fan Zi (M) [Style] (*lit.* Fluttering or Flying) a northern long-range fighting style that originated at the Shaolin Temple, Fan Zi has also been referred to as Fan Quan (Fluttering Fist) and Ba Shan Fan (Eight Dodge Fluttering)

fat sau (C) [Wihng Cheun] whisking arm

fei (M) [Common Usage] **1** lung **2** (*lit.* to Fly) a key movement in Zhang He

fei dou (C) [Weapon] throwing knives

Fei He (M) [Style] (*lit.* Flying Crane) one of the branches of Bai He, specializing in jumping movements to avoid an attacking opponent

Fei Hok (C) [Style] *see* Fei He

Fei Ngoh Jeuhng (C) [Chat Sing Tohng Lohng] (*lit.* Flying Goose Palm) a hand form

fei zao jia (M) [Medicine] the seed of this plant is used in Chinese herbal medicine

fen (M) [Common Usage] *see* fan

fen (M) [Qin Na] to divide; splitting or dividing an opponent's muscle

feng (M) [Qin Na] to seal

feng bae her yeh (M) [Xingyiquan] *see* feng bei he ye

feng bei he ye (M) [Xingyiquan] (*lit.* Wind Blows the Lotus Leaf) a series of circular hand movements combined with the shifting of stances to redirect an opponent's attack

feng chi (M) [Acupressure] a point located on the left side of the back of the neck

feng fu (M) [Acupressure] a point located on the back of the head at the base of the skull

feng wei (M) [Acupressure] a point located at the base of the shoulder blade

feng xian (M) [Common Usage] *see* fuhng hin

feng xiang quan fa (M) [Hong Jia Quan] *see* fung seung kyuhn faat

feng yan (M) [Acupressure] a point located above the shoulder blade

fennu (M) [Common Usage] to resent; resentment

Fo (M) [Common Usage] Buddha

fo chen (M) [Weapon] a club that is tipped with a long strand of animal hair

Fo fa (M) [Common Usage] Buddha dharma; Buddha doctrine; the power of Buddha

foh (C) [Common Usage] fire; one of the five elements of Chinese cosmology

Fo Han Quan (M) [Style] *see* Faht Hon Kyuhn

Fo Jia (M) [Style] *see* Faht Ga Kyuhn

Fo jing (M) [Common Usage] Buddhist scripture

Fo men (M) [Common Usage] the followers or disciples of Buddha

Fong Chat Neuhng (C) [Master] *see* Fang Qi Niang

fong chuan ho yeh (M) [Yang Taijiquan] *see* fang chuan he ye

fong foong (C) [Medicine] *see* fong fuhng

fong fuhng (C) [Medicine] a root used in Chinese medicine to expel cold and dampness from the body

fong gaan tahng (C) [Medicine] a root used in Chinese medicine for strengthening bones and tendons

fong gan tang (C) [Medicine] *see* fong gaan tahng

fong huang shuang chan chih (M) [Yang Taijiquan] *see* fang huang shuang chan chi

fong sao mei fua (M) [Yang Taijiquan] *see* fang sao mei hua

fong sung (C) [Common Usage] relax

fook sau (C) [Wihng Cheun] *see* fuhk sau

foon gun tang (C) [Medicine] *see* fun guhn tahng

Fo Shan (M) [Common Usage] *see* Faht Saan

Fo xue (M) [Common Usage] Buddhism, the study

fu (C) [Common Usage] *see* hei gun

fu (C) [Common Usage] *see* ku zi

fu (C) [Common Usage] *see* louh fu

fu (C) [Common Usage] tiger; one of the five animals found in Shaolin styles

fu (M) [Common Usage] **1** belly or abdomen **2** axe

fuai chung pao yueh (M) [Yang Taijiquan] *see* huai chong pao yue

fuantei (J) [Common Usage] unbalanced, disequilibrium

fuchi (J) [Weapon] a metal sleeve on the hilt of a Japanese sword; the *fuchi* and the *kashira* were usually paired and made by the same artisan

Fu Daaih Pah (C) [Huhng Ga] (*lit.* Tiger Big Fork) a weapons form using a trident

fude (J) [Common Usage] an ink brush used for calligraphy

fudo (J) [Common Usage] stability

fudo dachi (J) [Karate] a firm posture; a stance in which the feet are shoulder-width apart; also called *sochin dachi*

Fudogata (O) [Karate] a *kata* practiced in Kojo-ryu

fudo no seishin (J) [Zen] *see* fudoshin

fudoshin (J) [Ken-jutsu, Zen] immovable spirit; a state in which one is not moved or influenced by external forces

fudo shisei (J) [Karate] a ready position stance with the feet together

fudoza no kamae (J) [Nin-jutsu] a ninja *kamae* in which one sits in a half-kneeling position to allow one to stand quickly at any time

fu gwat (C) [Medicine] tiger bone; used in Chinese medicine to strengthen the bones of the body

fuh (C) [Common Usage] a seal used for protection and to ward off evil

fuhk fu chohng luhng (C) [Huhng Ga] (*lit.* Lying Tiger and Hidden Dragon) a movement consisting of an open-handed block thrusting downwards

Fuhk Fu Kyuhn (C) [Ying Jaau] (*lit.* Subduing the Tiger) a hand form

fuhk fu lihn jyu (C) [Huhng Ga] (*lit.* Lying Tiger Joining Pearl) a downward block using the palm while standing in a bow and arrow stance.

fuhk sau (C) [Wihng Cheun] bridge on arm

fuhng hin (C) [Common Usage] dedication

Fu Hohk Paai (C) [Style] (*lit.* Tiger Crane Style) a southern style that mimics the movements of the tiger and crane; commonly referred to as Naahm Kyuhn

Fu Hohk Seung Yihng Kyuhn (C) [Huhng Ga] (*lit.* Tiger Crane Double Form Fist) a hand form that mimics the fighting movements of the tiger and the crane

Fu Hua Qiu (M) [Master] a prominent master of baguazhang

fu hu cang long (M) [Hong Jia] *see* fuhk fu chohng luhng

fu hu lian zhu (M) [Hong Jia] *see* fuhk fu lihn jyu

fui (C) [Common Usage] to regret, to repent

fui fuhk (C) [Common Usage] *see* hui fu

fuijai (O) [Common Usage] left

fui sing tek dau (C) [Huhng Ga] (*lit.* A Streaking Star Kicking the Heavens) a crane stance with the hands forming tight fists at waist level

fu jaau (C) [Common Usage] tiger claw

Fu Jia Jian (M) [Fu Jia] (*lit.* Fu Family Sword) a weapons form using the straight sword

Fujian (M) [Common Usage] a province that is situated in the southeast coastal area of Mainland China

Fu Jia Quan (M) [Style] (*lit.* Fu Family Fist) a northern style of Chinese martial arts

Fuji-san (J) [Common Usage] Mount Fuji

Fujiwara (J) [Common Usage] a noble family which governed Japan from the ninth to twelfth century

fujubun (J) [Competitive Budo] a term used by a referee when a valid technique was not present

fuk (C) [Common Usage] *see* fu

Fukien (C) [Common Usage] *see* Fujian

fukiya (J) [Nin-jutsu] a blow gun used by ninja; often disguised as flutes or umbrellas, these blow guns would be used to shoot poisoned darts

fuk luhk sauh (C) [Common Usage] fortune, wisdom, longevity; the Gods of fortune, wisdom, longevity

fuku (O) [Common Usage] heart

fukubu (J) [Common Usage] abdomen

fukubu geri (J) [Karate] abdominal kick

Fukuda Hachinosuke (J) [Master] a master of Tenshin Shin-yo-ryu and one of Kano Jigoro's primary teachers

fukuju (J) [Common Usage] obedience

fukumi bari (J) [Nin-jutsu] small darts spat out from the mouth at the opponent's eyes

Fukuno-ryu (J) [Kempo] a school of kempo founded in the early Edo period by Fukuno Shichiroemon of the Kito-ryu

fukura (J) [Weapon] the curvature of the cutting edge at the point of a Japanese sword

fukuro (J) [Common Usage] bag

fukuro gaeshi no jutsu (J) [Nin-jutsu] a tactic used by ninja in which they seemingly leave their lord to be taken in by one of the rival lords, only to betray their new master in a time of crisis

fukuro shinai (J) [Kendo] leather or cloth covered *shinai* used in training in place of a *bokuto* or *katana*

fuku shidoin (J) [Aikido] (*lit.* Assistant Instructor) teaching license or certification given by the Aikikai to an aikido instructor ranked *nidan* or *sandan*

fukushin (J) [Competitive Budo] an assistant referee

fukushin shugo (J) [Competitive Budo] a term referring to when the head referee calls the assistant referee(s) toward him for discussion

Fukyugata (O) [Karate] a set of basic *kata* practiced in Matsubayashi Shorin-ryu

Fu Kyuhn (C) [Style] *see* Hu Quan

fu long bo (M) [Weapon] a set of earthenware bowls, decorated with dragon designs, that are used as weapons in some Chinese styles

fu lu shou (M) [Common Usage] *see* fuk luhk sauh

fu meih geuk (C) [Common Usage] Tiger Tail Kick

Fu Meih Saam Jit Gwan (C) [Chat Sing Tohng Lohng] (*lit.* Tiger Tail Three Section Staff) a weapons form using a three-section wooden staff

Fu Meih Saam Jit Gwan (C) [Ngh Jou Kyuhn] (*lit.* Tiger Tail Three Joint Staff) a weapons form using the three-section wooden staff

fumiashi (J) [Nin-jutsu, Suiei-jutsu] to tread water

fumi kiri (J) [Karate] a kick with the edge of the foot usually against the opponent's leg or knee

fumi komi (J) [Karate] stamping kick; a kick thrusting downwards using the heel or edge of the foot as the striking surface

fumikomu (J) [Common Usage] to step inside, to penetrate

fumiuchi (J) [Karate] a strike done while moving forward

fumu (J) [Common Usage] to move, to take a step

Funakoshi Gichin (J) [Karate] The founder of Shotokan karate and considered by many to be the "Father of Japanese karate." Born in Okinawa and a student of Shuri-te, he was one of the first Okinawans to demonstrate karate in mainland Japan, at the Kyoto Butokuden in 1917.

fundoshi (J) [Common Usage] a cotton loincloth worn by Japanese males

fung (C) [Kahm Na] *see* feng

fung seui si (C) [Common Usage] (*lit.* Wind Water Teacher) a geomancer; a person who studies the art of divination by means of the configuration of the earth

fung seung kyuhn faat (C) [Huhng Ga] (*lit.* Wind Box Fist) a straight punch attack using the right hand

fun guhn tahng (C) [Medicine] the whole plant is used in Chinese medicine to strengthen tendons

fun hei (C) [Common Usage] *see* shuan xi

fun yihng (C) [Common Usage] to welcome

fu pao tou (M) [Yang Taijiquan] (*lit.* Tiger Holds its Head) a movement in the Yang Taiji Sword form

fu pen zi (M) [Medicine] the fruit of this plant is used in Chinese herbal medicine

fureru (J) [Common Usage] to make contact, to touch

furikaburu (J) [Common Usage] to raise a weapon (especially a sword) over one's head

furikabute (J) [Iaido] preparatory movement made before cutting; the sword is raised forty-five degrees above the head with both hands, then swung down to execute the cut

furitsuki (J) [Karate] roundhouse punch

furoshiki (J) [Common Usage] a cloth used to wrap and carry small objects

furu (J) [Kendo] to swing the *shinai*

fu sau puhn (C) [Common Usage] the hand protective plate of a broadsword

fusenhai (J) [Competitive Budo] a loss by default

fusensho (J) [Competitive Budo] a win by default

Fu Sheng Yuan (M) [Master] a prominent master of Yang taijiquan

Fu Shi Baguazhang (M) [Style] a style of baguazhang created by Fu Zhen Song

futa ashi dachi (J) [Karate] two-legged stance

Futagoyama (J) [Sumo] a sumo *beya* located in Nakano Ward, Tokyo

futari (J) [Common Usage] two; used when referring to people

futaridori (J) [Karate] practice against multiple opponents

futatsu (J) [Common Usage] two; used as a general counter for most objects

fu tauh (C) [Weapon] axe

Fut Gar Kune (C) [Style] *see* Faht Ga Kyuhn

futokoro (J) [Common Usage] chest

futokoro teppo (J) [Weapon] a small pistol usually carried concealed in a pocket

Fu Ying Kyuhn (C) [Choy Leih Faht] (*lit.* Tiger Shape Form) a hand form

Fu Ying Kyuhn Deui Chuk Hok Ying Kyuhn (C) [Choy Leih Faht] (*lit.* Tiger Versus Crane) a two-man fighting form

Fu Zhen Song (M) [Master] the founder of Fu Shi baguazhang

Fu Zhong Wen (M) [Master] a prominent master of Yang taijiquan

— **G** —

ga (C) [Common Usage] family; commonly used in southern styles of Chinese martial arts to describe a particular family branch or style

gaai kyut (C) [Common Usage] to solve a problem

gaai sik (C) [Common Usage] to explain

gaai siuh (C) [Common Usage] to recommend

gaak (C) [Common Usage] skeleton

Gaam Jung Jaau (C) [Style] *see* jing zhong zhao

gaap (C) [Common Usage] nail, toenail

gaap gwat mahn (C) [Common Usage] oracle bone scripture; the earliest form of Chinese writing; found on pieces of turtle shells and animal bones

gaat lihng (C) [Common Usage] *see* jeung chihng

gaau (C) [Kahm Na] to twist

gaau fan (C) [Common Usage] lesson, lecture

gaau waaht (C) [Common Usage] sly, cunning, devious

gabyeopge ddwi da (K) [Common Usage] to skip

Gae Baek hyeong (K) [Taekwondo] *see* Kae Baek hyung

gaeshi (J) [Common Usage] *see* kaeshi

gaesok ha da (K) [Common Usage] to continue

gahn sau (C) [Wihng Cheun] splitting block

gai (C) [Common Usage] rooster

gai (M) [Nanquan] (*lit.* to cover) overhead punch; a key movement

gai juhk (C) [Common Usage] to continue

gaiwan (J) [Common Usage] outer forearm

gaji chigi (K) [Tae Kyon] strike to the neck with the blade of the hand

ga jihk (C) [Common Usage] worth, value

gakdo (K) [Common Usage] angle

gake (J) [Common Usage] *see* kake

gak gung (K) [Kung Do] bow

gakgweon (K) [Kuk Sool, Hapkido] backfist

Gak Jeo Chong (K) [Common Usage] tomb in Manchuria that contains ancient wall paintings of martial poses, created by Koreans when the Koguryo dynasty ruled the area

gak ji (K) [Kung Do] thumb ring for drawing a bow in archery practice

gakko (J) [Common Usage] school

gaku (J) [Common Usage] **1** a framed picture hung inside a dojo, usually of the style founder or a great *sensei* **2** the study of something; a science or academic discipline

galbi (K) [Common Usage] ribs

galbi bbyeo (K) [Common Usage] rib bone

gallyeo (K) [Taekwondo] command to "break" or "stop sparring"

gam (C) [Common Usage] gold; one of the five elements in Chinese cosmological theory

gaman (J) [Common Usage] persevere, endure

gam chihng (C) [Common Usage] *see* gan qing

gam chou (C) [Medicine] the root of this plant is used in

Chinese medicine to balance other herbal ingredients and as a germicidal agent

Gam Fa Cheung (C) [Ngh Jou Kyuhn] (*lit.* Golden Blossom Spear) a weapons form using the spear

Gam Gai Duhk Lahp Daan Dou (C) [Ngh Jou Kyuhn] (*lit.* Golden Chicken Standing Single Sword) a weapons form using the broadsword

gam gok (C) [Common Usage] to sense, to feel, to touch

gam gong cheut duhng (C) [Huhng Ga] (*lit.* Golden Strong Comes Out Of Cave) an open-handed upward block with the elbows slightly bent, executed while in a horse stance

Gam Gong Kyuhn (C) [Sai Chong Baahk Hok Kyuhn] a hand form

Gam Hok (C) [Fei Hok Kyuhn] *see* Jin He

gam jeh (C) [Common Usage] to thank

gam jeom (K) [Taekwondo] point deduction in sparring competition

gam kiuh seung dihng (C) [Huhng Ga] (*lit.* Golden Bridge Comes to a Stop) a blocking movement using both hands that is accomplished by sinking the elbows and the wrists with the fingers of the hands pointing upwards

gam luhng jaau (C) [Huhng Ga] (*lit.* Golden Dragon Claw) an empty-hand technique

gam ngaan chyun lihn (C) [Chyu Ga] *see* jin ya chuan lian

Gam Paau Kyuhn Deui Chuk Fu Ying Kyuhn (C) [Choy Leih Faht] (*lit.* Golden Leopard Versus Tiger) a two-man fighting form

gam sau (C) [Wihng Cheun] pinning hand

gam sik (C) [Common Usage] gold color

gam suhk (C) [Common Usage] metal

Gam Yihng Luhk Dau Sau Kyuhn (C) [Baahk Hok] (*lit.* Golden Shape Six Hand Fist) a hand form

gan (C) [Common Usage] **1** heel of the foot **2** tendon **3** to follow

gan (J) [Common Usage] eye

gan bei (M) [Common Usage] to empty one's glass or cup; toasting to someone or to someone's health

gan jeung (C) [Common Usage] nervous

gan jing (M) [Common Usage] clean

ganka (J) [Acupressure] a vital point located between the fifth and sixth rib

Gankaku (J) [Karate] (*lit.* Crane on a Rock) a karate *kata;* also known as Chinto

gan lan (M) [Medicine] the fruit of this plant is used in Chinese herbal medicine

ganmen (J) [Kendo] face; front of the head

Ganmen Ate (J) [Iaido] the fourth *kata* done from *iaihiza* in the Tachiai no Bu of the Zen Nihon Kendo Renmei Seitei Iai

ganmen zuki (J) [Karate] straight thrust to the face

gan qing (M) [Common Usage] feelings

ganseki otoshi (J) [Judo, Aikido] (*lit.* Stone Drop) a rarely used judo technique; in aikido, a type of *irimi nage*

gan shan (C) [Common Usage] careful, cautious

gan sui (M) [Medicine] the root of this plant is used to reduce swelling

gan xie (M) [Common Usage] *see* gam jeh

gan yuan bang (M) [Weapon] a club

gao (M) [Common Usage] *see* gou

Gao Yan Tao (M) [Master] a prominent master of Nan Quan

gapgweon (K) [Tang Soo Do] backfist

gar (C) [Common Usage] *see* ga

garami (J) [Judo, Aikido] *see* karami

garangi (K) [Common Usage] crotch, area between the legs

gari (J) [Judo] *see* kari

garo makgi (K) [Taekwondo, Tae Kyon] **1** a Taekwondo cross block **2** circular upward hand block in Tae Kyon

garo milgi (K) [Tae Kyon] upward pushing strike

gasae makgi (K) [Tae Kyon] cross block, X-block

gaseum (K) [Common Usage] chest

Gassan-ryu (J) [Naginata] a nineteenth-century school of *naginata*

Gassente (O) [Karate] a *kata* practiced in Motobu-ryu

gassho (J) [Zen] the act of placing both hands in front of the body vertically and touching, it is used in Zen to symbolize the unity of one's body and one's spirit

gassho kamae (J) [Shorinji Kempo] a salutation or greeting

gassho no kamae (J) [Nin-jutsu] a *kamae* used by ninja

ga tihng (C) [Common Usage] family

gau (C) [Common Usage] **1** dog **2** to save

Gau Bo Tui (C) [Baahk Meih] a hand form

Gau Duhk Kyuhn (C) [Huhng Ga] (*lit.* Nine Special Fist) a hand form

Gau Hyun Daaih Dou (C) [Choy Leih Faht] (*lit.* Nine-Ringed Long-Handled Broad Sword Form) a weapons form

Gau Kyuhn (C) [Style] *see* Gou Quan

gaun sau (C) [Wihng Cheun] *see* gahn sau

gawa (J) [Common Usage] side

gawimakgi (K) [Taekwondo] scissor block, X-block

gawi son ggeut (K) [Taekwondo] scissor spear-finger

ge (M) [Common Usage] armpit

gedan (J) [Common Usage] lower level

gedan barai (J) [Karate] downward block; lower-level sweeping block

gedan choku zuki (J) [Karate] a straight punch to the mid-section

gedan kake uke (J) [Karate] downward hooking block

gedan no kamae (J) [Kendo, Naginata] a low *kamae* used primarily for defensive movements

gedan tensho uke (J) [Karate] a low block with the heel of the hand

gedan tsuki (J) [Karate] lower-level punch or strike

gee ng diu tie ma (C) [Wihng Cheun] *see* ji ngh diu tai mah

gee ng ma (C) [Wihng Cheun] *see* ji ngh mah

gee yin tong (C) [Medicine] *see* ji yihn tong

gei (C) [Common Usage] *see* gei yuhk

gei cho (C) [Common Usage] *see* ji chu

gei dak (C) [Common Usage] to remember

gei gwaan (C) [Common Usage] trap

geih seuht (C) [Common Usage] *see* ji shu

geiko (J) [Common Usage] *see* keiko

gei yuhk (C) [Common Usage] muscle

gekiguan (O) [Weapon] a meter-long staff with a weighted chain attached to one end

Gekisai (O) [Karate] two basic *kata* practiced in Goju-ryu

gekken (J) [Kendo] a term used by the military during the Meiji era to refer to kendo

gen (M) [Common Usage] heel

gendai bu-jutsu (J) [Common Usage] modern martial arts; used in contrast to kobudo and kobu-jutsu

geng (C) [Common Usage] neck

geng (C) [Common Usage] *see* xia

genin (J) [Nin-jutsu] (*lit.* Lower Person) a ninja of low rank who was often used to carry out highly dangerous missions

Genkai-ryu (J) [style] a school of *yoroi kumiuchi*

Gensei-ryu (J) [Karate] a school of karate known for its tumbling exercises

genshi (J) [Common Usage] intuition; the ability to second guess the attacker's movements

geobuk seon (K) [Common Usage] turtle-shaped ironclad warship created by Admiral Yi Sun-Sin

geodeo chagi (K) [Tae Kyon] front kick that strikes with the toes

geodeup chagi (K) [Common Usage] double kick

geolchyeo chagi (K) [Taekwondo] hooking kick

geolchyeo makgi (K) [Taekwondo] hooking block

Geom Do (K) [Style] *see* kum do

geom gaek (K) [Kum Do] swordsman

geomjeong (K) [Common Usage] black

geomjeong ddi (K) [Common Usage] black belt

geommu (K) [Kum Do] ancient Korean sword dance

geommu hyeong (K) [Kuk Sool] sword-dance form

geom sul (k) [Style] *see* kum sool

geongang (K) [Common Usage] health

geongang ha da (K) [Common Usage] to be healthy

geopu ddanjuk (K) [Tae Kyon] ankle-level cross kick

georeo chagi (K) [Taekwondo] tackling kick

georeum (K) [Common Usage] walk, step

geri (J) [Common Usage] *see* keri

gesa gatame (J) [Judo] scarf hold

geta (J) [Common Usage] wooden clogs

geu jari dolgi (K) [Common Usage] stationary turn, turning in one place

geuk (C) [Common Usage] leg

geuk ji (C) [Common Usage] toe

geuk ji gaap (C) [Common Usage] *see* jyau ji jya

geuk jong (C) [Choy Leih Faht] leg dummy

geuk ngaahn (C) [Common Usage] ankle

geuman (K) [Common Usage] a command to "stop" or "break"

Geum Gang ap jireugi (K) [Taekwondo] diamond front punch

Geum Gang jangsa geup (K) [Ssi Rum] under 80-kilogram weight class of professional competition

Geum Gang pumse (K) [Taekwondo] *see* Kum Kang poomsae

Geum Gang Yeok Sa (K) [Common Usage] *see* Kum Kang Yuk Sa

geung woot (C) [Medicine] *see* geung wuht

geung wuht (C) [Medicine] the root of this plant is used in Chinese medicine to expel cold and dampness from the body

geunyuk (K) [Common Usage] muscle

geunyuk eul pyeo da (K) [Common Usage] to stretch the muscles

geup (K) [Taekwondo] grade under black belt

geup simsa pyo (K) [Taekwondo] grade testing form

geup so (K) [Taekwondo] vital point, vulnerable point

ggak eum geori (K) [Tae Kyon] stomping kick directed at the front of the shin

ggeokgi (K) [Hapkido] joint-locking technique

ggok dwi jipgi (K) [Ssi Rum] back-of-the-head grasping technique

Ggungssyangjwin hyeong (K) [Tang Soo Do] form named after a karate form composed of 134 movements

gi (J) [Common Usage] **1** uniform **2** justice, duty, honor, humility; one of the virtues of bushido

gi (K) [Common Usage] *see* ki

gibon (K) [Common Usage] basics

gibon dongjak (K) [Common Usage] basic movement

gibon hyeong (K) [Kuk Sool] basic form

gibon jase (K) [Kuk Sool] basic posture

gibon makgi (K) [Hapkido] basic block

gibon son gisul (K) [Common Usage] basic hand technique

gibon su (K) [Kuk Sool] basic hand technique

gibon suryeon (K) [Taekwondo] basic exercise, fundamental exercise

gibyeong (K) [Common Usage] cavalry

gibyeong do (K) [Common Usage] cavalry sword, saber

gibyeong janggyo (K) [Common Usage] cavalry soldier

gicho dongjak (K) [Common Usage] basic movement

gicho hyeong (K) [Kuk Sool, Tang Soo Do] fundamental form

gicho jjagi (K) [Kuk Sool] basic lower-abdominal breathing procedure

gicho undong (K) [Common Usage] basic exercise

gifa (O) [Common Usage] a decorative hairpin used by both men and women; used as a spike-like weapon

gigong (K) [Common Usage] *see* kikong

gihap (K) [Common Usage] *see* kihap

gihn chyuhn (C) [Common Usage] *see* gihn hong

gihng (C) [Common Usage] powerful, awesome

gihng (C) [Common Usage] *see* jing

gihn hong (C) [Common Usage] to be healthy, in good health

Giin (J) [Karate] a *kata* that concentrates on hand techniques, employing only one kick

gijeol ha da (K) [Common Usage] to be knocked out

gijeol siki da (K) [Common Usage] to knock out (someone)

gik (C) [Weapon] a spear head with a half crescent-shaped blade mounted on a staff

gik liht (C) [Common Usage] violent

gim (C) [Weapon] double-edged sword

gim (C) [Weapon] *see* jian

giman (K) [Common Usage] feint

giman ha da (K) [Common Usage] to feint

gimarip jase (K) [Tang Soo Do] horse-riding posture

gima seogi (K) [Taekwondo] horse-riding stance

gim bing (C) [Common Usage] straight sword handle

Gimbo (O) [Karate] one of five empty-hand *kata* introduced
    to the Meibukan Goju-ryu system by Yagi Meitoku

gim dau (C) [Common Usage] straight sword blade

gim gaak (C) [Common Usage] (*lit.* Sword Pattern) the mark-
    ing along the blade of a straight sword

gim jim (C) [Common Usage] straight sword tip

gim pou (C) [Common Usage] a book on sword forms

gim san (C) [Common Usage] (*lit.* Sword Body) the blade of
    a straight sword

gim sau (C) [Common Usage] (*lit.* Sword Head) the area at
    the end of the handle were tassels are attached

gin (C) [Common Usage] *see* jian

ging (C) [Common Usage] **1** shin **2** channel, meridian, a path-
    way for *qi*

ging chah (C) [Common Usage] to toast tea

ging fong (C) [Common Usage] *see* xia

ging gou (C) [Common Usage] warning

ging hei (C) [Common Usage] surprise; to be surprised; amaze-
    ment

ging jau (C) [Common Usage] to toast somebody

ging nga (C) [Common Usage] *see* jiu gya

ging syu (C) [Common Usage] Buddhist scripture or book

gin ji fu li shih (M) [Xingyiquan] *see* jin ji fu li xi

gin ji shang bu (M) [Xingyiquan] *see* jin ji shang bu

gin ji shang jia (M) [Xingyiquan] (*lit.* Golden Rooster on the
    Perch) a swinging of the arms commonly used to block
    attacks to the upper area of the body

gin ji shang jiah (M) [Xingyiquan] *see* gin ji shang jia

gin jong jaw (M) [Common Usage] *see* jing zhong zhao

Gi no Sho (J) [Sumo] (*lit.* Technique Prize) a prize awarded to the *rikishi* who displayed outstanding technique during a tournament

giri (J) [Bushido] a sense of duty or obligation arising from personal honor and pride

gisul (K) [Common Usage] technique, skill

giu (C) [Common Usage] to be proud; arrogant

giu ngouh (C) [Common Usage] proud

Giwaken (J) [Shorinji Kempo] a empty-hand *kata;* also called Tenchiken

go (J) [Common Usage] five

gobu no tsume (J) [Kyudo] the five final movements involved in tensing the bow

godan (J) [Common Usage] fifth-degree black belt rank, 5th Dan

godan ja (K) [Common Usage] a high-ranking black belt

godeun baljil (K) [Tae Kyon] walking kick

godeun dari (K) [Common Usage] straight leg

godeun jase (K) [Common Usage] erect posture

godeun meori (K) [Common Usage] erect head

godeun mom (K) [Common Usage] erect body

godeun pal (K) [Common Usage] straight arm

godo (J) [Zen] a keeper of a Zen dojo

gogeup (K) [Common Usage] high level

gogeup ban (K) [Kuk Sool] high-level course

gogeup hyeong (K) [Kuk Sool] high-level form

gogi (J) [Common Usage] consultation; this term is used when a center referee consults an arbitrator or other official prior to making a call

Goguryeo sidae (K) [Common Usage] *see* Koguryo sidae

Goguryeo wangjo (K) [Common Usage] *see* Koguryo wangjo

gogyo (J) [Common Usage] the five elements of Chinese cosmology: *ka* (fire), *sui* (water), *do* (earth), *moku* (wood), and *kin* (metal)

gogyo no kamae (J) [Kendo] five basic ready positions: *jodan, chudan, gedan, hasso no kamae,* and *waki gamae*

Gohakukai (O) [Style] a style of karate established by Toka-shiki Iken, an instructor of both Goju-ryu and Tomari-te

gohei (J) [Sumo] zigzag strips of white paper that hang from the *tsuna* of a Yokozuna

goho (J) [Shorinji Kempo] the "hard" or sparring techniques of the system; the striking, punching, and kicking techniques

gohon kumite (J) [Karate] an exercise consisting of five forward attacks coupled with five backward defenses

go hwan (K) [Common Usage] groin

gojeong seogi (K) [Taekwondo] fixed stance

go jo (J) [Bushido] the five virtues of a warrior: *chi* (wisdom), *gi* (justice), *jin* (benevolence), *rei* (courtesy), and *shin* (fidelity)

Goju-ryu (O) [Style] A style of Okinawan karate named and systematized by Miyagi Chojun. This Okinawan style concentrates on blending hard *(go)* and soft *(ju)* movements. The style's name was taken from a passage in the *Bubishi*.

Gojushiho (J) [Karate] (*lit.* Fifty-Four Steps) a pair of Okinawan *kata* derived from Useishi; individually the *kata* are called Gojushiho Sho and Gojushiho Dai

gojutai no waza (J) [Shorinji Kempo] basic breathing and stretching exercises

gokaku geiko (J) [Kendo, Naginata] practice sparring in a free-style manner

Gok Jin Kyuhn (C) [Baahk Hok] (*lit.* Horn Battle Fist) a hand form

gok ngh (C) [Common Usage] *see* jue wu

goko (J) [Weapon] a short stick-like weapon that has five points

gokseon (K) [Common Usage] curve

gok sut (C) [Common Usage] (*lit.* National Technique) martial arts

gokui (J) [Common Usage] techniques not usually revealed to the average student; sometimes referred to as hidden techniques

gokyo (J) [Judo, Aikido] **1** (*lit.* Five Categories of Technique) a set of forty techniques, divided into five equal categories, in

Kodokan judo **2** the fifth basic hold learned in the Aikikai school of aikido; also referred to as *tekubiosae*

gokyu (J) [Karate] fifth level or 5th Kyu

gom (K) [Common Usage] bear

Goma (J) [Common Usage] a fire ceremony for invocation of Buddhist deities, often performed for protection and special inspiration

gomen nasai (J) [Common Usage] sorry; pardon me

gom son (K) [Taekwondo] bear hand, bear claw

gon (C) [Common Usage] liver

gon (K) [Common Usage] club

gon bui (C) [Common Usage] *see* gan bei

gong (C) [Common Usage] **1** work; to achieve something **2** energy or work **3** Chinese bell; used in lion dance performances

gong (C) [Common Usage] *see* shuo

Gong Bang Beop (K) [Style] (*lit.* Attack Defense Way) ancient set of unsystematized Korean combat skills

gong bu (M) [Common Usage] bow stance

gongbu ha da (K) [Common Usage] to study

gong fu (M) [Common Usage] (*lit.* Hard Work) Chinese martial arts

gong gong (M) [Common Usage] public

gonggyeok (K) [Common Usage] attack, offense

gonggyeok bal chagi (K) [Common Usage] offensive kick

gonggyeok eul junghwa ha da (K) [Common Usage] to neutralize an attack

gonggyeok gakdo (K) [Common Usage] angle of attack

gonggyeok gi (K) [Taekwondo] attack technique

gonggyeok gisul (K) [Common Usage] attack technique

gonggyeok ha da (K) [Common Usage] to attack

gonggyeok ja (K) [Common Usage] attacker

gonggyeok jase (K) [Kuk Sool] offensive posture, attack posture

gonggyeok mit makgi bui (K) [Taekwondo] striking and blocking points

gonggyeok mugi (K) [Common Usage] offensive weapons

gong gyeong (K) [Common Usage] respect

Gong Ja (K) [Common Usage] Confucius

gong jeung (C) [Common Usage] uppercut palm thrust

gong ji (M) [Common Usage] *see* gung gik

gongjung deonjigi (K) [Ssi Rum] mid-air throwing technique

gongjung jebi (K) [Common Usage] somersault

gongjung nakbeop (K) [Kuk Sool] midair falling method; an aerial somersault followed by a controlled fall

gongjung yeop chagi (K) [Kuk Sool] midair side kick

Gong Lek Kyuhn (C) [Ying Jaau] (*lit.* Power Fist) a hand form

gong ping (M) [Common Usage] *see* gung pihng

Gong Su Do (K) [Style] *see* Kong Soo Do

gong sun (M) [Acupressure] a point located on the inner-edge of the foot

gong wuh (C) [Common Usage] martial arts society

gon jehng (C) [Common Usage] *see* gan jing

go no sen (J) [Common Usage] reactive or responsive initiative; to wait to perform a technique until after an attacker has launched his; also referred to as *go no saki*

Gorin no Sho (J) [Common Usage] *The Book of Five Rings;* written by Miyamoto Musashi, this book on strategy and philosophy is considered by many to be one of the greatest works on the subject ever written

Goryeo pumse (K) [Taekwondo] *see* Koryo poomsae

Goryeo sidae (K) [Common Usage] *see* Koryo sidae

Goryeo wangjo (K) [Common Usage] *see* Koryo wangjo

goshi (J) [Common Usage] *see* koshi

goshin (J) [Common Usage] self-defense

goshindo (J) [Common Usage] a modern manifestation of goshin-jutsu

goshin-jutsu (J) [Common Usage] self-defense techniques; a *kata* in Kodokan judo

Gosoku-ryu (J) [Karate] a modern system of karate developed by Kubota Takayuki in Los Angeles, California

goso nawa (J) [Hojo-jutsu] *see* inchi nawa

gotong eul cham da (K) [Common Usage] to endure pain

gottsuan (J) [Sumo] "thank you" in sumo slang

gou (C) [Common Usage] tall in height

gou (M) [Common Usage] hook

gou jong ma (C) [Common Usage] high horse stance

gou lian qiang (M) [Weapon] A spear with blades that resemble an inverted trident with its outer prongs curved outwards and tassels at the base of the trident blade. The spear is mounted on a wooden shaft and has a spearhead on the opposite end.

Gou Quan (M) [Style] (*lit.* Dog Fist) a southern Chinese style originating in China's Fujian Province that specializes in ground fighting; also known as Di Shu Quan

goyangi seogi (K) [Taekwondo] cat stance

goyu musul (K) [Common Usage] indigenous martial art

gu (C) [Common Usage] to guess, to speculate

gu (K) [Common Usage] nine

gu (M) [Common Usage] **1** thigh **2** to be strong **3** drum; an instrument used in lion dance performances

gu (M) [Common Usage] *see* daaih bei

gu (M) [Common Usage] *see* gwat

gua (M) [Qin Na] to hang up

Gua Dao (M) [Gou Quan] (*lit.* Trigram Sword) a weapons form using a broadsword

gua hong (M) [Common Usage] *see* gwa huhng

guai shoko (J) [Acupressure] a vital point on the back side of the fist

guan (M) [Common Usage] *see* gwun

Guan Fei Jiang (M) [Master] *see* Gwaan Fei Gong

Guangdong (C) [Common Usage] a province of southern China, commonly known as Canton

Guangdong Sahp Fu (C) [Common Usage] (*lit.* Ten Tigers of Guangdong) a group of Chinese masters reputed to have been the best fighters in all of southern China

guang rong (M) [Common Usage] *see* gwong wihng

guan xia (M) [Common Usage] *see* hung jai

gub da (K) [Common Usage] to be bent

gubeun (K) [Common Usage] curved, bent

gubeun dari (K) [Common Usage] bent leg

gubeun pal (K) [Common Usage] bent arm

gubhi da (K) [Common Usage] to flex, to bend (something)

guburigi (K) [Common Usage] flexion

gudan (K) [Common Usage] ninth-degree black belt

gui (M) [Common Usage] spirit or ghost

guih (C) [Common Usage] exhausted, tired

gui tou da dao (M) [Weapon] A broadsword with the point
  curved into a swirl that is mounted on the head of a staff. The
  opposite end of the shaft has a small spear point.

gui tou dan dao (M) [Weapon] a broadsword with a blade tip
  so flexible that it forms a coil that can be used to whip

gui ze (M) [Common Usage] **1** rules **2** strength

gu jap (C) [Common Usage] stubborn

gu jeung (C) [Common Usage] to applaud; applause

guji (J) [Shinto] the chief Shinto priest of a shrine

guk (K) [Common Usage] nation

gukgi (K) [Common Usage] flag

gukgi bae rye (K) [Common Usage] a command to "salute
  the flag"

Guk Gi Do (K) [Style] *see* Kuk Ki Do

gukgi e daehayeo gyeongnye (K) [Common Usage] a command to "bow to the flag"

Guk Gi Weon (K) [Taekwondo] *see* Kuk Ki Won

guk gung (C) [Common Usage] to bow, the act of paying
  respects

Guk Gung (K) [Style] (*lit.* National Archery) Korean archery

guksa (K) [Buddhism] a title meaning "highest-ranking monk
  in the nation"

Guk Sul (K) [Style] *see* Kuk Sool

gu laih (C) [Common Usage] to support, to cheer on

gulleo ap chagi (K) [Taekwondo] rolling front snap kick

gulleo chagi (K) [Taekwondo] rolling kick

gulleo dollyeo chagi (K) [Taekwondo] rolling roundhouse kick

gulleo yeop chagi (K) [Taekwondo] rolling side kick

gum chihn chaan (C) [Weapon] (*lit.* Golden Coin Shovel) a weapon consisting of a staff with a large metallic circular plate on one end, resembling a Chinese coin

gum cho (C) [Medicine] *see* gam chou

gum sau (C) [Wihng Cheun] *see* gam sau

gun (M) [Common Usage] *see* gwan

gun (M) [Weapon] staff

gunbai (J) [Sumo] a war fan; a fan used by the *gyoji* in a sumo match

gung (C) [Common Usage] energy or work

gung do (K) [Style] *see* kung do

gung douh (C) [Common Usage] fair

gung fu (C) [Common Usage] (*lit.* Hard Work) Chinese martial arts

gung gik (C) [Common Usage] to attack

gung git (K) [Kung Do] feathers on an arrow

gun gi (K) [Common Usage] discipline

Gung Jih Fuhk Fu Kyuhn (C) [Huhng Ga] (*lit.* Subduing the Tiger Fist) the oldest hand form in this style, it was developed by Huhng Hei Gun and contains all the basic movements of the Huhng Ga style

gung jung (C) [Common Usage] *see* gong gong

Gung Jung Musul (K) [Style] (*lit.* Palace Martial Skill) a set of martial skills purportedly used by palace guards prior to the twentieth century

gung pihng (C) [Common Usage] justice, fairness, equal

gung su (K) [Kung Do] archer

gung sul (K) [Style] *see* kung sool

gung sul ga (K) [Kung Do] archer

gun gwan (C) [Common Usage] first-place winner

gun haht (C) [Common Usage] *see* hung jai

gun jung (C) [Common Usage] spectators

gunki (J) [Common Usage] military discipline

gunpo (J) [Common Usage] military strategy

gunsa hak (K) [Common Usage] military science

gunsa hullyeon (K) [Common Usage] military training

guntai (J) [Common Usage] military troops

gunto (J) [Common Usage] military-issue *katana*

gun yam (C) [Common Usage] goddess of mercy

gun zhn bao dao (M) [Weapon] a specialized broadsword used as a weapon in Shaolin-based gong fu

guo (M) [Common Usage] a nation, a country, an empire

guo shu (M) [Common Usage] National art; the Chinese martial arts; this term was first used to denote Chinese martial arts in 1928 at the founding of the Nanjing Central Guoshu Institute

Guo Yun Shen (M) [Master] a prominent master of baguazhang and a fourth-generation disciple

gu pan (M) [Common Usage] pelvis, hips

gu sahn (C) [Common Usage] to look after the body; an exercise that strengthens and stabilizes the spirit

gusan jo (O) [Weapon] a heavy short staff with an ovoid cross section, approximately one meter in length

gusip (K) [Common Usage] ninety

gusip do (K) [Common Usage] ninety-degree angle

gusip do dolgi (K) [Common Usage] ninety-degree turn

gu zhi (M) [Common Usage] *see* gu jap

gwa (C) [Kahm Na] *see* gua

gwaai (C) [Common Usage] obedient, good

gwaai ji (C) [Medicine] a stem of a plant used in Chinese medicine to expel cold and dampness from the body

gwaan dou (C) [Weapon] a crescent-shaped halberd named after Gwaan Gung

Gwaan Fei Gong (C) [Master] a prominent Huhng Ga master who was taught by Dang Fong

Gwaan Gung (C) [Common Usage] General Gwaan, a military leader during the Three Kingdoms period who is now considered to be a god of war

Gwa Dou (C) [Gau Kyuhn] *see* Gua Dao

gwa huhng (C) [Common Usage] *(lit.* to Hang the Red) a red ribbon with a bow and a small metal mirror to reflect evil spirits, usually tied on the horn of a new lion at the ceremony to welcome the new lion into a traditional Chinese martial arts school

gwai (C) [Common Usage] ghost

gwai (C) [Common Usage] *see* gui

gwai gee (C) [Medicine] *see* gwaai ji

gwai gwan (C) [Common Usage] second-place winner

gwaih (C) [Common Usage] to kneel

gwaih dai (C) [Common Usage] to kneel down

gwai hei (C) [Common Usage] ghost energy, the residual energy of a ghost

gwaih ma (C) [Common Usage] a cross horse stance

gwai jaan (C) [Wihng Cheun] a downward elbow strike

gwai sik (C) [Hei Gung] (*lit*. Turtle Breathing) the ability to breathe through the skin in *qigong*

Gwai Tauh Dou (C) [Choy Leih Faht] (*lit*. Ghost Head Broadsword Form) a weapons form

gwan (C) [Common Usage] to roll

gwan (C) [Weapon] *see* gun

Gwan Daaih Dihn Sau Kyuhn (C) [Baahk Hok] a hand form

Gwang Gae hyeong (K) [Taekwondo] *see* Kwang Gae hyung

gwan hyeok (K) [Kung Do] archery target

gwanja nori (K) [Common Usage] temple (side of the head)

gwanjeol (K) [Common Usage] joint

gwanjeolgi (K) [Kuk Sool] joint-manipulation technique

gwan jong (C) [Choy Leih Faht] staff dummy; a training aid that is used to develop staff techniques

gwan mah (C) [Wihng Cheun] pole stance

gwan sau (C) [Wihng Cheun] rotating arms

gwansu (K) [Common Usage] spearhand

gwansu jireugi (K) [Hapkido] spearhand thrust

gwat (C) [Common Usage] bone

gwat soi bouh (C) [Medicine] the root of this plant is commonly used in Chinese medicine to heal bone injuries

gwat soy bow (C) [Medicine] *see* gwat soi bouh

gweon (K) [Common Usage] *see* kwon

Gweon Beop (K) [Style] *see* Kwon Bup

gweon chong (K) [Common Usage] handgun, pistol

gweondo (K) [Tang Soo Do] hammerfist

Gweon Gyeok Do (K) [Style] *see* Kun Gek Do

gweontu (K) [Common Usage] boxing

gweontu ha da (K) [Common Usage] to box

gweontu ring (K) [Common Usage] boxing ring

gwi (K) [Common Usage] ear

gwibap (K) [Common Usage] earlobe

gwok (C) [Common Usage] *see* guo

gwok ga (C) [Common Usage] *see* guo

gwok seuht (C) [Common Usage] *see* guo shu

Gwong Tit Fu (C) [Master] a prominent master of Huhng Ga

gwong wihng (C) [Common Usage] glory

gwo sau (C) [Wihng Cheun] fighting practice/exercise

gwun (C) [Common Usage] a school, or place of training for the practice of traditional Chinese martial arts

gyaku (J) [Common Usage] opposite, reverse

gyaku hanmi (J) [Aikido] a ready position in which the opponents have opposite feet forward

gyaku hanmi katatedori (J) [Aikido] to grab the opponent's wrist on the opposite side (*e.g.,* left hand grabs right and right hand grabs the left wrist)

gyaku juji jime (J) [Judo] a strangulation hold done with the hands crossed over in an X-shape

gyaku mawashi geri (J) [Karate] a reverse roundhouse kick

gyaku soto uke (J) [Karate] reverse outside block

gyaku taka no ha (J) [Weapon] inverted V-shaped file marks on the tang of a *katana*

Gyakute Inyo Shintai (J) [Iaido] the eleventh *kata* in the Muso Shinden-ryu Omori-ryu Shoden series, which is done from *seiza*

Gyakuto (J) [Iaido] the eighth *kata* in the Muso Shinden-ryu Omori-ryu Shoden series, which is done from *seiza*

gyaku tsuki (J) [Karate] a reverse punch

gyaku waza (J) [Ju-jutsu] techniques done against the natural movement of a joint

gyeodeurangi (K) [Common Usage] armpit

gyeokpa (K) [Common Usage] breaking

gyeokpa hyeong (K) [Kuk Sool] breaking form

gyeoktu (K) [Common Usage] combat

Gyeok Tu Gi (K) [Style] *see* Kyuk Too Ki

gyeoktu ha da (K) [Common Usage] to engage in combat

gyeolhu (K) [Common Usage] Adam's apple

gyeolseung jeon (K) [Taekwondo] final match in sparring competition

gyeondi da (K) [Common Usage] to endure

gyeong (K) [Common Usage] Buddhist scripture

gyeonggi (K) [Common Usage] contest

gyeonggi jang (K) [Common Usage] competition area

gyeonggi sigan (K) [Common Usage] contest duration

gyeonggo (K) [Common Usage] warning during sparring

gyeonggol (K) [Common Usage] tibia, shinbone

gyeonggye seon (K) [Common Usage] boundary line of a sparring ring

gyeonghoweon (K) [Common Usage] bodyguard

gyeongjaeng (K) [Common Usage] competition

gyeongjaeng ja (K) [Common Usage] competitor

gyeongnye (K) [Common Usage] command to "bow" or "salute"

gyeongnye ha da (K) [Common Usage] to bow, to salute

gyeon jugi (K) [Taekwondo, Tae Kyon] **1** sparring **2** advanced level of Tae Kyon training that involves sparring with a partner

gyeorugi jase (K) [Taekwondo] sparring posture

gyesok (K) [Common Usage] command to "continue"

gyesok ha da (K) [Common Usage] to continue

gyo (J) [Common Usage] a ritual of purification undertaken by sword smiths in order to produce a better blade

gyobon (K) [Common Usage] instructional text

gyocha seogi (K) [Taekwondo] cross stance, X-stance

gyocha sudo (K) [Taekwondo] crossed knifehand

gyodae (K) [Common Usage] command to "change"

gyoji (J) [Sumo] referee; his rank is identified by the color of the rope on his *gunbai* and the rosettes of his costume

gyunhyeong (K) [Common Usage] balance

gyunhyeong eul yuji ha da (K) [Common Usage] to keep one's balance

— H —

ha (J) [Common Usage] blade of a *katana*

haahng (C) [Common Usage] to walk

haaih (C) [Common Usage] *see* xie

haak (C) [Common Usage] *see* xia

haak fuhk (C) [Common Usage] *see* ke fu

Haak Ga Tiu Gwan (C) [Luhng Yihng Kyuhn] (*lit.* Haak Family Shoulder Staff) a weapons form using the staff

haak sik (C) [Common Usage] black

Haap Ga (C) [Style] Founded by Wohng Yihm Luhm who had originally studied the Si Ji Haau style. This system of Chinese martial arts is characterized by its long- and short-range fist techniques derived from animals: ape, snake, tiger, and crane, and emphasizes training on the *muih fa jong.*

haau (C) [Common Usage] **1** to knock, to strike, to drum upon **2** to test

haau ging (C) [Common Usage] to pay respects

haau seuhn (C) [Common Usage] filial

haau touh (C) [Common Usage] obedient student

habaki (J) [Kendo] the sleeve or collar that fits over the blade of a sword at its juncture with the guard *(tsuba)*

habansin (K) [Taekwondo] parts of the foot

hachi (J) [Common Usage] eight

hachi dan (J) [Common Usage] eighth-degree black belt; 8th Dan

hachiji dachi (J) [Karate] figure-eight stance

hachi kyu (J) [Common Usage] eighth class, 8th Kyu

hachimaki (J) [Kendo, Naginata] a cloth worn over the head underneath the *men*

hachinoji dachi (J) [Karate] stationary position

hada (J) [Common Usage] skin

hadaka (J) [Common Usage] nude, bare

hadaka jime (J) [Judo] naked strangle; a strangulation done without the use of the *keikogi*

hadan bangeo (K) [Common Usage] low-level defense

hadan chagi (K) [Kuk Sool] low-level kick

hadan dora chagi (K) [Kuk Sool] dropping spinning kick

hadan dwi dora chagi (K) [Kuk Sool] dropping back-spinning kick

hadan jireugi (K) [Taekwondo] low-level punch

hadan jumeok (K) [Taekwondo] low-level fist, low-level punch

hadan makgi (K) [Tang Soo Do] low-level block

Hae Dong (K) [Common Usage] (*lit.* East Sea) an old name for Korea

Hae Dong Geom Do (K) [Style] *see* Hae Dong Kum Do

Hae Dong kum do (K) [Style] (*lit.* Korean Sword Way) Korean fencing

haengjeong chigi (K) [Tae Kyon] open-handed hammerfist strike

ha eui (K) [Common Usage] uniform bottom, pants

ha gaeshi (J) [Naginata] the ability to quickly reverse the blade of the *naginata*

Hagakure (J) [Common Usage] a literary work by Yamamoto Tsunemono in the eighteenth century; considered by many as one of the classics of budo

hah (C) [Common Usage] low, lower

hah gam sau (C) [Wihng Cheun] back pinning hand

hah loh (C) [Wihng Cheun] lower level; the region of the body below the groin and above the ankles

hahm (C) [Common Usage] *see* xian

hahm hoih (C) [Common Usage] to set someone up

hahm jihng (C) [Common Usage] trap

Hahng Jieh Paahng Deui Chuk Fong Tihn Waahk Gik (C) [Choy Leih Faht] (*lit.* Monkey Staff Versus Fong Tien Waahk Gik) a two-man fighting form

Hahng Kyuhn (C) [Huhng Kyuhn] *see* Xing Quan

Hahng Kyuhn (C) [Ying Jaau] (*lit.* Walking Fist) a hand form

hahng sam (C) [Common Usage] *see* heng xin

hahp (C) [Common Usage] *see* he

hah tin (C) [Common Usage] summer season

hai (J) [Common Usage] lung

hai (J) [Common Usage] yes

hai (M) [Common Usage] sea, ocean

haigyo (J) [Sumo] to quit the sumo world

hairi kata (J) [Judo] techniques used to enter the opponent's guard

hairu (J) [Common Usage] to enter

haishin undo (J) [Aikido] an exercise used for making the back more flexible

haishu (J) [Common Usage] the back of the hand

haishu uchi (J) [Karate] an open backhand strike

haishu uke (J) [Karate] backhand block

Haitorei (J) [Common Usage] legal statutes enacted in the 1870s prohibiting the carrying of weapons in everyday life that effectively ended feudalism

haito uchi (J) [Karate] a ridgehand strike; a technique that uses the index finger side of the open hand as the striking surface

haiwan (J) [Common Usage] back of the arm

haiwan nagashi uke (J) [Karate] back of the arm sweeping block

haiwan uke (J) [Karate] a forearm block

hajime (J) [Common Usage] to start; a command used by referees to begin a match

hak (K) [Common Usage] crane

hakama (J) [Common Usage] traditional Japanese trousers with seven pleats, five of which are in the front and two in the back; usually colored either black, blue, or white

hak dari seogi (K) [Taekwondo] crane-leg stance

Hak Fu Gaau Cha Kyuhn (C) [Chat Sing Tohng Lohng] (*lit.* Black Tiger Hands Over the Fork) a hand form

hak fu jaau (C) [Huhng Ga] black tiger claw

hak fu tau sam (C) [Huhng Ga] (*lit.* Black Tiger Steals the Heart) a palm strike to the opponent's heart

Hakkaku (J) [Sumo] a sumo *beya* located in Sumida Ward, Tokyo

hakkaku bo (J) [Weapon] an octagonal staff

hakke yoi (J) [Sumo] (*lit.* Keep Going) an encouragement shouted by referees during a match

hakko (J) [Karate] *see* Sochin

Hakko-ryu (J) [Aikido] a style of aiki-jutsu founded by Okuyama Yoshiharu

hak saeng (K) [Common Usage] student

Hakutaru no Kon (O) [Kobudo] a staff *kata* practiced in Ryukyu Kobudo

Hakutsuru (O) [Karate] a White Crane form from southern China practiced in Matsumura Orthodox Shorin-ryu, Matayoshi Kobudo, and Kojo-ryu

halla jangsa geup (K) [Ssi Rum] 80.1-kilogram to 95-kilogram weight class of professional competition

Hamahiga no Jo (O) [Kobudo] a *jo kata* practiced in Ryukyu Kobudo

hambo (J) [Weapon] half staff; a short bo used in bo-jutsu

hana (J) [Common Usage] nose

hana (K) [Common Usage] one

Hanakago (J) [Sumo] a sumo *beya* located in Yamanashi Prefecture

hanamichi (J) [Sumo] (*lit.* Flower Path) a corridor from the dressing room area to the *dohyo* by which the *rikishi* make their entrance

hanare (J) [Kyudo] (*lit.* Separation) to shoot an arrow; the seventh position in kyudo

Hanaregoma (J) [Sumo] a sumo *beya* located in Suginami Ward, Tokyo

Hanashiro Chomo (O) [Master] a master of Shuri-te who studied under Matsumura Sokon; he specialized in the Jion *kata*

hanazumo (J) [Sumo] any sumo performance other than the six official tournaments

han ballo seogi jase (K) [Tang Soo Do] one-leg stance

hanbeon gyeorugi (K) [Taekwondo] one-step sparring

hanbok (K) [Tae Kyon] traditional Korean worker's clothes, now worn by students of Tae Kyon as a uniform

hanbon gyeorugi (K) [Taekwondo] one-step sparring

Han Dai (M) [Common Usage] Han Imperial dynasty, which ruled China from 206 B.C. to. A.D 220

hando (J) [Common Usage] reaction

hane (J) [Common Usage] **1** feather **2** spring, jump

hane goshi (J) [Judo] spinning hip throw

hane maki komi (J) [Judo] a type of circular hip throw

hangeoreum geot da (K) [Common Usage] to take one step

hangeoreum giri (K) [Common Usage] a length of one step

Hangetsu (J) [Karate] *see* Seisan

hangetsu barai uke (J) [Karate] half-moon sweeping foot block

hangetsu dachi (J) [Karate] half-moon stance, wide hourglass stance

hangeul (K) [Common Usage] Korea's phonetic script, the creation of which was ordered by King Sejong and completed in 1443

hang jeong chigi (K) [Tae Kyon] strike to the back of the neck with the blade of the hand

Hang Jyeh Paang (C) [Choy Leih Faht] (*lit.* Monkey Staff Form) a weapons form using the staff

Han Guk (K) [Common Usage] *see* Hankook

Han Guk Gweon Gyeok Do Hyeophoi (K) [Common Usage] Korea Kun Gek Do Association

Han Guk Jeontong Tae Kyon Yeongu Hoi (K) [Common Usage] Korea Traditional Tae Kyon Research Association

Han Guk Su Bak Do Hoi (K) [Common Usage] Korea Soo Bahk Do Association

Han Guk Yu Sul Hyeophoi (K) [Common Usage] Korea Yoo Sool Association

han heiko dachi (J) [Karate] a stance with the feet parallel, and closer together than the regular *heiko dachi*

hanja (K) [Common Usage] Korea's non-phonetic script based on the Chinese writing system, also called *hanmun*

hanjeong sigan (K) [Common Usage] time limit in sparring competition

Hanko (J) [Karate] the original name Mabuni Kenwa gave his style of karate, later called Shito-ryu

Hankook (K) [Common Usage] Korea

hankyu (J) [Nin-jutsu] (*lit.* Half-Bow) a small bow used by ninja to shoot arrows or incendiary devices at enemy encampments

hanmato (J) [Kyudo] an eighty-one centimeter target used in shooting practice

hanmi (J) [Common Usage] a ready position in which the feet are staggered and the body is slightly turned to the side, at a forty-five-degree angle

hanmi no neko dachi (J) [Karate] half-view cat stance; a cat stance position with the body is slightly turned to the side, at a forty-five-degree angle

hanmun (K) [Common Usage] Korea's non-phonetic script based on the Chinese system of writing, also called *hanja*

hanpan (K) [Common Usage] a round in sparring competition

hanshi (J) [Common Usage] **1** master; a title given to some eighth- to tenth-degree black belts; the highest of three teaching ranks **2** a title given to some Japanese aristocracy in the Edo period

hansoku (J) [Competitive Budo] rule infraction; foul

hansoku chui (J) [Competitive Budo] a warning given to a competitor for an infraction of the rules

hansoku gachi (J) [Competitive Budo] winner by disqualification

hansoku make (J) [Competitive Budo] a disqualification for committing an infraction of the rules

hanson geulggi (K) [Tae Kyon] strike in which the extended arm moves horizontally from the outside to the inside and the fingertips strike

hanson ggeut (K) [Taekwondo] single spear-finger

hanson hechigi (K) [Tae Kyon] block in which the hand travels in an arc in front of the waist

hanson jeochigi (K) [Tae Kyon] strike in which the extended arm moves horizontally from the inside to the outside and the fingertips strike

Hansu pumse (K) [Taekwondo] Eighth-Degree form

hantai (J) [Common Usage] opposite

hantei (J) [Common Usage] judgment, a referees' decision

hantei gachi (J) [Competitive Budo] a winner by referees' decision

hantei shimasu (J) [Common Usage] an announcement made by a referee that the judges will determine the winner of a match

Han Xing (M) [Style] *see* Hon Sihng

hanza handachi waza (J) [Aikido] pair techniques practiced with one person sitting in *seiza* and the opponent in standing position; also called *hanmi handachi waza*

hao qi xin (M) [Common Usage] *see* hou keih sam

haori (J) [Common Usage] a traditional coat worn over a kimono

Hao taijiquan (M) [Style] a style of taijiquan developed by Wu Yu Xiang characterized by upright stances and by slow and soft movements

Hapgido (K) [Style] *see* Hapkido

Hap Gi Muye Do (K) [Style] *see* Hap Ki Muye Do

Hapkido (K) [Style] (*lit.* Coordinated Internal Energy Way) a martial art that uses joint-locks, throws, punches, and kicks to turn an attacker's strength against him

Hap Ki Muye Do (K) [Style] (*lit.* Coordinated Internal Energy Martial Art Way) Korean version of aikido

happi (J) [Common Usage] eight directions

happo giri (J) [Iaido] an exercise in which cuts to the eight cardinal directions are made

happo undo (J) [Aikido] a movement exercise in which the student moves toward all eight cardinal points; performed to develop the ability to move smoothly in any direction

happo zanshin (J) [Aikido, Kendo] *zanshin* in eight directions

hara (J) [Common Usage] abdomen, belly; an area a few centimeters below the navel; considered the place where the vital energy is stored and generated

haragei (J) [Common Usage] personality; psychology

harai (J) [Common Usage] **1** sweep, as in *ashi barai,* leg sweep **2** a sweeping movement of the blade of the weapon

harai do (J) [Kendo, Naginata] an attack pushing the opponent's weapon upward and to the right, then striking the opponent's torso *(do)*

harai goshi (J) [Judo] sweeping hip throw

harai makikomi (J) [Judo] binding sweeping hip throw

harai men (J) [Kendo, Naginata] an attack to the opponent's head that is performed by sweeping the opponent's weapon out of the way and then striking the head *(men)*

harai te (J) [Karate] a sweep with the hand

harai tsuki (J) [Kendo, Naginata] an attack to the opponent's head that is performed by sweeping the opponent's weapon out of the way and then thrusting to the opponent's throat *(tsuki)*

harai waza (J) [Kendo, Naginata] sweeping movements used in offense and defense

harak ap chagi (K) [Taekwondo] dropping front kick

harak ap dollyeo chagi (K) [Taekwondo] dropping roundhouse kick

harakiri (J) [Bushido] *(lit.* Cutting the Abdomen) samurai ritual suicide in which the abdomen was sliced open with a short sword; more correctly referred to in Japanese as *seppuku*

harak yeop chagi (K) [Taekwondo] dropping side kick

harau (J) [Common Usage] to brush aside; to sweep

hareru (J) [Common Usage] to swell up

harikitte (J) [Common Usage] a state of alertness, or vigilance

har lo (C) [Wihng Cheun] *see* hah loh

hasaki (J) [Common Usage] the point of a bladed weapon

hasami (J) [Common Usage] scissors

hasami jime (J) [Judo] a scissors hold or strangle

hasami tsuki (J) [Karate] scissor punch; a circular technique in which both hands hit simultaneously, one striking the front of the target, the other the back of it

Hasegawa Eishin-ryu (J) [Iaido] the second level of teachings in Muso Shinden-ryu iaido

hashiru (J) [Common Usage] to run

hasso kamae (J) [Kendo, Naginata] a ready position in which the weapon is held tip pointing up against the side of the body

hata (J) [Common Usage] a flag used by judges and referees

hataki komi (J) [Sumo] slap down; after sidestepping his opponent's charge, the *rikishi* smacks his off-balanced opponent down with a slap on the back

hatamoto (J) [Common Usage] flag bearer

Hatsu Geiko (J) [Common Usage] the first training session of the year

Hatsumi Masaaki (J) [Master] the thirty-fourth-generation head of Togakure-ryu nin-jutsu

hat yih yahn (C) [Chyu Ga] (*lit.* Beggar's Hand) an on-guard position with the hands slightly stretched out and the elbows tucked in to protect the vital organs of the body

hau (C) [Common Usage] mouth

hau gum sau (C) [Wihng Cheun] *see* hah gam sau

hauh (C) [Common Usage] back, behind

hauh (C) [Common Usage] *see* hou zi

hauh saang (C) [Common Usage] young

Hauh Ying Kyuhn (C) [Choy Leih Faht] (*lit.* Monkey Hand Form) a hand form

hayagake-jutsu (J) [Nin-jutsu] the art of walking and running; for enduring long marches

hayai (J) [Common Usage] fast, rapid

Hayashizaki Jinsuke Shigenobu (J) [Master] A sixteenth-century master of sword-fighting sometimes referred to as "Hojo" Jinsuke Shigenobu, he founded the Junpaku Den style of swordsmanship and is considered by most to be the father of iaido. His successors renamed his system Shin Muso Hayashizaki-ryu, and it is noted for its use of extremely long swords

hazushi uke (J) [Karate] evading block; dodging block

he (M) [Common Usage] **1** crane **2** to gather

he (M) [Common Usage] *see* yam

hebi geup (K) [Taekwondo] heavyweight class in sparring competition

he cai (M) [Common Usage] *see* gu jeung

hechyeo makgi (K) [Taekwondo] spreading block, wedging block

hegu (M) [Acupressure] a point located between the forefinger and thumb

he hao (M) [Common Usage] to reconcile

he hua (M) [Common Usage] *see* lihn fa

hei (C) [Common Usage] energy

hei (J) [Common Usage] army, soldier

Heian (J) [Karate] *see* Pinan

Heian jidai (J) [Common Usage] (*lit.* Period of Tranquillity) a period in Japanese history from 794 to 1192, comparable to the European early middle ages; during this period Zen was introduced to Japan

hei foh (C) [Common Usage] to build a fire

hei gun (C) [Common Usage] organ

hei gung (C) [Common Usage] internal energy of the body and mind; a reserve of energy that can be used at any point of time

heiho (J) [Common Usage] **1** military strategy or tactics **2** ken-jutsu

hei hu chu dong (M) [Xingyiquan] (*lit.* Black Tiger Exits from Cave) a vertical fist strike executed with one hand as the other hand is retracted back to the waist

hei hwu chu dong (M) [Xingyiquan] *see* hei hu chu dong

Heijo Muteki-ryu (J) [Ken-jutsu] a school of ken-jutsu founded by Yamanouchi Renshinsai

heijoshin (J) [Bushido] (*lit.* Ordinary Mind) a state of spiritual calm during combat or a stressful moment; the state of mind one has doing ordinary, routine tasks

heiken (J) [Common Usage] fist

heiki (J) [Common Usage] weapons; arms

heiko (J) [Common Usage] parallel

heiko dachi (J) [Karate] a stance in which the feet are kept parallel

heiko tsuki (J) [Karate] parallel punch; a strike in which both arms are parallel to each other and the ground

Heiku (O) [Karate] a *kata* practiced in Ryuei-ryu

hei se (M) [Common Usage] *see* haak sik

Heisei jidai (J) [Common Usage] the present era of Japanese history; it started in 1989

heishi (J) [Common Usage] soldier(s), troops

hei si (C) [Common Usage] (*lit.* Raise the Lion) the part of a lion dance when the lion is raised from its slumber

heisoku (J) [Common Usage] the top of the foot

heisoku dachi (J) [Karate] attention stance; the feet and toes are together

he jie (M) [Common Usage] *see* he hao

He Ji Kui (M) [Master] a prominent master of baguazhang

he jiu (M) [Common Usage] *see* ging jau

Heki-ryu (J) [Kyudo] one of the first schools of Japanese archery, it was founded in the tenth century by Heki Danjo Masatsugu

heng xin (M) [Common Usage] patience; a virtue taught to those who study martial arts

henka (J) [Common Usage] change, variation

hensho-jutsu (J) [Nin-jutsu] the ninja art of disguise and impersonation

heobeokji (K) [Common Usage] thigh

heollyeo makgi (K) [Taekwondo] sweeping block

heori (K) [Common Usage] hip

heori ggeokkgi (K) [Ssi Rum] waist-locking technique

heori gubhigi (K) [Common Usage] lean forward

heori jaegi (K) [Tae Kyon] hip-circling exercise

heori reul apeuro (K) [Common Usage] hips forward

heori reul dolli da (K) [Common Usage] to turn the hips

heori teulgi (K) [Common Usage] hip twisting

hetsu kagami (J) [Shinto] a form of meditation practiced in many sects of Shinto

heuin ddi (K) [Common Usage] white belt

heuinsaek (K) [Common Usage] white color

heuk (K) [Common Usage] black

heuk ddi (K) [Common Usage] black belt

heuk saek (K) [Common Usage] black color

heung (C) [Common Usage] incense used during ceremonies

heung louh (C) [Common Usage] incense holder

heya (J) [Sumo] a sumo stable

heya gashira (J) [Sumo] the highest-ranked *rikishi* in a *beya*

He Zhao Zhan Wei (M) [Bai He] (*lit.* Crane Claw Spread Might) a hand form in Su He

hi (J) [Weapon] the grooves on the blade of a weapon

hichu (J) [Acupressure] a vital point located below the throat on the suprasternal notch

hidari (J) [Common Usage] left

hidari ashi (J) [Common Usage] left leg

hidari kokutsu dachi (J) [Karate] back-stance with the left leg in front

hidari men (J) [Kendo, Naginata] the left side of the head

hidari neko ashi dachi (J) [Karate] cat stance with the left leg in front

hidari shizentai (J) [Kendo, Karate] natural position with the left leg forward

hidari sumi (J) [Common Usage] left corner

hidari te (J) [Common Usage] left hand

hidari tsuki (J) [Karate] left punch

hidari yokomen (J) [Kendo, Naginata] strike to the left side of the head *(men)*

hidari zenkutsu dachi (J) [Karate] front stance with the left leg in front

Higa Seiko (O) [Master] a master of Goju-ryu who studied under Miyagi Chojun; a former president of the Okinawa Karate-do Federation

Higa Seitoku (O) [Master] founder of the Bugeikan; a student of Shorin-ryu under Chibana Choshin, Okinawa Te under Uehara Sekichi, and Yamani-ryu bo-jutsu under Chinen Masami

higashi (J) [Common Usage] east

higashi gawa (J) [Sumo] (*lit.* East Side) the more prestigious side of the ring or stadium

Higashionna Kanryo (O) [Karate] a master of Naha-te, and the principal teacher of Miyagi Chojun, he studied the Okinawan martial arts under Arakaki Seisho and the Chinese martial arts in Fujian Province, China, under Ryu Ru Ko

Higa Yuchoku (O) [Master] An early pioneer of both Goju-ryu and Shorin-ryu, he was the senior heir of Chibana Choshin's Shorin-ryu (Kobayashi-ryu). He founded the Kyudokan and eventually took over the chairmanship of the All Okinawa Karate-Do Federation.

hiji (J) [Common Usage] elbow

hijiate (J) [Karate] to strike with the elbow

hiji gatame (J) [Judo] an elbow lock

hijikimeosae (J) [Aikido] an elbow lock

hiji otoshi (J) [Aikido] a pin using the elbow as a means to control the opponent

hiji suri uke (J) [Karate] elbow sliding block

hiji uchi (J) [Karate] elbow strike

hikae rikishi (J) [Sumo] the *rikishi* sitting around the sides of the *dohyo* waiting for their turn to enter the ring

Hikida Bungoro (J) [Master] a master swordsman and founder of the Hikida Kage-ryu; one of the "Four Kings" (*Shi Tenno*) of Japanese swordsmanship

Hikida Kage-ryu (J) [Style] a school of ken-jutsu founded by Hikida Bungoro

hikime (J) [Kyudo] an arrow with a wooden ball rather than a point at the tip

hikimi (J) [Shorinji Kempo] a method of pulling the midsection of the body away to avoid an attack to the body

hiki otoshi (J) [Sumo] a pushing technique used to oust the opponent after freeing oneself from an attempted throw

hikitate geiko (J) [Kendo, Naginata] when partners of different skill levels train together

hikitate oyobi (J) [Taiho-jutsu] the art of physically controlling the opponent, used by police in Japan

hikite (J) [Karate] the retractor; the arm going in the opposite direction as the technique being executed

hikiwake (J) [Competitive Budo] a draw

hikiwaza (J) [Kendo] technique performed while stepping backward

hiku (J) [Common Usage] to pull

hikui (J) [Common Usage] low

him (C) [Common Usage] to be modest, to be humble

him (K) [Common Usage] strength

Himagoi (J) [Iaido] a seated *kata* included in the Muso Shinden-ryu Okuden Tachiwaza series, which is done from a standing position; there are a total of three variations of this kata in this series

him eul jipjung ha da (K) [Common Usage] to concentrate force at one point

him heui (C) [Common Usage] *see* him

him i itneun (K) [Common Usage] with power

him itge gureu da (K) [Common Usage] to stomp

himjul (K) [Common Usage] tendon

himo (J) [Kendo, Naginata] the cords used to tie *bogu,* the protective equipment used in free pratice

hin (C) [Kahm Na] *see* qian

hinawaju (J) [Weapon] a matchlock musket

hinerite (J) [Ju-jutsu] a hand-lock done by twisting the hand

hing (C) [Common Usage] *see* xiong

hing gung (C) [Common Usage] the mythical ability to levitate or make great leaps and jumps

hing juk (C) [Common Usage] *see* qing zhu

hinin (J) [Nin-jutsu] (*lit.* Non-human) a term used for ninjas and torturers of the *bakufu*

hip (C) [Common Usage] *see* xie

hip (C) [Kahm Na] *see* jia

hira (J) [Common Usage] (*lit.* Flat) the flat of the hand or foot when used as a striking surface

hiraken tsuki (J) [Karate] a fore-knuckle punch usually striking below the nose, the temple, or the ribcage

hiraken uchi (J) [Karate] fore-knuckle strike

hiraki (J) [Common Usage] opening

hiraki ashi (J) [Kendo, Naginata] a side-step done by first moving the foot on the side to which one is going, then following with the other foot

hira zukuri (J) [Weapon] the shape of blade most common on a short sword

hiriki (J) [Aikido] elbow power

Hiroi Tsuneji (J) [Master] a master of classical jo-jutsu and keijo-jutsu

hishiryo (J) [Zen] action taken without thought

hitai (J) [Common Usage] forehead

hito washi (J) [Nin-jutsu] (*lit.* Human Eagle) a glider made of bamboo and cloth used by ninja to glide over walls, giving the illusion of flight

hitsu (J) [Weapon] the grip section of a *kozuka*

hittsui (J) [Common Usage] a strike with the knee

Hiwatari Matsuri (J) [Common Usage] a ceremony that involves walking over red hot coals as a test of self-control

hiza (J) [Common Usage] knee

hiza gashira (J) [Common Usage] kneecap

hiza gatame (J) [Judo] a technique that uses the knee to control the opponent's elbow

hiza geri (J) [Karate] a kick with the knee

hiza jime (J) [Judo] a strangulation in which the knee is used to apply pressure

hiza kansetsu (J) [Common Usage] knee joint

hizamazuku (J) [Common Usage] to kneel

hiza uke (J) [Karate] a block using the knee

hizo (J) [Common Usage] spleen

ho (J) [Common Usage] cheek

hocho (J) [Weapon] soft steel used in sword making that contains less then half a percent of carbon

hodoku (J) [Kendo] the act of separating the blades or *shinai* of two opponents after a clash

hogen (J) [Common Usage] dialect

hogu (K) [Taekwondo, Hapkido] **1** chest protector **2** striking surface located between the thumb and index finger

Ho Guk Muye (K) [Style] (*lit.* National Defense Martial Art) alternative name for Kuk Sool

hoheup beop (K) [Common Usage] breathing method

hoheup ha da (K) [Common Usage] to breathe

hoheup jojeol (K) [Common Usage] breath control

hohk (C) [Common Usage] *see* he

hohk (C) [Common Usage] to learn

Hoh Lahp Tihn (C) [Master] a prominent Huhng Ga master who was taught by Dang Fong

hohn (C) [Common Usage] sweat

hoi (C) [Common Usage] **1** sea, ocean **2** to open

hoi cheuih (C) [Common Usage] *see* juhk cheut

hoi gong dim ngahn (C) [Common Usage] (*lit.* Opening the Light by Dotting the Eyes) a ceremony to anoint a new lion by dotting the eyes, eyelids, mouth, and tongue with red ink, which symbolizes bringing it to life. The ink that is used for this ceremony is held in a cup made from a hollow ginseng root, and is applied with a new brush. This ceremony must be performed before the lion can be used for lion dances.

hoi gung sau (C) [Hei Gung] *see* kai gong shou

hoih sing (C) [Common Usage] *see* yan

hoijang (K) [Common Usage] chairman of an association or organization

hoijeon ap dollyeo chagi (K) [Kuk Sool] spinning roundhouse kick

hoijeon bal chagi (K) [Kuk Sool] spinning kick

hoijeon cheukbang nakbeop (K) [Hapkido] spinning side-falling technique

hoijeon gisul (K) [Kuk Sool] spinning technique

hoijeon ha da (K) [Common Usage] to spin, to turn

Hoi Jeon Musul (K) [Style] (*lit.* Turning Martial Skill) a soft martial art similar to aikido; it uses mostly circular techniques

hoijeon nakbeop (K) [Kuk Sool] spinning falling technique, forward roll

hoijeon yeop chagi (K) [Kuk Sool] spinning side kick

hoi jeung (C) [Common Usage] opening; a term use to describe an opening of a school, business, or association

hoi jong (C) [Choi Leh Faht] (*lit.* Open Hands Technique) these movements originated as secret identification signals among Choy Leih Faht revolutionaries during the Qing dynasty

hoi mah (C) [Wihng Cheun] preparing stance

hoipi ha da (K) [Common Usage] to evade

hoi sam (C) [Common Usage] happy

hoi yeuhng (C) [Common Usage] ocean

hojo-jutsu (J) [Style] the art of tying an opponent

hojo undo (J) [Karate, Judo] supplemental training

ho-jutsu (J) [Style] (*lit.* Art of Gunnery) gunnery; marksmanship with matchlock firearms

hok cho (C) [Medicine] *see* sihn hok chou

hoken (J) [Common Usage] a ceremonial temple sword

hoko (J) [Weapon] a long spear with a wide blade on the end

Hokushin Itto-ryu (J) [Ken-jutsu] a school of ken-jutsu founded by Chiba Shusaku in the eighteenth century

hok yihk (C) [Huhng Ga] crane wing

Hok Ying Kyuhn (C) [Choy Leih Faht] (*lit.* Crane Hand Form) a hand form

hombu (J) [Common Usage] main office, head branch; the school where the head of a style teaches

homi geolgi (K) [Ssi Rum] hoe-hooking technique to the ankle

hon (M) [Common Usage] *see* hohn

hon basho (J) [Sumo] the six fifteen-day official tournaments held in different parts of Japan each year

hone (J) [Common Usage] bone

hong (K) [Common Usage] red

hongaku no kamae (J) [Kendo] a combative stance specific to the Ono-ha Itto-ryu, with the sword held at throat level, parallel to the ground

hong ddi (K) [Common Usage] red belt

Hong Jia (M) [Style] *see* Huhng Ga

hong men (M) [Common Usage] vast gate

Hong Men Quan (M) [Style] Vast Gate Fist

Hong Quan (M) [Style] **1** Red Fist **2** Vast Fist

hong saek (K) [Common Usage] red color

hong se (M) [Common Usage] *see* huhng sik

honja (K) [Common Usage] alone

honja ikhigi (K) [Tae Kyon] beginning level of training practiced without a partner

honja suryeon (K) [Common Usage] solo training

Hon Kyuhn (C) [Ying Jaau] (*lit.* Walking Fist) a hand form

ho no ki (J) [Common Usage] a type of magnolia wood used for making scabbards

Honshin-ryu (O) [Style] a kobudo preservation society established by Miyagi Masakazu

Hon Sihng (C) [Style] (*lit.* Strong Winning) the original style of southern Choy Leih Faht

hontai (J) [Zen] one's original essence; a state of awareness of this absolute or original condition

horangi (K) [Common Usage] tiger

horangi bal (K) [Common Usage] tiger claw

hosin (K) [Common Usage] self-defense

Ho Sin Do (K) [Style] (*lit.* Self-Defense Way) a martial art that primarily utilizes pressure points

hosin ha da (K) [Common Usage] to protect oneself

hosin sul (K) [Common Usage] self-defense skill

Hosso-shu (J) [Common Usage] one of the first Buddhist sects introduced to Japan, in A.D. 654

hossu (J) [Buddhism] a fly whisk used by Buddhist masters as a symbol of authority; a Buddhist high priest or abbot

hot choi (C) [Common Usage] *see* gu jeung

hotoke gamae (J) [Karate] (*lit.* Buddha-Hand Fighting Posture) a position with one hand in *jodan tate uke* and the other in *gedan barai*

hou keih sam (C) [Common Usage] curiosity, the desire to know

Hou Quan (M) [Style] (*lit.* Monkey Fist) a northern style of Chinese martial arts

hou seui (C) [Common Usage] *see* kou shui

hou zi (M) [Common Usage] monkey

Hozoin-ryu (J) [Style] a school of so-jutsu founded in sixteenth century by a priest at the Kofuku-ji temple in Nara

hsiao kuai hsing (M) [Yang Taijiquan] *see* xiao guai xing

hsien jen chih lu (M) [Yang Taijiquan] *see* xian ren zhi lu

Hsing I (M) [Style] *see* xingyiquan

Hsing Yi Chuan (M) [Style] *see* xingyiquan

hsi nieu wang yueh (M) [Yang Taijiquan] *see* xi niu wang yue

hsu tuan (M) [Medicine] teasel; a brownish-red root bark used to strengthen tendon and bone

hu (M) [Common Usage] *see* louh fu

hua (M) [Common Usage] **1** flower **2** to transform

hua (M) [Common Usage] *see* wa

huai chong pao yue (M) [Yang Taijiquan] (*lit.* Holding the Moon Against the Chest) a movement in the Taiji Sword form

huai yi (M) [Common Usage] suspicion; to be suspicious

huai zhong biao ye (M) [Xingyiquan] (*lit.* Embrace the Moon on the Chest) both hands are brought back to the abdomen level and one fist hits the palm of the other hand as one foot stamps down in front of the other

huang (M) [Common Usage] yellow

huang chi (M) [Medicine] vetch; a medicinal herb used to strengthen the immune system and to regulate the flow of *qi*

Huang Fei Hong (C) [Master] *see* Wohng Fei Huhng

Huang Jiu Qaun (M) [Master] *see* Wohng Gau Chuhn

huang se (M) [Common Usage] yellow color

huang ting (M) [Common Usage] *see* wohng ting

Huang Ying Jia (M) [Hong Quan] (*lit.* Yellow Nightingale Shelf) a hand form

Hua Quan (M) [Style] **1** Brilliant Fist; a northern Chinese style that emphasizes the cultivation of *qi, jing,* and *shen.* These three energies are referred to as *San Hua,* the Three Brilliancies. This style has also been called Xi Yu Hua Quan (Hua Fist of West Mountain), where it is said to have been created. **2** Sliding Fist

Hua Tuo (M) [Common Usage] a famous doctor of the second century A.D., he developed a set of therapeutic exercises based on the movements of animals and is credited with the development of acupuncture

hubae (K) [Common Usage] junior classmate

hubang gureugi (K) [Common Usage] backward roll

hubang nakbeop (K) [Hapkido, Kuk Sool] rear-falling technique

Hu Bao Quan (M) [Style] Tiger Leopard Fist

Hu Die Quan (M) [Style] Butterfly Fist

huen bo (C) [Wihng Cheun] *see* hyun bo

huen got sau (C) [Wihng Cheun] *see* hyun got sau

huen sau (C) [Wihng Cheun] *see* hyun sau

huet git (C) [Medicine] *see* hyut giht

hugul jase (K) [Tang Soo Do] back posture

hugul seogi (K) [Taekwondo] back stance

Hu He Pai (M) [Style] *see* Fu Hohk Paai

Hu He Shuang Xing Quan (M) [Hong Jia] *see* Fu Hohk Seung Yihng Kyuhn

huhng (C) [Common Usage] bear

huhng fa (C) [Medicine] the flower of this plant is commonly used in Chinese medicine to increase blood circulation and to reduce bruising

Huhng Faht (C) [Style] a hybrid southern style that combines Huhng Ga and Choy Leih Faht

Huhng Ga (C) [Style] (*lit.* Huhng Family Fist) A style developed by Huhng Hei Gun, it is known for its use of isometric breathing exercises, low strong stances, and powerful hand techniques, which stress the use of the entire body to create strong powerful strikes. The fighting methods are based on the movements of the five animals, which consist of the Dragon, Tiger, Crane, Snake, and Leopard. The Huhng Ga style is known for its various weapons such as the staff, *gwaan dou,* trident, and butterfly swords, and hand forms such as the Fu Hohk Seung Yihng Kyuhn, Gung Jih Fuhk Fu Kyuhn, Ngh Yihng Kyuhn, and Tit Sin Kyuhn.

Huhng Hei Gun (C) [Master] the founder of Huhng Ga, who

learned his art directly from the abbot of the Southern Shaolin Temple, Jih Sihn Sim Si

huhng sik (C) [Common Usage] red

Huhng Sing (C) [Style] *see* Hon Sihng

Huhng Sing Choi Leh Faht (C) [Style] Southern Choy Leih Faht

Huhng Yahn Baatgwa Kyuhn (C) [Choy Leih Faht] (*lit.* Bear-Man Eight Trigram Hand Form) a hand form

Huhng Ying Cheung Deui Chuk Gwaan Dou (C) [Choy Leih Faht] (*lit.* Spear Versus Gwaan Dou) a two-man fighting form

Huhng Yuht Dou (C) [Huhng Ga] (*lit.* Walking Moon Sword) a weapons form using a broadsword

hui (M) [Common Usage] *see* fui

hui da (M) [Common Usage] *see* daap

hui fu (M) [Common Usage] to recover

huin ying (M) [Common Usage] *see* fun yihng

Hui Si Shu (M) [Master] a student of Fang Qi Niang and a second-generation disciple of the Bai He style

hui yin (M) [Acupressure] a point located beneath the groin

huk (K) [Common Usage] hook punch

hullyeon (K) [Common Usage] drill

hullyeon ha da (K) [Common Usage] to drill, to train

hung (C) [Common Usage] chest

Hung Gar (C) [Style] *see* Huhng Ga

hung haak (C) [Common Usage] to threaten

hung jai (C) [Common Usage] to control; control

Hung Ji (C) [Common Usage] Confucius

Hung Kune (C) [Style] *see* Huhng Ga

Hung Sau Gaap Seung Pei Sau (C) [Choy Leih Faht] (*lit.* Empty Hands Versus Double Daggers) a two-man fighting form

huo (M) [Common Usage] *see* foh

Huo Yuan Chia (M) [Master] *see* Huo Yuan Jia

Huo Yuan Jia (M) [Master] a prominent master of Mi Zong Yi, or Labyrinthine Boxing, and founder of the Jing Wu Athletic Association in Shanghai

Hu Quan (M) [Style] (*lit.* Tiger Fist) a southern Chinese style originating in Fujian Province

huryeo chagi (K) [Taekwondo, Tae Kyon] **1** a Taekwondo slapping kick, whipping kick **2** roundhouse kick in Tae Kyon

hu shou yue (M) [Weapon] crescent-shaped axes usually used in pairs with short handles

hutoi ha da (K) [Common Usage] to retreat

Hu Wei San Jie Gun (M) [Wu Zu Quan] *see* Fu Meih Saam Jit Gwan

Hu Xing Ba Gua Quan (M) [Style] Tiger Eight Trigram Fist

hwai jong biao yeuh (M) [Xingyiquan] *see* huai zhong biao ye

hwal (K) [Kung Do] archer's bow

hwal eul ireukineun bang beop (K) [Kung Do] bow-stringing method

hwal ssogi (K) [Kung Do] archery

hwal teo (K) [Kung Do] archery practice place

hwang (K) [Common Usage] yellow

hwang ddi (K) [Common Usage] yellow belt

Hwang Kee (K) [Master] founder of modern Soo Bahk Do

hwang saek (K) [Common Usage] yellow color

hwangso makgi (K) [Taekwondo] (*lit.* Bull Block) high forearm block

hwang ting (C) [Common Usage] (*lit.* Yellow Yard or Hall) a meditation hall where Taoist priests wore yellow robes

hwang tyng (C) [Common Usage] *see* hwang ting

Hwarang (K) [Common Usage] (*lit.* Flowering Men) a military youth group of the Silla dynasty period, often credited with helping unify Paekche, Silla, and Koguryo

Hwarangdo (K) [Common Usage] (*lit.* Way of the Hwarang) a moral and ethical code heavily influenced by Buddhism

Hwarang hyung (K) [Taekwondo] form named after the Silla dynasty military youth group

Hwarang Segi (K) [Common Usage] (*lit.* Records of the Hwarang) a book describing the exploits of the Hwarang warriors

hwasal (K) [Kung Do] arrow

hwasal chok (K) [Kung Do] arrowhead

hyakurai ju (J) [Nin-jutsu] an explosive device used by ninja to distract or confuse the enemy

hyeo (K) [Common Usage] tongue

hyeol (K) [Common Usage] acupuncture region

hyeong (K) [Common Usage] *see* hyung

hyeophoi (K) [Common Usage] association

hyeophoi gi (K) [Common Usage] association flag

hyeorap (K) [Common Usage] blood pressure

hyodo (J) [Common Usage] an alternative name for swords-manship in particular, and budo in general

Hyosho-shiki (J) [Sumo] award ceremony held after the con-clusion of a tournament

hyun (C) [Kahm Na] *see* quan

hyun bo (C) [Wihng Cheun] circling steps

hyung (K) [Common Usage] form, prearranged sequence of movements

hyungbu (K) [Common Usage] upper body

hyun got sau (C) [Wihng Cheun] circling cut

Hyun Kyuhn (C) [Style] a southern style that has its origins in the Fujian province that specializes in ground-fighting techniques and attacks to vital points of the body

hyun sau (C) [Wihng Cheun] circling hand

hyut (C) [Common Usage] blood

hyut giht (C) [Medicine] a sap or resin used in Chinese med-icine to reduce pain, stop bleeding, heal cuts, and speed healing

hyut gun (C) [Common Usage] arteries

— I —

i (K) [Common Usage] two, tooth

iai (J) [Iaido] the art of drawing and striking with the sword in a single movement

iaido (J) [Style] (*lit.* The Way of Drawing the Sword) an art

that aims to teach self-cultivation and self-perfection through
the technique of drawing, cutting, cleaning, and sheathing the
sword; it is derived from iai-jutsu

iaigoshi (J) [Iai-jutsu, Karate] **1** kneeling stance preparatory
to drawing the sword **2** kneeling stance used in self-defense
training exercises

iaihiza (J) [Iaido, Kendo] half-seated, half-kneeling position

Iaihiza no Bu (J) [Iaido] a section of the Zen Nihon Kendo
Renmei Seitei Iai comprised of one technique done from a
half-seated, half-kneeling position

iai-jutsu (J) [Style] *see* iaido

iaito (J) [Iaido] a metal practice sword with a rebated edge

iawasu (J) [Iaido] an alternative name for iaido

ibi (O) [Common Usage] finger

ibo daeryeon (K) [Taekwondo] two-step sparring

ibo jayu daeryeon (K) [Taekwondo] two-step free sparring

ibo omgyeo didigi (K) [Taekwondo] double step

ibo omgyeo didimyeo dolgi (K) [Taekwondo] double-step
turn

ibuki (J) [Karate] to breathe out hard from the lower abdomen

ibukuro (J) [Common Usage] stomach

ichi (J) [Common Usage] one

ichiban (J) [Common Usage] number one, the best, the best
quality

Ichiden-ryu (J) [Ken-jutsu] a school of ken-jutsu, bo-jutsu,
and kusarigama-jutsu founded in the Tokugawa period

Ichimonjigata (O) [Karate] a *kata* practiced in Kojo-ryu

idan (K) [Common Usage] second-degree black belt

idanap chagi (K) [Taekwondo] jumping front kick

idan dollyeo chagi (K) [Taekwondo] jumping roundhouse kick

idan dwi dollyeo chagi (K) [Taekwondo] jump spinning back
kick

ido (J) [Common Usage] movement, travel

idori (J) [Judo, Ju-jutsu] a series of eight self-defense movements done from a kneeling position; techniques performed
from a seated or kneeling position

idubakgeun (K) [Common Usage] biceps

igadama (J) [Weapon] caltrop; sometimes used as a throwing weapon; also known as *tetsubishi*

Iga-ryu (J) [Style] a school of nin-jutsu

i geup (K) [Common Usage] second rank under black belt

igi da (K) [Common Usage] to win

iie (J) [Common Usage] "No!"

ijiggeut chigi (K) [Hapkido] technique in which the tips of index and middle fingers are used to strike

iji gwansu (K) [Taekwondo] two spear-finger

Ijo sidae (K) [Common Usage] Yi-dynasty period

Ijo wangjo (K) [Common Usage] Yi dynasty

ijung (K) [Common Usage] double

ijung chagi (K) [Common Usage] double kick

ijung ddwieo ap chagi (K) [Taekwondo] double jumping front kick

ijung makgi (K) [Taekwondo] double block

ikebana (J) [Common Usage] the Art of Flower Arrangement; some styles of this are heavily influenced by Zen Buddhism

iki (J) [Common Usage] breath

ikioi (J) [Common Usage] **1** impetus; momentum **2** the breath of life

ikkajo (J) [Aikido] the first immobilization technique of aikido; also known as *ikkyo* or *ude osae*

Ikkaku-ryu (J) [Style] a seventeenth-century school specializing in the *jutte,* or iron truncheon

ikkyo (J) [Aikido] see *ikkajo*

ikkyu (J) [Common Usage] first class, 1st Kyu

il (K) [Common Usage] one

ilbo daeryeon (K) [Taekwondo] one-step sparring

ilbo jayu daeryeon (K) [Taekwondo] one-step free sparring

Ilbon (K) [Common Usage] Japan

Ilbon musul (K) [Common Usage] Japanese martial art

il dae il eui ssaum (K) [Common Usage] one-to-one combat

ildan (K) [Common Usage] first-degree black belt

il geup (K) [Common Usage] first rank under black belt

ilgop (K) [Common Usage] seven

il hoi (K) [Common Usage] a round in sparring competition

ilji gwansu (K) [Taekwondo] single spear-finger

ilji gweon (K) [Kuk Sool, Taekwondo] raised first-knuckle fist

il su sik daeryeon (K) [Common Usage] one-step sparring

il yeo pumse (K) [Taekwondo] ninth-degree form

ima (J) [Common Usage] now; of the moment

ima (K) [Common Usage] forehead

ima jaegi (K) [Tae Kyon] palm strike to the forehead

inagashi (J) [Kyudo] a standard distance (about fifty-five meters) from which the long-range style of kyudo is practiced

Inamine Seijin (O) [Master] a student of Shimabuku Eizo and the founder of the Ryukyu Shorin-ryu Karate Association

inatobi (J) [Suiei-jutsu] a technique of jumping out of the water, an important combat tactic developed in suiei-jutsu

Inazuma (J) [Iaido, Acupressure] **1** the third iaido *kata* in the Muso Shinden-ryu Hasegawa Eishin-ryu Chuden series, which is done from *tatehiza* **2** the liver, an important vital point

inchi nawa (J) [Hojo-jutsu] a method of tying an opponent from behind

in ibuki (J) [Karate] internal breathing, common to many martial arts, especially in Goju-ryu

inja (K) [Common Usage] ninja

inji (K) [Common Usage] index finger

inji gweon (K) [Taekwondo, Hapkido] protruding first-knuckle fist

in jung (K) [Acupressure] philtrum, vital point on the upper lip

innaeryeok (K) [Common Usage] endurance

insa (K) [Common Usage] greeting

insa ha da (K) [Common Usage] to greet

intai (J) [Sumo] the act of retiring from competitive sumo and becoming a coach

inuou mono (J) [Kyudo] an ancient target practice exercise; dogs were used as targets and chased by mounted archers

in yo (J) [Common Usage] yin-yang

Inyo Shintai (J) [Iaido] the fifth *kata* in the Muso Shinden-ryu Omori-ryu Shoden series, which is done from *seiza*

ip (K) [Common Usage] mouth

ipgim (K) [Common Usage] bad breath

ippatsu (J) [Common Usage] a single blow

ippon gachi (J) [Common Usage] a contest in which victory is decided by a single full point

ippon ken (J) [Karate] a fist with a single knuckle protruding and used as the striking surface

ippon ken tsuki (J) [Karate] a thrust with the middle knuckle protruding and used as the striking surface

ippon kumite (J) [Karate] a sparring match involving a single full point

ippon seoi nage (J) [Judo] one-arm front shoulder throw

ipsul (K) [Common Usage] lip

ireona (K) [Common Usage] a command to "stand up"

ireru (J) [Common Usage] to put in, to place inside

irimi (J) [Common Usage] entering; an entering movement

iriminage (J) [Aikido] a throw in which the person performing the technique "enters" or closes with the opponent and throws with a cutting or thrusting movement

Irumagawa (J) [Sumo] a sumo *beya* located in Yono City, Saitama Prefecture

isamiashi (J) [Sumo] a situation in which a *rikishi* who is apparently about to win a match loses because he has inadvertently stepped out of bounds before his opponent does so or is thrown down

Isegahama (J) [Sumo] a sumo *beya* located in Kashiwa City, Chiba Prefecture

Isenoumi (J) [Sumo] a sumo *beya* located in Edogawa Ward, Tokyo

ishibukuro (O) [Karate] (*lit.* A Bag of Rocks) a supplemental training device

Ishimine-ryu (O) [Style] a relatively small style of the Shurite

isip (K) [Common Usage] twenty

Iso Mataemon (J) [Master] founder of Tenshin Shinyo-ryu ju-jutsu

Isshin Itto (J) [Ken-jutsu] (*lit.* One Spirit One Sword) a motto used by Ito Ittosai Kagehisa, founder of the Itto-ryu

Isshin-ryu (O) [Style] a hybrid style of Okinawan karate developed by Tatsuo Shimabuku in 1954; a combination of Goju-ryu and Shorin-ryu

issoku (J) [Common Usage] **1** a pair (of shoes of sandals) **2** a single step

issoku itto no ma (J) [Kendo, Naginata] a distance or interval where one can attack the opponent after taking a single step

itame hada (J) [Weapon] wood grain, a commonly seen pattern on sword blades

itami wake (J) [Competitive Budo] a ruling of "no contest" is given by the referee when a competitor is unable to fight due to injury, or upon a doctor's advice

Ito Ittosai Kagehisa (J) [Master] the founder of Itto-ryu ken-jutsu

itomeru (J) [Kyudo] to kill someone with an arrow

ito suguha (J) [Weapon] a narrow, straight temper line on a blade

Itosu Yasutsune (O) [Master] a master of Shuri-te who studied under Matsumura Sokon; the teacher of Chibana Choshin, Mabuni Kenwa, Funakoshi Gichin, Yabu Kentsu, and Hanashiro Chomo; also known as "Ankoh" Itosu

Itsutsu no Kata (J) [Judo] one of the official *kata* of Kodokan judo, it is considered unfinished and its techniques do not have any names; the techniques are said to represent the fundamental principles of judo throwing techniques

Ittatsu-ryu (J) [Style] a school of hojo-jutsu famous for being used to immobilize suspects by the Japan police force, which now trains its members in the basic techniques of this art as an alternative to handcuffing

Itto-ryu (J) [Style] a school of ken-jutsu founded in the sixteenth century by Itto Kagehisa and said to have been developed from the concept that a single technique, the *kiri otoshi*, constitutes the essence of all techniques and can be adapted to meet any situation

Iwanami (J) [Iaido] the sixth *kata* in the Muso Shinden-ryu Hasegawa Eishin-ryu Chuden series, which is done from *tatehiza*

Izutsu (J) [Sumo] a sumo *beya* located in Sumida Ward, Tokyo

— J —

jaak beih (C) [Common Usage] to reproach, to reprimand

jaat laan (C) [Medicine] the leaves and branches of this plant are used in Chinese medicine to increase blood circulation and to reduce bruising

jaau (C) [Common Usage] broom

jaau (C) [Common Usage] *see* zhou

jabadaegi (K) [Tae Kyon] kick-defense in which the heel is trapped

jaban dwijigi (K) [Ssi Rum] technique in which an opponent on one's back is flipped to the side and taken down

jaejuneom da (K) [Common Usage] to do a somersault

jaejuneomgi (K) [Common Usage] somersault

jai zhi (M) [Common Usage] *see* ga jihk

jajeonbal (K) [Taekwondo] foot shuffling

jajeonbal omgyeo didigi (K) [Taekwondo] shifting step, a change of foot positions

jam (C) [Common Usage] to pour

Ja Ma Dou (C) [Weapon] (*lit.* Horse-Cutting Sword) a weapon used for cutting a horse's legs in battle

jam chah (C) [Common Usage] to pour tea; to offer tea; a part of many ceremonies

jami (J) [Weapon] steel of medium hardness used in making a sword

jam sau (C) [Wihng Cheun] sinking block

jan (C) [Baahk Hok] *see* zhan

jang (K) [Common Usage] long

jangbi (K) [Common Usage] equipment

jang bong (K) [Common Usage] long staff

jang geom ssanggeom hyeong (K) [Kuk Sool] double long-sword form

jang gweon (K) [Taekwondo] palm heel

jang hahn (C) [Common Usage] hate

jang jeo (K) [Tae Kyon] palm heel

jang leuhn (C) [Common Usage] dispute

jang mugi (K) [Common Usage] long weapon

jangsa geup (K) [Ssi Rum] 90.1-kilogram and over adult weight class of amateur competition

japchaegi (K) [Ssi Rum] technique in which the opponent's sash is pulled and the hip is thrust against the opponent's abdomen before he is thrown

jap da (K) [Common Usage] to hold, to grab

japgi (K) [Kuk Sool] grappling technique

jareu da (K) [Common Usage] to cut

jase (K) [Common Usage] posture

jat lan (C) [Medicine] *see* jaat laan

jau (C) [Common Usage] *see* zou

jauh leuih chohng fa (C) [Huhng Ga] (*lit.* Flower Hidden in Sleeves) an open palm push across the body of the practitioner

jayu (K) [Common Usage] free, freedom

jayu daeryeon (K) [Common Usage] free sparring

Jayu Jung Gong (K) [Common Usage] (*lit.* Free China) Taiwan

je (C) [Weapon] umbrella

jebipum mok chigi (K) [Taekwondo] swallow-shaped neck strike

jechin pyeonson ggeut (K) [Taekwondo] palm-upward spearfingers

jechyeo jireugi (K) [Taekwondo] upper punch

jeja (K) [Common Usage] follower, student

jek gwat (C) [Common Usage] vertebrae

jeogi chagi (K) [Tae Kyon] kick in which the heel travels out and up, then retracts horizontally to strike

jeol (K) [Common Usage] **1** religious temple **2** standing bow in Tae Kyon

jeol gwansu (K) [Hapkido] bent-knuckle spearhand

Jeol Musul (K) [Style] (*lit.* Temple Martial Skill) the martial arts taught in select Buddhist temples

jeom (K) [Common Usage] point awarded in sparring competition

jeonbang gureugi (K) [Common Usage] forward roll

jeonbang nakbeop (K) [Hapkido, Kuk Sool] forward-falling technique

Jeong Do-mo (K) [Master] founder of Kun Gek Do

jeonggangi (K) [Common Usage] shin

jeonggangi chagi (K) [Common Usage] shin kick

jeonggangi dae (K) [Common Usage] shin pad

jeonggangi makgi (K) [Common Usage] shin block

Jeong Geom hyeong (K) [Kuk Sool] (*lit.* Straight-Hold Sword Form) a weapons form using the sword

jeong gwansu (K) [Taekwondo] straight spear-finger

jeonggweon (K) [Common Usage] straight punch

jeonggweon chigi (K) [Hapkido] *see* jeonggweon

jeong hwak (K) [Common Usage] accuracy

jeong jeok in (K) [Common Usage] static, stationary

jeongsin (K) [Common Usage] mind, spirit

jeongsin tongil (K) [Common Usage] spirit unification

Jeong Tong Muye Do (K) [Style] (*lit.* Original Martial Art Way) a martial art derived from Hapkido

jeongul baro jireugi (K) [Taekwondo] forward stance lunge punch

jeongul jase (K) [Tang Soo Do] forward posture

jeongul seogi (K) [Taekwondo] forward stance

jeon jaeng (K) [Common Usage] war

jeonjin ha da (K) [Common Usage] to advance

jeon mun ga (K) [Common Usage] expert

jeonsi (K) [Common Usage] demonstration, exhibition

jeonsi ha da (K) [Common Usage] to demonstrate, to exhibit

jeon tong (K) [Common Usage] tradition

Jeontong Mudo (K) [Style] (*lit.* Traditional Martial Way) a collective term for traditional self-defense skills combined with philosophical teachings

Jeontong Musul (K) [Style] (*lit.* Traditional Martial Skill) a collective term for traditional self-defense skills with less emphasis on philosophy

Jeontong Muye (K) [Style] (*lit.* Traditional Martial Art) often used to refer to Tae Kyon

jeontu (K) [Common Usage] battle, combat

jeontu ha da (K) [Common Usage] to engage in combat, to fight

jeopgeunjeon gweontu (K) [Common Usage] infighting

jeopjilli da (K) [Common Usage] to sprain

jeopjillim (K) [Common Usage] sprain

jeotggokji (K) [Common Usage] nipple

jeuhng (C) [Common Usage] elephant

jeui (C) [Common Usage] lips

jeuih (C) [Common Usage] guilt

Jeui Kyuhn (C) [Style] *see* Zui Quan

jeui seuhn (C) [Common Usage] *see* jeui

jeuk (C) [Common Usage] to pour wine, to toast, or to feast

jeung (C) [Common Usage] puffy, swollen

jeung bui (C) [Common Usage] trophy cup

jeung chihng (C) [Common Usage] regulations

jeung gam (C) [Common Usage] monetary award

jeung gwan (C) [Common Usage] general of an army

jeung myeong seo (K) [Common Usage] certificate

Jeung Yihm (C) [Master] a prominent Choy Leih Faht master and a second-generation disciple of Chahn Heung

jeun mah cheut jeung (C) [Huhng Ga] (*lit.* Forward Horse Striking Palm) a palm strike to the side at kidney level while in a bow and arrow stance

ji (C) [Common Usage] limbs

ji (C) [Common Usage] *see* miu

ji (J) [Weapon] the surface of the blade of a weapon

ji (M) [Common Usage] *see* gai

ji (M) [Common Usage] **1** muscle **2** press; a posture in taijiquan that is used as primary action in an exercise called push-hands *(tui shou)*

jia (M) [Common Usage] *see* ga

jia (M) [Qin Na] to hold under the arm

jian (M) [Common Usage] **1** shoulders **2** double-edged straight sword

jian ding (M) [Common Usage] *see* pai pihng

jiang (M) [Common Usage] to award; award or prize

jiang bei (M) [Common Usage] *see* jeung bui

Jiang Rang Qiao (M) [Master] a prominent master of ba-guazhang

jiang tai (M) [Acupressure] a point located at the upper area of the pectoral muscle

jian jing (M) [Acupressure] a point located on the top of the trapezius muscle

jian quan (M) [Common Usage] *see* gihn hong

jiao (M) [Common Usage] **1** foot **2** to teach **3** to twist

jiao (M) [Common Usage] *see* giu

jiao ao (M) [Common Usage] *see* giu ngouh

jiao bo (M) [Common Usage] heel of foot

jiao hua (M) [Common Usage] *see* gaau waaht

jiao xun (M) [Common Usage] *see* gaau fan

jiap sul (K) [Kuk Sool] pressure-point technique

jiap yo beop (K) [Common Usage] acupressure

ji bouh bui liah (C) [Baahk Meih] the salute prior to starting the Baahk Meih Pah form

Jichin (O) [Karate] a *kata* practiced in the Bugeikan style

ji chu (M) [Common Usage] foundation

ji de (M) [Common Usage] *see* gei dak

ji dihng jung yuhn (C) [Huhng Ga] (*lit.* Pulling Out the Single Candle) an open-handed block across the body using the *kiuh sau*

jie (M) [Common Usage] *see* jit

jiei (J) [Common Usage] self-defense

jie jue (M) [Common Usage] *see* gaai kyut

jie shao (M) [Common Usage] *see* gaai siuh

jigeiko (J) [Judo, Kendo, Naginata] free training; training without direct instruction

Jigen no Jo (O) [Kobudo] a *jo kata* practiced in Ryukyu Kobudo

Jigen-ryu (J) [Style] a school of ken-jutsu founded by Togo Hizen no Kami Jui known for its strong, aggressive technique

jigi (K) [Common Usage] internal energy received from the earth

jigo hontai (J) [Judo] a defensive stance with the feet shoulder-width apart and the hips lowered to give the exponent more stability

ji gok (C) [Common Usage] *see* gan qing

Jigoro Kano (J) [Judo] *see* Kano Jigoro

jigotai (J) [Judo, Karate] **1** a defensive judo stance with the feet in a wide position and the hips lowered **2** a karate stance in which the legs are bent with the front foot pointing forward and the back foot pointing to the side

ji gweon (K) [Taekwondo] knuckle fist

jih (C) [Common Usage] *see* yi

ji hada (J) [Weapon] the structural layering of the metals in the blade of a *katana, naginata,* or *yari*

jihng (C) [Common Usage] quiet, calm

Jih Sihn Sim Si (C) [Master] *see* Huhng Ga

ji hsing shyr baa (M) [Xingyiquan] *see* ji xing shi ba

Jiht Kyuhn (C) [Ying Jaau] intercepting fist, or quick fist form

Jiin (O) [Karate] a *kata* in Shuri-te

ji jeon tong (K) [Kung Do] quiver

jikan (J) [Competitive Budo] time out

ji lie (M) [Common Usage] *see* gik liht

Ji Long Feng (M) [Master] a prominent master and potential founder of xingyiquan

jiman (J) [Kyudo] the fifth position in kyudo

jime (J) [Judo, Ju-jutsu] *see* shime

ji meih chaang tin (C) [Huhng Ga] (*lit.* Fingertips Supporting the Heavens) a blocking movement using the base of the hand with the fingers pointing upwards

ji mihng (C) [Common Usage] *see* ji ming

ji mihng seung (C) [Common Usage] fatal or mortal wound

ji ming (M) [Common Usage] fatal, mortal

ji ming shang (M) [Common Usage] *see* ji mihng seung

jim ji pek cheuih (C) [Common Usage] short, diagonal blow to the area between the fist and the first half of the forearm

ji mouh dou (C) [Huhng Ga] *see* wu dip dou

Ji Mouh Kyuhn (C) [Ying Jaau] (*lit.* Son Mother Fist) a hand form

jin (C) [Baahk Hok] *see* zhan

jin (J) [Common Usage] **1** tendons or muscles **2** the Confucian concept of benevolence

Jin Chao Dai (M) [Common Usage] Jin Imperial dynasty, which ruled China from A.D. 265 to 420

jin cheuih (C) [Common Usage] arrow fist; a flat fist with the back of the hand facing up

jinchu (J) [Acupressure] the pressure point above the upper lip at the base of the nose

jindachi (J) [Weapon] a type of mounting used by mounted warriors, sometimes called *tachi*

jindachi zukuri (J) [Weapon] a type of Japanese sword, worn hanging from the hip

Jinddoi hyeong (K) [Tang Soo Do] form named after a karate form composed of fifty-four movements

jin fei cao (M) [Medicine] a root used in Chinese herbal medicine

jing (C) [Hei Gung] essence

jing (M) [Common Usage] **1** shin **2** a power in which *qi* has energized the muscles in order for them to reach their maximum potential

jing (M) [Common Usage] *see* ging

Jin Gang Ba Shi (M) [Bajiquan] (*lit.* Eight Exercises of the Buddha's Warrior Attendant) a routine in the Bajiquan style

jin gang chu dong (M) [Hong Jia] *see* gam gong cheut duhng

jin gang liang bi (M) [Qigong] (*lit.* Diamond Bright Arms) a Taoist breathing exercise in Shi San Tai Bao Gong

jin gang zao (M) [Weapon] chisel-shaped weapons usually used in pairs

jing chaih (C) [Common Usage] *see* chaih jing

jing chu (M) [Acupressure] a point located on the lower back near the kidneys

jing da ji (M) [Medicine] a root used in Chinese herbal medicine

jingeup (K) [Common Usage] promotion

jingeup jeung (K) [Common Usage] promotion certificate

jingeup siheom (K) [Common Usage] promotion test

jing gao (M) [Common Usage] *see* ging gou

ji ngh diu taih mah (C) [Wihng Cheun] (*lit.* Meridian Half-Hanging Stance) a stance that allows the practitioner to distribute his weight

Ji Ngh Gim (C) [Chat Sing Tohng Lohng] (*lit.* Son Noon Sword) a weapons form using a straight sword

ji ngh jyu kiuh (C) [Huhng Ga] (*lit.* Pearl Bridge at Noon) a circular block using the *kiuh sau* in a bow and arrow stance

ji ngh mah (C) [Wihng Cheun] meridian stance

jing huang (M) [Common Usage] *see* xia

jing kok (C) [Common Usage] correct, accurate

Jingluo (M) [Common Usage] the meridian system; the network of fourteen energy pathways along which *qi* travels through the body

ji ng ma (C) [Common Usage] *see* dihng jih ma

Jing Mo (M) [School] *see* Jing Wu

jingnip han (K) [Common Usage] upright

jing qi (M) [Common Usage] *see* ging hei

Jing Wu (M) [School] a famous martial arts academy in Shanghai founded by Huo Yuan Jia

jing zhong zhao (M) [Common Usage] (*lit.* Golden Bell Cover) a training method for invulnerability, also known as "iron shirt/vest"

Jin He (M) [Bai He] (*lit.* Golden Crane) a hand form in Fei He

jin hua chui (M) [Weapon] hand-held weapons usually used in pairs consisting of oval-shaped metal balls decorated with flower patterns mounted at the end of short shafts

Jin Hua Qiang (M) [Wu Zu Quan] *see* Gam Fa Cheung

jinja (J) [Shinto] a Shinto shrine

jin ji du li (M) [Bai Mei] (*lit.* Golden Cockerel Stands on Single Leg) a stance or posture in which one leg is raised protecting the groin area while the other supports the weight and one arm blocks high and the other low

Jin Ji Du Li Dan Dao (M) [Wu Zu Quan] *see* Gam Gai Duhk Lahp Daan Dou

jin ji fu li xi (M) [Xingyiquan] (*lit.* Golden Rooster Stands on One Leg) a movement performed while balanced on one leg

jin ji shang bu (M) [Xingyiquan] (*lit.* Golden Rooster Steps Forward) an advancing technique in this internal martial art

jin long he kou (M) [Qigong] (*lit.* Golden Dragon Closes its Mouth) a breathing exercise in Shi San Tai Bao Gong

jin ma chu dong (M) [Hong Jia] *see* jeun mah cheut jeung

jin qiao xiang ding (M) [Hong Jia] *see* gam kiuh seung dihng

Jin Quan (M) [Style] Gold Fist

jin se (M) [Common Usage] *see* gam sik

Jin Shin Do (J) [Common Usage] a type of massage

Jin Shi Quan (M) [Style] Golden Lion Fist

jin ya chuan lian (M) [Zhu Jia] (*lit.* Golden Duck Ascends from the Lotus Leaf) a form or exercise that is used to develop short powerful phoenix eye fist punches, strikes, and blocks in a way that is deceptive to an opponent

jinzo (J) [Common Usage] kidney

Jion (O) [Karate] a *kata* in Shuri-te

Jion hyeong (K) [Tang Soo Do] form named after a karate form composed of one hundred movements

jip (C) [Common Usage] to catch

jipangi (K) [Common Usage] walking cane

jipangi sul (K) [Hapkido, Kuk Sool Won] cane technique

jipge jumeok (K) [Taekwondo] pincer fist

jipge son (K) [Tang Soo Do] pincer hand

jipge songarak (K) [Common Usage] index finger

jipjung (K) [Common Usage] concentration

jipjung ha da (K) [Common Usage] to focus, to concentrate

jippon kumite (J) [Karate] sparring practice in which one person does ten consecutive attacks while the other defends

jip sauh (C) [Common Usage] to approve, to accept

jip sin (K) [Tae Kyon] traditional Korean sandals made of woven rice straw, now worn by students of Tae Kyon as part of their uniform

ji quan (M) [Acupressure] a point located at the armpit

jirai (J) [Nin-jutsu] a type of fused land mine used by ninja

jireugi (K) [Taekwondo] punch, thrust

jireumyeo chagi (K) [Taekwondo] combination technique involving a punch and a kick

ji rou (M) [Common Usage] *see* gei yuhk

ji sai (C) [Common Usage] posture, action, movement, or gesture

ji samurai (J) [Common Usage] farmer-warriors living and farming their own land in the countryside

ji shu (M) [Common Usage] technique

ji sik (C) [Common Usage] *see* zi se

jissen kumite (J) [Karate] real combat; a training bout approximating a real fight

jit (C) [Common Usage] joint

Ji Tae pumse (K) [Taekwondo] Sixth-Degree form

jita kyoei (J) [Judo] Mutual Prosperity and Welfare; a phrase coined by Kano Jigoro to define one of the goals of judo training

jit fu cheuih (C) [Common Usage] blocking tiger fist

Jitte (O) [Karate] a *kata* in Shuri-te

jiu (M) [Common Usage] nine

jiu chi ding ba (M) [Weapon] a rake consisting of a series of long spikes on a round surface supported by a long shaft

jiu geng sau (C) [Huhng Ga] (*lit.* Shiny Mirror Hand) a blocking technique using an open palm

Jiu Gong San Pan Zhang (M) [Style] (*lit.* Nine Unit Three Plate Palm) a style of baguazhang

jiu gya (M) [Common Usage] surprise

jiu huan jin bei da dao (M) [Weapon] A long broad sword

mounted at the head of a staff. The blade has nine rings attached to the serrated edge of the back of the blade, and there is a spear head at the opposite end of the staff.

Jiu Long Baguazhang (M) [Style] (*lit.* Nine Dragon Eight Trigram Palm) a style of baguazhang

jiu long tao (M) [Weapon] hand-held weapons usually used in pairs consisting of metal rods with a spear head at one end, and a circular ring on the other

jiu xi (M) [Common Usage] *see* yan xi

Jiu Yuan Ting (M) [Master] a prominent master of xingyi-quan

jiu za jin qiang (M) [Qigong] (*lit.* Thrusting the Golden Spears) a breathing exercise in Shi San Tai Bao Gong

Jixiao Xinshu (M) [Common Usage] an eighteen-chapter treatise on military tactics by the sixteenth-century general Qi Jiguan; it included illustrations of armed and unarmed combat techniques

ji xing shi ba (M) [Xingyiquan] a pushing technique that is executed while advancing forward

ji xu (M) [Common Usage] *see* gai juhk

ji yihn tong (C) [Medicine] a mineral commonly used in Chinese medicine to heal bone injuries

jiyu (J) [Common Usage] free; freedom, liberty

jiyu ippon kumite (J) [Karate] free sparring match in which the first to make a valid point wins the bout

jiyu kumite (J) [Karate] free sparring

jiyu renshu (J) [Common Usage] free practice

jiyu waza (J) [Aikido] free technique or practice, similar to either judo randori or karate *jiyu kumite*

jja da (K) [Common Usage] to squeeze

jjae (K) [Tae Kyon] Tae Kwon's equivalent of the *geup* rankings of other Korean martial arts

jjae chagi (K) [Tae Kyon] modified front kick that is angled from the inside to the outside

jjigeo chagi (K) [Common Usage] hook kick

jjigeo chagi (K) [Hapkido] chopping kick

jjikgi (K) [Kuk Sool] axe kick, chopping kick

Jjindo hyeong (K) [Tang Soo Do] a form named after a karate form composed of eighty-six movements

jjireu da (K) [Common Usage] to stab

jjireugi (K) [Common Usage] stab, thrust

jo (C) [Common Usage] left, left side

jo (J) [Weapon] a stick or short staff used in aikido, jo-jutsu, and Okinawan kobudo

joba (J) [Common Usage] horse(back) riding; on horseback

joba-jutsu (J) [Style] the art of military horsemanship; mounted combat

jo chaan (C) [Common Usage] breakfast

jodan (J) [Kendo, Naginata] upper-level *kamae*

jodan age uke (J) [Karate] upper-level block

jodan kosa uke (J) [Karate] a upper-level cross block

jodan tsuki (J) [Karate] upper-level punch

jodan uchi shuto uke (J) [Karate] an upper-level inner knife-hand block

jodo (J) [Common Usage] **1** (*lit.* The Way of the Stick, Stick Way) a form of weapons training in which a stick is used against a sword; it is similar to iaido and kendo in that the purpose of such training is self-cultivation, and spiritual and physical discipline rather than combative effect or self-defense **2** one of the most widespread sect of Japanese Buddhism, with over 29,000 temples in Japan

jogai (J) [Competitive Budo] out of bounds

jogai chui (J) [Competitive Budo] a warning for repeatedly going out of bounds

joge buri (J) [Kendo, Naginata] a vertical swinging movement, raising the weapon from *chudan kamae* over one's head and back to a mid- or low-level position

johap gonggyeok (K) [Common Usage] combination attack

joh diu geuk ma (C) [Common Usage] hanging leg stance

joh ma (C) [Common Usage] *see* joh sei pihng ma

joh mah daan kiuh (C) [Huhng Ga] (*lit.* Sitting Horse Single Bridge) a *kiuh sau* block to the side while in a horse stance

joh sei pihng ma (C) [Common Usage] left square horse stance

jo hwa (K) [Common Usage] harmony

joi jouh (C) [Common Usage] *see* zai zuo

joi syut (C) [Common Usage] *see* zai zuo

jojeong (K) [Common Usage] coordination

jojik (K) [Common Usage] organization

Jo Jin Kyuhn (C) [Ngh Jou Kyuhn] (*lit.* Left Side Battle Fist) a form

jo-jutsu (J) [Style] (*lit.* Stick Art, Stick-Fighting) the first school in this art was the Shinto Muso-ryu; it was founded by Muso Gonnosuke Katsuyoshi, who had trained in the Tenshin Shoden Katori Shinto-ryu and was famous for his use of the *rokushaku bo* (a staff 198 centimeters in length)

jok (K) [Common Usage] foot

jok bangeo sul (K) [Kuk Sool] counterkick technique, kick-defense technique

jokdo (K) [Taekwondo] foot sword, knife edge of the foot

jokdo natgecha dolligi (K) [Hapkido] low spinning kick in which the blade of the foot is used as a striking surface

jokdo seweo chanaerigi (K) [Hapkido] push kick in which the blade of the foot strikes in a downward motion

jokdo seweo milgi (K) [Hapkido] push kick in which the blade of the foot is used as a striking surface

jokgi (K) [Taekwondo, Tang Soo Do] foot technique

jokgi beop (K) [Tang Soo Do] foot technique

jokgi daeryeon (K) [Taekwondo] foot-technique sparring, kick sparring

jok sul (K) [Common Usage] foot skill

Jok Sul Do (K) [Style] (*lit.* Foot Skill Way) a martial art composed of several thousand kicks and combinations

jong (C) [Common Usage] **1** uppercut **2** wooden piles or dummy

jongari (K) [Common Usage] lower rear part of the leg, calf

jongari bbyeo (K) [Common Usage] fibula

jong heung (C) [Common Usage] to place incense into an urn

jongji bbyeo (K) [Common Usage] kneecap

Jonidan (J) [Sumo] the second lowest of the six divisions of sumo

jonin (J) [Nin-jutsu] a leader or high-ranking member of a ninja group

Jonokuchi (J) [Sumo] the lowest division in sumo

jook duen (C) [Medicine] *see* juhk dyun

jo sau po paaih (C) [Huhng Ga] (*lit.* Left Hand Breaking Ribs) a movement that traps the opponent's arm with one hand while striking the rib cage with the other

joseki (J) [Common Usage] (*lit.* Upper Seat) a place of honor in a room or dojo; the more highly regarded side of the room, farthest from the entrance

Joseon sidae (K) [Common Usage] *see* Chosun sidae

Joseon wangjo (K) [Common Usage] *see* Chosun wangjo

Joshi Goshin-ho (J) [Judo] a set of self-defense techniques mainly practiced by female judoka

joshiki (J) [Common Usage] common sense

josokutei (J) [Common Usage] the ball of the foot

jouh gong fu (C) [Common Usage] to perform martial arts

jou sahn (C) [Common Usage] early morning, good morning

jou si (C) [Common Usage] the name given to the founder of a style or system of Chinese martial arts

jou sin (C) [Common Usage] ancestors

jou sin daahn (C) [Common Usage] ancestral anniversary celebration

jou tauh (C) [Common Usage] early rest, good night, or good evening

jo wahn yauh kiuh (C) [Huhng Ga] (*lit.* Left Delivering the Soft Bridge) a blocking movement to the side of the body with both hands

Jo Yauh Daaih Pah (C) [Baahk Meih] (*lit.* Left Right Big Trident) a weapons form using the trident

joza (J) [Common Usage] *see* kamiza

jozu (J) [Common Usage] skillful

ju (J) [Common Usage] ten

ju cheung (C) [Wihng Cheun] *see* jyu cheung

juchum seogi (K) [Taekwondo] riding stance

judan (J) [Common Usage] tenth-degree black belt, 10th Dan; the highest attainable rank in many martial arts

judo (J) [Style] (*lit.* Gentle Way) A sport founded by Kano Jigoro in 1882, derived from the fighting techniques of ju-jutsu. In 1964 judo was recognized as an Olympic sport and is now a regular feature in virtually all international sporting events.

judogi (J) [Judo] the training uniform worn in judo

judojo (J) [Judo] a judo training hall

judoka (J) [Common Usage] someone who studies judo

jue ding (M) [Common Usage] *see* kyut dihng

jue wu (M) [Common Usage] awareness

jugu (M) [Acupressure] a point located on the top part of the shoulder

ju gum sau (C) [Wihng Cheun] *see* jyu gam sau

juhk cheut (C) [Common Usage] to exile, to expel

juhk dyun (C) [Medicine] the root of this plant is commonly used in Chinese medicine to heal bone injuries

juhk ga daih ji (C) [Common Usage] (*lit.* Common Family Students) laymen who were allowed to learn the martial arts at the Shaolin Temple after the Qing dynasty

juho (J) [Shorinji Kempo] the "soft" or grappling techniques in the system, consisting of throwing, pinning, joint-locking, and escaping techniques

juh sun mah (C) [Wihng Cheun] diagonal stance

juichidan (J) [Judo] eleventh-degree black belt, 11th Dan; the only person ever to reach this rank was Kano Jigoro, the founder of Kodokan judo

juji (J) [Common Usage] cross

juji uke (J) [Karate] cross or X-block

ju jue (M) [Common Usage] *see* keuih jyuht

ju-jutsu (J) [Style] (*lit.* Flexible Way, Way of Flexibility) Techniques for close combat, including throwing, pinning, joint-locking, striking and kicking, and choking and strangling, which were used by *bushi*. The roots of this art have been traced to before the eleventh century. Today, many different branches and styles exist, as well as modern derivatives such as aikido and judo.

juk (C) [Common Usage] bamboo

juk (C) [Common Usage] *see* jip

juk do (K) [Kum Do] bamboo sword used in practice, similar to Japanese *shinai*

juken (J) [Common Usage] bayonet

jukendo (J) [Style] a modern form of juken-jutsu; practiced for physical and spiritual discipline rather than combative effectiveness

juken-jutsu (J) [Style] the art of bayonet combat; it was developed during the Meiji era, based on the traditional spear-fighting techniques of so-jutsu

juk jyuh (C) [Common Usage] *see* juk

juk lahm jong (C) [Choy Leih Faht] (*lit.* Bamboo Forest Dummy) a training tool used to develop and strengthen hand and foot techniques

juk saan (C) [Common Usage] *see* juk

juku gashira (J) [Common Usage] the senior student of a dojo or teacher; often, the one who will receive all the teaching and technical knowledge the master has to offer

jukuren (J) [Common Usage] mastery

Jukyo (J) [Common Usage] Confucianism

jumeok (K) [Common Usage] fist

jumeok dallyeon (K) [Taekwondo] fist training

jumeok him (K) [Common Usage] punching power

jumeok jwineun beop (K) [Common Usage] fist-making method

jumeok meori (K) [Tae Kyon] knuckle striking area of the fist

jumeok moseori (K) [Tae Kyon] hand-edge striking area of the fist

jumeok ssaum (K) [Common Usage] fistfight

jumonji (J) [Bushido] the act of turning the blade and cutting upwards during *seppuku;* considered a sign of honor and valor because of the pain it involved

Jumonjigata (O) [Karate] a *kata* practiced in Kojo-ryu

jumonji no kamae (J) [Nin-jutsu] a *kamae* in which the legs are bent and the arms crossed in front of the face

---

jum sau (C) [Wihng Cheun] *see* jam sau

junbi (K) [Common Usage] a command to "get ready"

junbi ha da (K) [Common Usage] to get ready

junbi jase (K) [Taekwondo, Tang Soo Do] ready posture

junbi seogi (K) [Taekwondo] ready stance

junbi taiso (J) [Common Usage] *see* junbi undo

junbi undo (J) [Common Usage] preparatory movements; warm-up training

junbi undong (K) [Common Usage] warm-up exercise

jung (C) [Common Usage] **1** middle **2** loyal, just

jung (K) [Common Usage] monk

jungbae geori (K) [Tae Kyon] foot sweep directed at the opponent's calf area

jung bong (K) [Common Usage] middle-length staff

jung bong hyeong (K) [Kuk Sool] (*lit.* Middle-Length Staff Form) a weapons form using the staff

jung daan tihn (C) [Common Usage] center of the body; an energy center

jungdan bangeo (K) [Common Usage] middle-level defense

jungdan makgi (K) [Tang Soo Do] middle-level block

Jung Geun hyeong (K) [Taekwondo] *see* Chung Gun hyung

junggeup ban (K) [Kuk Sool] middle-level course

junggeup hyeong (K) [Kuk Sool] middle-level form

Jung Gong (K) [Common Usage] Communist China

Jungguk (K) [Common Usage] (*lit.* Middle Country) China

Jungguk musul (K) [Common Usage] Chinese martial art

Jung Gwun Kyuhn (C) [Ngh Jou Kyuhn] (*lit.* Middle Pipe Fist) a hand form

Jung Hok Kyuhn (C) [Style] *see* Bai He

junghwa ha da (K) [Common Usage] to neutralize

jungji (K) [Common Usage] middle finger

jungji gweon (K) [Kuk Sool, Taekwondo] raised middle-knuckle fist

Jung Kwaang (C) [Mihng Hok Kyuhn] *see* Zhong Kuang

jung laahn chi pah (C) [Baahk Meih] a striking movement in the Baahk Meih Pah form countering an opponent's attack

jung lo (C) [Wihng Cheun] mid-level; a region of the body located below the sternum and above the groin

jung saam sin (C) [Wihng Cheun] centerline or median line; a vertical line through the center of the body

jung sam (C) [Common Usage] (*lit.* Middle Heart) someone who is loyal or true from the heart

jungsim (K) [Common Usage] center

jungsim gyunhyeong (K) [Common Usage] center of balance

jungsim seon (K) [Common Usage] centerline

jung sin (C) [Wihng Cheun] *see* jung saam sin

jun gyeolseung (K) [Common Usage] semifinal

jungyo (J) [Sumo] exhibition tours that follow the fifteen-day official tournaments; these tours give people in the country-side a chance to see sumo up close and meet the *rikishi* in a more informal setting

junidan (J) [Judo] twelfth-degree black belt, 12th Dan; the highest rank possible in judo; the only person ever to attain this rank was Kano Jigoro, the founder of modern judo

junin gake (J) [Judo, Karate] a training exercise where one person fights ten consecutive opponents

jun jun gyeolseung (K) [Common Usage] quarterfinal

Ju no Kata (J) [Judo] (*lit.* Forms of Flexibility) one of the official Kodokan judo kata, emphasizing flexibility of move-ment in response to an attack and done slowly, without any sudden, rapid movements

Junto (J) [Iaido] the seventh *kata* in the Muso Shinden-ryu Omori-ryu Shoden series, which is done from *seiza*

Juryo (J) [Sumo] second-highest division of the six levels of sumo; the first of the salaried division; at this point the *rikishi* is called a *sekitori*

ju sun kuen (C) [Wihng Cheun] *see* jyu sun kyuhn

ju sun ma (C) [Wihng Cheun] *see* juh sun mah

jut sau (C) [Wihng Cheun] *see* jyut sau

jutsu (J) [Common Usage] art; used to distinguish between the older martial arts intended for combat and more contem-porary ones whose purpose is self-cultivation

jutte (J) [Weapon] a metal truncheon used by police of the Tokugawa period; it had a projecting tine that was used to block and trap sword or knife attacks

ju xiang (M) [Medicine] frankincense; a grainy resin used to enhance circulation and stimulate blood flow

jwa (K) [Common Usage] left

jwagi (K) [Kuk Sool, Hapkido] seated techniques

jwa jase (K) [Hapkido] left posture

jwarye (K) [Taekwondo] seated bow

jwaseon (K) [Common Usage] seated meditation

jwaseon ha da (K) [Common Usage] to meditate

jwineun beop (K) [Common Usage] fist-clenching method

jyan (C) [Common Usage] *see* geuk

jyang bang (C) [Common Usage] *see* jian

jyau ji (C) [Common Usage] *see* geuk ji

jyau ji jya (C) [Common Usage] toenail

jyu (C) [Common Usage] pig

jyu (C) [Common Usage] *see* zhu

jyu cheung (C) [Wihng Cheun] side palm

Jyu Ga (C) [Style] *see* Zhu Jia

jyu gam sau (C) [Wihng Cheun] side-pinning hand

jyuh juhng (C) [Common Usage] to respect

jyun (C) [Common Usage] to drill, go through

jyun gwai (C) [Common Usage] honorable

jyun jung yahn (C) [Common Usage] to respect someone

jyun sam (C) [Common Usage] dedicated; committed

Jyu roku (O) [Karate] a *kata* in Shuri-te

jyu sun kyuhn (C) [Wihng Cheun] diagonal punch

jyu sun mah (C) [Wihng Cheun] sidelong stance

jyut sau (C) [Wihng Cheun] jerk hand

— **K** —

kaau (C) [Kahm Na] *see* kao

kaau bo (C) [Wihng Cheun] *see* kau bo

kaau sau (C) [Wihng Cheun] *see* kau sau

Kabe Zoe (J) [Iaido] the ninth *kata* in the Muso Shinden-ryu Okuden Tachiwaza series, which is done from a standing position

kabuki (J) [Common Usage] a traditional form of Japanese theater that often features exaggerated scenes of combat

kabuto (J) [Armor] helmet

Kabutoyama (J) [Sumo] a sumo *beya* located in Bunkyo Ward, Tokyo

kachikoshi (J) [Sumo] winning record; more wins than losses in a sumo tournament

kachinuki (J) [Competitive Budo] a training drill in which one trainee faces consecutive attacks from a series of opponents and fights until defeated; he is then replaced by one of his opponents, who faces all those present until his defeat

kachinuki shiai (J) [Competitive Budo] *see* kachinuki

kadoban (J) [Sumo] An Ozeki put on probation for losing more bouts than he won in a tournament. If he fails to get a winning record in the following tournament, he will be demoted in rank.

Kado Iri (J) [Iaido] the eighth *kata* in the Muso Shinden-ryu Okuden Tachiwaza series, which is done from a standing position

Kae Baek hyung (K) [Taekwondo] a form named after a Paekche-dynasty general

kaeshi (J) [Common Usage] a counter technique

Kaeshide (O) [Karate] a *kata* practiced in Motobu-ryu

kagami (J) [Common Usage] mirror; used in Shinto to symbolize one's own soul; often found inside a Shinto altar

kagami biraki (J) [Common Usage] a ceremony held during the New Year at a dojo, during which *kagami mochi* (round rice cakes) are cut into pieces and served along with a sweet soup made of red beans

Kagamiyama (J) [Sumo] a sumo *beya* located in Edogawa Ward, Tokyo

kagi tsuki (J) [Karate] a hook punch; a short punch in which the fist moves in a circular, hooking motion

kagiyari (J) [Weapon] spear with a cross-bar

Kahm Na (C) [Style] *see* Qin Na

kahn lihk (C) [Common Usage] *see* qin li

kaho (J) [Common Usage] form training, an emphasis on *kata* in the teaching and training of a particular art

kai (J) [Common Usage] **1** association **2** a wooden boat oar used as a weapon, much like a spear or staff **3** the sixth position in Japanese archery; the position from which the arrow is released

kaiaku (J) [Acupressure] a pressure point located on the hand

Kaibara Ekken (J) [Master] a scholar of the seventeenth century; he was the first to define *kiai*

kai chu (M) [Common Usage] *see* juhk cheut

kaiden (J) [Common Usage] (*lit.* Complete Transmission) one of the highest-level licenses or instructor's rank awarded in the classical martial arts

kai gong she diao (M) [Qigong] (*lit.* Draw Back Your Bow and Shoot the Vulture) a breathing exercise in Shi San Tai Bao Gong

kai gong shou (M) [Zhu Jia] (*lit.* Bow Drawing Hand) a form that combines leg and stance movements with hand techniques to develop hand and arm strength

kaigun to (J) [Weapon] a modern Japanese naval sword

kaiho gyo (J) [Common Usage] an exercise done by Buddhist monks of the Shingon and Tendai esoteric sects, consisting of long daily hikes

kaiken (J) [Weapon] a short dagger carried by women of the *bushi* class; sometimes used to commit ritual suicide

Kai Men Bajiquan (M) [Style] *see* Bajiquan

kaina hineri (J) [Sumo] (*lit.* Arm Twisting) arm twist-down throw, a technique where the *rikishi* twists or pulls his opponent's arms around and throws him

kaishakunin (J) [Bushido] the second, or assistant in *seppuku* who would chop off the victim's head after he stabbed himself

kaishu (J) [Karate] an open-hand strike in which the baby finger-edge of the hand is used as the striking surface

kaiten (J) [Common Usage] spin, turn, revolve

kaiten jun zuki (J) [Karate] a combination turn and thrusting attack

kaji (J) [Common Usage] a smith specializing in making *katana* and other weapons

kakato (J) [Common Usage] heel

kakato fumikomi (J) [Karate] stomping heel kick

kakato geri (J) [Karate] heel kick

kake (J) [Common Usage] a hooking action

kake dachi (J) [Karate] hook stance

kake geri (J) [Karate] hook kick

kakegoe (J) [Kendo, Naginata] a yell used while attacking in which the target of an attack is called out

kake shuto uke (J) [Karate] hooking knifehand block

kakete (J) [Karate] a hooking hand technique

kake uke (J) [Karate] hook block

kakiwake uke (J) [Karate] reverse wedge block

kakushi buki (J) [Weapon] a concealed weapon

kakuto (J) [Common Usage] **1** a fight; hand-to-hand combat **2** bent wrist, the top surface of the wrist

kakuto uke (J) [Karate] bent-wrist block

kal (K) [Common Usage] sword, knife

kal chum (K) [Common Usage] traditional Korean sword dance

kal ggeut (K) [Kum Do] tip of the sword blade

kal jaguk (K) [Kum Do] cut, incision

kal jebi (K) [Tae Kyon] open-handed strike to the neck using the area between the thumb and index finger

kal jegi (K) [Tae Kyon] upward neck strike

kaljip (K) [Kum Do] scabbard, sheath

kaljipe neot da (K) [Kum Do] to sheathe a sword

kaljipeseo bbae da (K) [Kum Do] to unsheathe sword

kallo be da (K) [Kum Do] to slash with a sword

kallo chi da (K) [Kum Do] to chop with a sword

kama (J) [Weapon] sickle

kamae (J) [Common Usage] combative engagement stance or posture

kamae kata (J) [Common Usage] methods of assuming and holding *kamae*

kama ikada (J) [Nin-jutsu] a one-person collapsible raft carried by ninja

Kamakura jidai (J) [Common Usage] a period of Japanese history, 1192 to 1233, when Japan was ruled by a line of shoguns from the Minamoto clan

Kameshima Shinei (O) [Master] a student of his father, Kameshima Shinbi, and Ishimine *Pechin,* he established the Ishimine-ryu lineage of Shuri-te

kami (J) [Common Usage] **1** Shinto deity **2** hair

kami basami (J) [Judo] scissors throw

kamidana (J) [Shinto] (*lit.* God Shelf) a Shinto altar; usually placed on the front wall of the dojo

kamikaze (J) [Common Usage] (*lit.* Divine Wind) the name given to a typhoon that prevented the Mongol invasion of Japan in 1280

kamikaze (J) [Common Usage] a name given to the suicide pilots of the *Tokotai* (Special Attack Units) of World War II

kami shiho gatame (J) [Judo] upper four-corner hold

kamishimo (J) [Common Usage] (*lit.* Upper-Lower) a garment worn over the kimono on formal occasions

kami tori (J) [Aikido, Judo, Ju-jutsu] seizing the opponent by the hair

kamiza (J) [Common Usage] (*lit.* Upper Seat) a position of respect; this term is often used to refer to the front wall of a dojo, where a Shinto altar, scroll, or picture of a former teacher or founder of the art is placed

kampo (J) [Common Usage] Chinese medicine

kam sau (C) [Common Usage] covering palm

kan (J) [Common Usage] intuition

Kanchin (O) [Karate] a *kata* practiced in Uechi-ryu

kancho (J) [Common Usage] the title sometimes given to the head of a dojo or organization

kanden no metsuke (J) [Common Usage] seeing with both the eyes and the spirit

Kanemaki Jisai (J) [Master] the founder of Kanemaki-ryu ken-jutsu

Kanemaki-ryu (J) [Style] a school of ken-jutsu established in the sixteenth century

kan geiko (J) [Common Usage] (*lit.* Cold Training) special winter training sessions, held outdoors or in dojos with the windows open during the coldest part of the year, to improve trainees' fortitude and fighting spirit

kanji (J) [Common Usage] Chinese ideograms used in Japanese writing

kanjin sumo (J) [Common Usage] a charity sumo exhibition used for fund-raising at a Shinto shrine

Kanku (J) [Karate] *see* Kusanku

kankyaku (J) [Common Usage] spectator

Kano Jigoro (J) [Master] the founder of Kodokan judo; an educator and student of Tenshin Shinyo-ryu and Kito-ryu ju-jutsu, he removed the more dangerous techniques of ju-jutsu, revised the training methods, and developed judo as a safe method of physical, mental, and spiritual training

kansetsu geri (J) [Karate] a kick to a joint

kansetsu waza (J) [Judo, Aikido] joint-locking techniques

Kanshiwa (O) [Karate] a *kata* practiced in Uechi-ryu

Kanshu (O) [Karate] a *kata* practiced in Uechi-ryu; also called Dai-Ni Seisan

kanteika (J) [Common Usage] an appraiser; usually refers to someone specializing in swords and other traditional weapons

Kanto Sho (J) [Sumo] (*lit.* Fighting Spirit Prize) a prize given to the fighter who showed the strongest fighting spirit in a tournament

kanzashi (J) [Common Usage] a hairpin worn by women, sometimes used as a throwing or stabbing weapon

kanzo (J) [Common Usage] liver

kao (M) [Common Usage] **1** to test **2** leaning

kap cheuih (C) [Common Usage] (*lit.* Stamping Fist) a circular downward strike using the first two knuckles of the fist

karami (J) [Judo, Aikido] to entwine; a twisting or curling action used when immobilizing the opponent

Karamite (O) [Karate] a *kata* practiced in Motobu-ryu

karate (J) [Style] (*lit.* Empty Hand) The Okinawan form of unarmed self-defense that was introduced to Japan in the early twentieth century. Today there are countless styles, most of which trace their roots to one of two traditional Okinawan lineages of karate-jutsu, Shuri-te and Naha-te.

karate-jutsu (J) [Style] an alternative reading of tode-jutsu

karate ni sente nashi (J) [Karate] There is No First Strike in Karate; a saying attributed to Gichin Funakoshi, which means that karate is essentially defensive in nature

kari (J) [Judo] a reaping technique done with the leg

Kasugano (J) [Sumo] a sumo *beya* located in Sumida Ward, Tokyo

kasumi (J) [Common Usage] temples; the vital point located above and in front of the ears

Kasumi (J) [Iaido] the first *kata* in the Muso Shinden-ryu Okuden Suwariwaza series, which is done from *tatehiza*

kata (J) [Common Usage] **1** shoulder **2** formal training exercise set

kata ashi dori (J) [Judo] a single-leg hold

kata gatame (J) [Judo] a shoulder hold

kata guruma (J) [Judo] shoulder wheel; a technique derived from the Fireman's Carry of freestyle wrestling

kata ha jime (J) [Judo] a single-wing choke

kata juji jime (J) [Judo] a half-cross stranglehold

kataki (J) [Common Usage] enemy; rival

kataki uchi (J) [Common Usage] vengeance; vendetta

kata mawashi (J) [Judo] shoulder turning

katame (J) [Judo, Ju-jutsu] defense, stable, rooted

katame jime (J) [Judo] strangulation using the hands

Katame no Kata (J) [Judo] (*lit.* Forms of Grappling) one of the official Kodokan *kata* including representative pinning, strangling, and joint-locking techniques

katameru (J) [Common Usage] to strengthen, harden, fortify, reinforce

katame waza (J) [Judo] grappling techniques

katana (J) [Weapon] a Japanese sword

katana kake (J) [Common Usage] a wooden stand used to hold a sword for display

katana mei (J) [Weapon] the sword smith's signature on the tang of the *katana*

katana zutsu (J) [Common Usage] a box in which a *katana* is stored

Kataonami (J) [Sumo] a sumo *beya* located in Sumida Ward, Tokyo

kata oshi (J) [Judo] shoulder push

kata sukashi (J) [Sumo] a throwing technique similar to *zubu neri,* with the exception that in order to control the opponent's fall the two combatant's arms are inter-locked, thus giving the opponent some support

katate (J) [Common Usage] one-handed; using only one hand

katate age (J) [Judo] to raise the hand in order to strike

katate dori (J) [Aikido] to grab one of the opponent's hand with a single hand

katatedori ryotemochi (J) [Aikido] to seize one hand or wrist with both hands

katate uchi (J) [Kendo] a single-handed strike; almost invariably uses the left hand to hold the *shinai* and striking to the right side of the opponent's head

katate waza (J) [Kendo] techniques in which the *shinai* is held in one hand

katchu (J) [Common Usage] armor

katsu (J) [Common Usage] **1** to win, be victorious **2** the art of resuscitation

katsujin no ken (J) [Kendo] (*lit.* Sword that Gives Life; Life-Giving Sword) it represents the act of overcoming the desire to kill or to be victorious; waiting for an opponent to launch his attack before doing anything, as opposed to *satsujin to*

kau (C) [Kahm Na] to hold

kau bo (C) [Wihng Cheun] dragging steps

kauh (C) [Common Usage] to beg, to beseech, to ask for

kauh sik (C) [Wihng Cheun] pre-fight posture

kau sau (C) [Wihng Cheun] circling block

kawa (J) [Common Usage] **1** side **2** leather

kawasu (J) [Common Usage] to change, to alter

kayaku-jutsu (J) [Nin-jutsu] the ninja art of fire and explosives

kazami (J) [Karate] to jab

ke (J) [Common Usage] hair

ke fu (M) [Common Usage] to conquer; conquer

kega (J) [Common Usage] injury, lesion

keh mah sik (C) [Saandong Hak Fu Paai] *see* qi ma shi

keibo (J) [Weapon] a baton or billy club usually sixty centimeters in length used by the Japanese police; not to be confused with the *tokushu keibo,* which is a collapsible baton

keibo-soho (J) [Style] the art of using the police club or truncheon

keichu (J) [Acupressure] a vital point located on the nape of the neck

keih (C) [Common Usage] flag

keijo (J) [Weapon] riot baton; a stick about 130 centimeters in length made of white oak

keijo-jutsu (J) [Style] a method of combat using the *keijo* that is presently practiced by the Japanese police

keiko (J) [Common Usage] training, instruction

keikogi (J) [Common Usage] training uniform

keikoku (J) [Common Usage] a warning, as in a referee warning a competitor

keimyaku-iho (J) [Common Usage] the study of pressure points on the body

keiraku hiko (J) [Shorinji Kempo] pressure point manipulation; there are said to be 708 such points

keirei (J) [Common Usage] a traditional bow or salutation

kei sau cheuih (C) [Common Usage] traveling hand strike

keito (J) [Karate] chicken-beak strike; a pecking strike with the bunched fingertips

keito uke (J) [Karate] chicken-head wrist block

Ke Jia Tiao Gun (M) [Long Xing Quan] *see* Haak Ga Tiu Gwan

kekomi (J) [Karate] a thrust; usually referring to a low thrusting kick

kempo (J) [Style] (*lit.* Fist Method/Law) Chinese-influenced unarmed fighting systems; the same characters are read *quan fa* or *kyuhn faat* in Chinese

ken (J) [Common Usage] **1** an old-style straight two-edged sword usually about three *shaku* (one meter) in length **2** vision; process of seeing

kendo (J) [Style] (*lit.* Way of the Sword) A modern interpretation of ken-jutsu that traditionally focused more on the spiritual development of its disciples than the art of combative swordsmanship. Today the focus has shifted more toward the competitive aspects of the art.

kendo gi (J) [Common Usage] kendo uniform

kendo gu (J) [Kendo] the protective armor worn by *kendoka* consisting of the *men, do, tare,* and *kote*

kendoka (J) [Common Usage] someone who follows the Way of the Sword

kengi (J) [Kendo] sword technique

kengo (J) [Kendo] master swordsman

ken-jutsu (J) [Style] (*lit.* Art of the Sword) combative swordsmanship; it differs from iaido in that it does not involve sword-drawing techniques, instead emphasizing fighting techniques with the sword already drawn

kenkyaku (J) [Ken-jutsu] master swordsman

Ken no Michi (J) [Style] *see* kendo

ken o korosu (J) [Kendo] to attack and control the opponent's *shinai* in order to execute a technique

kensaki (J) [Weapon] *see* kissaki

kensen (J) [Kendo] the line or trajectory of the sword as it is being held or swung

kenshi (J) [Ken-jutsu] a swordsman

kensho godo (J) [Zen] a concept of universal understanding of nature

kenshokin (J) [Sumo] bonus prize money provided to senior winning Makunouchi-ranked *rikishi* by private corporations or citizens

kenshusei (J) [Common Usage] (*lit.* Research Student) a term used in reference to a student who is being groomed to become an instructor

kento (J) [Common Usage] to fight; boxing

kentsui (J) [Karate] *see* tettsui

keppan (J) [Common Usage] (*lit.* Blood Seal) a vow or oath taken by a student before being accepted as a disciple in a traditional or classical school of martial arts

keri (J) [Common Usage] kick

keri age (J) [Karate] rising kick

keri kata (J) [Karate] way of kicking

keri waza (J) [Karate] kicking techniques

kesa gatame (J) [Judo] scarf hold; a basic pinning technique

kesa geri (J) [Karate] diagonal kick

Kesagiri (J) [Iaido] the first *kata* done from *iaihiza* in the Tachiai no Bu of the Zen Nihon Kendo Renmei Seitei Iai

kesho mawashi (J) [Sumo] the ceremonial apron worn by *rikishi* of Juryo and Makunouchi rank

kesho yasuri (J) [Weapon] decorative file markings on the tang of a sword

keuhng (C) [Common Usage] strong

keuih jyuht (C) [Common Usage] to reject, to resist, to refuse

keun jeol (K) [Tae Kyon] kneeling bow

ke zaya (J) [Weapon] an ancient type of scabbard, which had the tip wrapped in animal fur

ki (J) [Common Usage] the energy of life, breath, intention; referred to as *qi* in Chinese

ki (K) [Common Usage] **1** internal energy, vital energy (actually pronounced "gi") **2** person's height

ki (O) [Common Usage] hair

kiai (J) [Common Usage] unification of the energy/vital spirit; usually done by means of a loud shout while performing a technique

kiai-jutsu (J) [Style] (*lit.* Art of Kiai) an ancient art that concentrated on the development and accurate use of the *kiai;* sometimes called toate-jutsu

kiarasoi (J) [Bushido] fighting spirit

kiba dachi (J) [Karate] straddle-leg or horse-riding stance

kiba sen (J) [Ba-jutsu] combat on horseback

Ki Do Hoi (K) [Common Usage] (*lit.* Internal Energy Way Association) Korean martial arts organization

kihap (K) [Common Usage] internal-energy coordination, shout; *kiai* in Japanese

kihon (J) [Common Usage] basic, elementary, fundamental

kihon dosa (J) [Common Usage] fundamental movements

kihon kata (J) [Common Usage] basic form(s)

kihon kumite (J) [Karate] basic sparring practice

kihon renshu (J) [Common Usage] basic training

kihon waza (J) [Common Usage] basic technique

kikboksing (K) [Style] kickboxing

kiki (J) [Common Usage] pull

kikong (K) [Common Usage] internal-energy cultivation method, *qigong (chi kung)* in Chinese

kimarite (J) [Sumo] any techniques used to win a sumo match; there are seventy such techniques recognized by the Japan Sumo Association

kime (J) [Common Usage] the combination of focus and explosive energy required to deliver a decisive technique

Kime no Kata (J) [Judo] (*lit.* Forms of Decision) one of the official Kodokan judo *kata,* it incorporates throwing, striking, joint-locking, and pinning techniques for use in self-defense

kime shiki (J) [Judo] *see* Kime no Kata

kimochi (J) [Common Usage] feeling, sensation

kimono (J) [Common Usage] traditional Japanese dress worn by both men and women

kimusubi (J) [Aikido] to be in harmony with another person's *ki* energy

kingeri (J) [Karate] kick to the groin

kinniku (J) [Common Usage] muscle

ki no nagare (J) [Aikido] to use one's *ki* energy in a flowing manner while performing techniques

kintama (J) [Common Usage] testicles

kinteki (J) [Common Usage] groin; testicles

ki o tsuke (J) [Common Usage] Command to "Pay Attention!" or "Stand at attention!"

kiri (J) [Common Usage] a cutting attack

kiribo (J) [Weapon] a *bo* with either a spear head or cutting blade at the tip

kirigami (J) [Common Usage] a low-level license given by a master to a student in some classical martial arts schools

kiri hiraku (J) [Aikido] to cut and open; an expression used for the symbolic aiki sword cuts intended to cut away blemishes or flaws in character and action, while opening one's heart to spiritual progress

kiri kaeshi (J) [Sumo] a take-down done by lifting the opponent up and pulling him backward throwing him up and over one's leg

kiri komi (J) [Ken-jutsu, Kendo] to cut with a weapon

kiri otoshi (J) [Iaido] to cut from the top down with the sword; one of the fundamentals of the Itto-ryu

kiri tsuke (J) [Iaido, Kendo] the act of cutting with the sword; the blade is raised to its ready position and swung down at maximum speed to the point of impact

kiru (J) [Common Usage] to cut

Kise (J) [Sumo] a sumo *beya* located in Bunkyo Ward, Tokyo

kisha hasamu mono (J) [Ba-jutsu] techniques used for shooting arrows from the back of a galloping horse at the armor of the opponent's horse

kiso (J) [Common Usage] base; foundation; basic(s); fundamental(s)

kissaki (J) [Weapon] the point of a sword, dagger, or other weapon

kita (J) [Common Usage] north

kitae (J) [Common Usage] methods of combining metals to be used for making a sword

Kitanoumi (J) [Sumo] a sumo *beya* located in Koto Ward, Tokyo

kito gan (J) [Nin-jutsu] a pill used by ninja to suppress thirst, sometime for several days at a time

Kito-ryu (J) [Ju-jutsu] a school founded by Ibaragi Toshifusa;

it was one of the precursors to Kodokan judo and was noted for its throwing techniques and freestyle training methods

kiuh (C) [Common Usage] bridge

kiuh sau (C) [Common Usage] **1** (*lit.* Bridge Hand) connecting between two opponents, the hand literally bridging the distance between oneself and an opponent **2** (*lit.* Bridge Hand) A hand position similar to a tiger claw but with the index finger fully extended pointing toward the sky. This technique, which is a trademark of Huhng Ga, can be used for blocking as well as for isometric breathing exercises.

kiu sau (C) [Wihng Cheun] *see* kiuh sau

kizami tsuki (J) [Karate] jabbing punch

kizu (J) [Ken-jutsu] defects in a sword blade caused at the time of forging or by poor maintenance

ko (K) [Common Usage] nose

koan (J) [Zen] a conundrum or riddle used to provoke non-discursive insight in the study of Zen

Kobayashi-ryu (O) [Karate] Considered by many to be the pure line of Sui Di or Shuri-te. Although the lineage can be traced back to the Okinawan royal family and throughout Okinawan history, the name, which is an alternate reading of the characters for Shorin-ryu, is relatively new. It was so named by Chibana Choshin in the 1940s and is presently taught by Onaga Yoshimitsu, Nakazato Shigoro, and Miyahira Katsuya.

kobo itchi (J) [Common Usage] a combative concept in which the distinction between defense and attack disappears, and all defenses are intended to inflict damage

kobudo (J) [Style] (*lit.* Ancient/Classical Martial Ways) although this term literally refers to all the classical warrior arts, which include yabusame, kyu-jutsu, ken-jutsu, and others, in the West it is often used when referring to Okinawan weapons arts such as the *bo, jo, tonfa, sai, ekku,* and *kama*

kobu-jutsu (J) [Style] *see* kobudo

Kobukan (J) [Aikido] the name of Ueshiba Morihei's first dojo in Tokyo

Kobusho (J) [Common Usage] a government-run martial arts academy of the Tokugawa *bakufu,* in the early part of the nineteenth century

kodachi (J) [Weapon] short sword; another term for the *waki-zashi*

kodansha (J) [Judo] a senior black belt, usually 6th Dan or higher

ko dogu (J) [Weapon] sword furnishings

Kodokan (J) [Judo] the world judo headquarters located in Tokyo; the governing body for judo through out the world

koen kai (J) [Sumo] a support or fan club for a particular *rikishi* or sumo *beya*

kogai (J) [Weapon] a metal rod attached to a sword sheath

Koga-ryu (J) [Style] a school of nin-jutsu

Koguryo sidae (K) [Common Usage] Koguryo-dynasty period (37 B.C.–A.D. 668)

Koguryo wangjo (K) [Common Usage] Koguryo dynasty, a political entity that ruled the northern part of the Korean peninsula and much of Manchuria

kohai (J) [Common Usage] junior; someone of lower rank than yourself; the opposite of a *sempai*

koho ukemi (J) [Common Usage] back(ward) fall

koi guchi (J) [Weapon] (*lit.* Carp's Mouth) the opening or mouth of a sword scabbard from which the blade is drawn

Kojo no Jo (O) [Kobudo] a *jo kata* practiced in Ryukyu Kobudo

Kokonoe (J) [Sumo] a sumo *beya* located in Sumida Ward, Tokyo

kokoro (J) [Common Usage] heart, spirit, soul

kokutsu dachi (J) [Karate] back stance

kokyu (J) [Aikido] breath, breathe

kokyu ho (J) [Common Usage] training methods to control one's breathing and to develop efficient use of power; the ability to control one's internal energy by regulating one's breathing; a training method frequently used in aikido

kokyu nage (J) [Aikido] a throw in which *kokyu ryoku* is used to generate the power to throw the opponent

kokyu ryoku (J) [Aikido] breath power; ability to control one's energy through specialized breathing patterns

komata sukui (J) [Sumo] a throw in which the opponent's thigh is trapped under the forearm and used to push the opponent back, forcing him to the *dohyo* floor

Komeagawa no Kon (O) [Kobudo] a staff *kata* practiced in Ryukyu Kobudo

komuso (J) [Common Usage] a mendicant Zen priest wearing a basket-like hat and playing a *shakuhachi;* often used as a disguise by ninja

Komusubi (J) [Sumo] the fourth-highest rank in sumo

kon (O) [Weapon] a staff usually measuring about 190 centimeters in length

kong ggeokkgi (K) [Ssi Rum] two-handed knee-grasping technique

kong hu (M) [Common Usage] *see* hung haak

Kongo Zen (J) [Shorinji Kempo] the Zen philosophy developed by So Doshin

kongpat (K) [Common Usage] kidney

Kong Soo Do (K) [Style] (*lit.* Empty Hand Way) a system very similar to karate-do

kong zhi (M) [Common Usage] *see* hung jai

Kong Zi (M) [Common Usage] Confucius

konsaibo (J) [Weapon] a metal reinforced wooden staff

koon (C) [Common Usage] *see* gwun

koppo (J) [Nin-jutsu] ninja bone-breaking techniques

Koranto (J) [Iaido] the tenth *kata* in the Muso Shinden-ryu Omori-ryu Shoden series, which is done from *seiza*

koreisai (J) [Acupressure] a vital point located on the top of the foot

koromo (J) [Common Usage] monk's robes

korosu (J) [Common Usage] to contain, to control, to kill

Koryo poomsae (K) [Taekwondo] first-degree form named after the Koryo dynasty

Koryo sidae (K) [Common Usage] Koryo dynasty period (918–1392)

Koryo wangjo (K) [Common Usage] Koryo dynasty, a political entity that ruled most of the Korean peninsula after the fall of the United Silla dynasty

koryu (J) [Bu-jutsu] classical martial arts traditions or schools

koshi (J) [Common Usage] waist, hips

koshi guruma (J) [Judo] hip wheel; the attacker grabs the opponent around the neck and executes a hip throw

koshi ita (J) [Common Usage] a stiff support that is attached to the back of the *hakama* and placed on the lower back

koshiki (J) [Common Usage] old-style; archaic

Koshiki karate-do (J) [Style] a form of sport karate developed by Hisataka Masayuki in which the competitors wear Supersafe body armor and headgear, allowing them to strike one other solidly without risking serious injury

Koshiki no Kata (J) [Common Usage] (*lit.* Forms of Antiquity) also called Kito-ryu no Kata; one of the official Kodokan judo *kata,* based on Kito-ryu ju-jutsu; a series of throwing and grappling techniques performed as though wearing armor

koshi nage (J) [Common Usage] hip throw

koshirae (J) [Weapon] sword mountings or fittings

koshi sabaki (J) [Common Usage] hip movement

koshiwari (J) [Sumo] stretching exercises

koshi waza (J) [Common Usage] hip techniques

kosho seido (J) [Sumo] the public injury system; allows a *rikishi* who has been injured in a public tournament to sit out the next tourney without having any effect on his rank

Kosokun Sho (O) [Karate] *see* Kusanku

ko soto gake (J) [Judo] small outside hook; used to break the opponent's balance, in preparation for another move

kotae (J) [Common Usage] answer, reply

kote (J) [Common Usage] forearm

kote gaeshi (J) [Aikido] a technique in which the opponent's wrist is twisted outward in order to throw him to the ground

kote nage (J) [Sumo] a throwing technique similar to *sukui nage,* but instead of holding the opponent's back, his arm is grasped as a means of control

kotmaru (K) [Common Usage] bridge of the nose

koto (J) [Common Usage] **1** a stringed instrument played like a horizontal harp **2** an old sword; a blade made before 1596

kotodama (J) [Shinto] sacred words and sounds that originate in the ancient Shinto belief that some sounds have divine properties

kou (M) [Common Usage] *see* hau

kou (M) [Qin Na] to hold

ko uchi gake (J) [Judo] small inner hook; often used by a smaller man against a long-legged opponent

kou she cao (M) [Medicine] a plant used to kill intestinal parasites

kou shui (M) [Common Usage] saliva

kozuka (J) [Weapon] a utility knife inserted in the scabbard of a sword

ku (J) [Common Usage] nine

kua hu lan (M) [Weapon] a woven basket with a crescent shaped handle in the center

kuai (M) [Common Usage] **1** quick, fast **2** chopsticks

kuai le (M) [Common Usage] *see* hoi sam

kuai man (M) [Common Usage] *see* su du

kuai shan shuang jue (M) [Weapons] hand-held sickles usually used in pairs

Kuai Tao (M) [Pi Gua Quan] *see* Faai Tou

kubi (J) [Common Usage] neck

kubi jime (J) [Aikido] a holding technique in which the lapels are used to apply pressure on the opponent's neck

kubi nage (J) [Sumo] a neck throw

kuchiki taoshi (J) [Judo] one-hand drop; a throwing technique resembling a single-leg take-down in wrestling

kudan (J) [Common Usage] ninth-degree black belt, 9th Dan

kuda yari (J) [Weapon] a spear used with a tube-like sleeve to enable rapid movements in thrusting and withdrawing

kuen to (C) [Common Usage] *see* kyuhn tou

kui xing ti dou (M) [Hong Jia] *see* fui sing tek dau

kuji kiri (J) [Common Usage] ritual hand gestures made by followers of Esoteric Buddhism and some martial artists in order to calm themselves and concentrate their power

kuki nage (J) [Judo] a timing throw similar to a *kokyu nage*

Kukje Hapkido Yeonmaeng (K) [Common Usage] International Hapkido Federation, an organization that promotes and controls Hap Ki Muye Do

Kuk Ki Do (K) [Style] (*lit.* National Internal Energy Way) a modern martial art that uses joint-locks, pressure-point strikes, punches, kicks, and weapons; probably derived from Kuk Sool

Kuk Ki Won (K) [Taekwondo] National Taekwondo Headquarters in Seoul, South Korea

Kuk Sool (K) [Style] (*lit.* National Skill) a martial art that combines Hapkido-like joint-locks and throws with Taekwondo-like kicks and numerous weapons techniques

Kuk Sool Won (K) [Kuk Sool] Korean organization that promotes and controls the art of Kuk Sool

kumade (J) [Karate] bear paw; a hand position in which the fingers and thumb are partially clenched, creating a flat striking surface on the palm of the hand

kumade (J) [Nin-jutsu] a collapsible climbing pole used by ninja, made of bamboo and rope

kumade uchi (J) [Karate] bear claw strike using the palm of the hand with the fingers bent, used to jab into the opponent's soft tissue

Kumagatani (J) [Sumo] a sumo *beya* located in Edogawa Ward, Tokyo

kum do (K) [Style] (*lit.* Sword Way) Asian fencing, Korean version of Japanese kendo

kumijo (J) [Aikido] techniques for *jo* against *jo*

kumikata (J) [Judo] (*lit.* Methods of Gripping) methods of obtaining an advantageous grip to perform a technique or counter an attack

kumitachi (J) [Aikido] techniques of *bokken* against *bokken*

kumite (J) [Common Usage] sparring

kumiuchi (J) [Style] the art of close combat while wearing armor

Kum Kang poomsae (K) [Taekwondo] second-degree diamond form

Kum Kang Yuk Sa (K) [Common Usage] Vajradhara statues located in Gyeongju, South Korea that supposedly show ancient martial poses

kum sool (K) [Style] (*lit.* Sword Skill) Asian fencing

kum sul (K) [Style] *see* kum sool

kune (C) [Common Usage] *see* kyuhn

kung do (K) [Style] (*lit.* Bow Way) archery

Kun Gek Do (K) [Style] (*lit.* Fist Attack Way) a modern martial art that mixes Taekwondo hand and foot techniques with kickboxing

kung fu (C) [Common Usage] *see* gung fu

Kung Hu (K) [Style] *gong fu*

Kung Jung Musul (K) [Style] *see* Gung Jung Musul

kung sool (K) [Style] (*lit.* Bow Skill) archery

kung sul (K) [Style] *see* kung sool

Kun Na (M) [Bai He] (*lit.* Bind and Hold) a hand form practiced in Fei He

kun nan (M) [Common Usage] difficult

kunoichi (J) [Nin-jutsu] a term used to refer to female ninja

Ku no Kata (O) [Karate] a *kata* practiced in Kojo-ryu

kuo (M) [Taijiquan] shoulder strike; a strike using the shoulder that generates the necessary power from the motions of the hips

kuo shu (M) [Common Usage] *see* guo shu

Kuo Yun Shen (M) [Master] *see* Guo Yun Shen

kurigata (J) [Weapon] a small protruding knob on the scabbard of a *katana,* where the *sageo* is passed through before being attached to the *obi*

kuroboshi (J) [Sumo] a black star, a loss

kuro obi (J) [Common Usage] black belt

Kururunfa (O) [Karate] a *kata* practiced in Goju-ryu

kurushimeru (J) [Common Usage] to torture; to torment

Kusanku (O) [Karate] a Shuri-te *kata* named after a Chinese military attaché who briefly stayed in Okinawa and taught *quan fa* there; it is divided into two parts, Kusanku no Dai and Kusanku no Sho; often called Kanku in Japanese karate

kusari (J) [Weapon] chain

kusari fundo (J) [Weapon] weighted chain; also called *ryo-fundo* and *manrikigusari*

kusarigama (J) [Weapon] a sickle attached to a chain ranging from seventy-five centimeters to over 2.7 meters in length

kusarigama-jutsu (J) [Style] the art of using the *kusarigama*

ku sui pu (M) [Medicine] drynaria; a medicinal herb that strengthens tendons and bones

kuwa (O) [Kobudo] a broad-bladed hoe or mattock

ku zi (M) [Common Usage] pants, trousers

kuzure kami shiho gatame (J) [Judo] irregular upper-four corner hold

kuzushi (J) [Common Usage] disequilibrium, to break the opponent's balance

kwa cheuih (C) [Common Usage] backfist; a vertical strike using the back of the fist

Kwahn Yeung Gwun (C) [Ying Jaau] (*lit.* Shepherd's Staff) a weapons form using the staff

kwai (C) [Common Usage] *see* laih

kwai jak (C) [Common Usage] *see* gui ze

kwai jarn (C) [Wihng Cheun] *see* gwai jaan

Kwang Gae hyung (K) [Taekwondo] a form named after a Koguryo-dynasty king

Kwan Na (C) [Fei Hok Kyuhn] *see* Kun Na

kwan naahn (C) [Common Usage] *see* kun nan

kwa teui (C) [Common Usage] outside crescent kick

kwon (K) [Common Usage] fist, punch

Kwon Bup (K) [Style] (*lit.* Fist Method) an ancient martial art described in the *Muye Dobo Tongji* text; other than basic hand techniques for offense and defense, very little is known of the art's techniques

Kwong Tit Fu (C) [Master] *see* Gwong Tit Fu

kwun ma (C) [Wihng Cheun] *see* gwan mah

kwun sau (C) [Wihng Cheun] *see* gwan sau

Kyan Chotoku (O) [Master] the founder of the Shobayashi lineage of Shorin-ryu and teacher of Shimabuku Eizo, Chitose Tsuyoshi, and the Kadena Police Force, through which he met Nagamine Shoshin

kyobako fune (J) [Nin-jutsu] a chest-like device covered with fur used for crossing lakes and rivers

kyobu (J) [Common Usage] chest

kyogi judo (J) [Judo] (*lit.* Competitive Judo) a term first coined by Kano Jigoro, referring to those students who were mistakenly interested only in the sportive aspects of judo

kyoketsu shogei (J) [Weapon] a sickle with an additional short blade protruding from the large blade and a weighted rope or chain attached to the other end

Kyokushinkai (J) [Style] *see* Kyokushin karate-do

Kyokushin karate-do (J) [Karate] A style founded by Oyama Masutatsu, well known for its strong basic techniques and its heavy emphasis on "bare-knuckle" full contact competition. It has become one of the leading styles of modern karate in the world.

kyokutsu (J) [Common Usage] the sternum, the breastbone

kyoshi (J) [Common Usage] **1** the second of three instructor ranks; usually given only to those who have 7th Dan rank or no less than seven years after receiving *renshi* **2** behavior

kyu (J) [Common Usage] level, class, rank; used to indicate ranks below black belt; many styles start at nine or ten and work up to one, although most begin at 6th Kyu

kyuba (J) [Kyudo] bow and arrow techniques from horseback

Kyuba no Michi (J) [Style] (*lit.* The Way of Mounted Archery) a term for warrior life; it referred to the life of the warrior who used a bow from horseback

kyubu geri (J) [Karate] chest kick

kyudo (J) [Style] (*lit.* The Way of the Bow) the art of archery applied as a form of self-improvement and austere training focusing on relaxation, meditation, and concentration

kyudojo (J) [Kyudo] place where one practices Kyudo

Kyudokan (O) [Karate] the school of Shorin-ryu (Kobayashi) founded by Higa Yuchoku

kyudo yosoku (J) [Kyudo] the guiding principles of kyudo

kyuhn (C) [Common Usage] fist

kyuhn faat (C) [Common Usage] fist technique; a method of fighting with the fists

kyuhn tauh (C) [Common Usage] *see* cheuih

kyuhn tou (C) [Common Usage] fist or form

kyujo (J) [Sumo] absence from a tournament

kyu-jutsu (J) [Style] (*lit.* The Art of Archery) the art of combative archery, it is more concerned with developing the technique of hitting the target with the arrow than with spiritual development or expression

kyukei (J) [Common Usage] a break, a pause

Kyuk Too Ki (K) [Style] (*lit.* Combat Techniques) a modern martial art that mixes traditional Korean hand and foot techniques with the elbow, knee, and leg-kicking attacks of Muay Thai

kyushaku bo (J) [Weapon] long staff; a 297-centimeter staff used in combat, intended to give more reach than the regular *rokushaku bo*

kyushin (J) [Judo] a theory of judo that dictates that body movements must be natural rather than forceful, and loose not stressed

Kyushin-ryu (J) [Style] an early school of ju-jutsu

kyusho (J) [Common Usage] vital point

kyut dihng (C) [Common Usage] resoluteness, firmness, determination

— L —

la (M) [Common Usage] wax

laahm sik (C) [Common Usage] blue

laahn (C) [Common Usage] obstruct, to block

laahn jeung (C) [Common Usage] *see* lan zhang

Laahn Jit Kyuhn (C) [Chat Sing Tohng Lohng] (*lit.* Orchid Section Fist) a hand form

Laahn Sau Muhn (C) [Style] (*lit.* Obstructing Hand Gate) a northern style of Chinese martial arts

laahp (C) [Common Usage] *see* la

laahp juk (C) [Common Usage] candle

laaih (C) [Common Usage] to blame

laang jihng (C) [Common Usage] to be calm

laan sau (C) [Wihng Cheun] bar arm

laap sau (C) [Wihng Cheun] deflecting arm

laat taaht (C) [Common Usage] dirty

laau gaauh (C) [Common Usage] untidy, messy

laauh kiuh (C) [Common Usage] scooping fist

Lahm Fuk Sang (C) [Master] a student of Tit Kiuh Saam, and a third-generation disciple of Huhng Ga

Lahm Gwok Gei (C) [Master] a prominent master of Luhng Yihng Kyuhn

Lahm Sai Wihng (C) [Master] A master of Huhng Ga who was famous for modernizing and popularizing this style in Hong Kong in the early twentieth century. He was taught directly by Wohng Fei Huhng and was the first to write several instructional manuals on Huhng Ga.

Lahm Yiu Kwaih (C) [Master] the first layman to be taught the Dragon style by Daaih Yuhk, he popularized the style

laih (C) [Common Usage] rules, regulations

laih sih (C) [Common Usage] gift of luck; within Chinese communities, this is usually of money and is presented in a red envelope

lai maauh (C) [Common Usage] manners, politeness

lai maht (C) [Common Usage] gifts, presents

lait geup (K) [Taekwondo] lightweight class in sparring competition

lam (C) [Common Usage] to think

Lama (C) [Common Usage] a Buddhist monk from Tibet

Lama Paai (C) [Style] A style of Tibetan Chinese martial arts derived from an older system called Si Ji Haau that was founded by Hoh Da Do in the fourteenth century. Si Ji Haau is based on eight fighting methods, which consist of: eight fists, eight kicks, eight stances, eight finger attacks, eight palm strikes, eight foot sweeps, and eight gripping methods. The style was passed down to Wohng Luhm Hoi, and later was referred to as Lama Paai. This style was eventually taught to the imperial guards of the Qing dynasty.

Lama Pai (C) [Style] *see* Lama Paai

lam cheuih (C) [Common Usage] upper roundhouse punch

lan (M) [Common Usage] *see* laahm sik

lan (M) [Common Usage] *see* laahn

lang ya bang (M) [Weapon] hand-held weapons usually used in pairs consisting of barbed metal pine cone-shaped balls mounted at the ends of short shafts

Lan Shou Men (M) [Style] *see* Laahn Sau Muhn

lan zhang (M) [Common Usage] blocking palm

Lao Jia Quan (M) [Hong Quan] (*lit.* Old Shelf Fist) a hand form

lao long gui dong (M) [Hong Jia] *see* yiuh luhng gwai duhng

lao ying zhu shi (M) [Qigong] (*lit.* Hawk Capturing Its Prey) a breathing exercise in Shi San Tai Bao Gong

Lao Zi (M) [Common Usage] the reputed writer of the *Dao De Jing* and founder of Taoism; also known as Li Er

Lau Fat Mang (C) [Master] *see* Lauh Faat Maahng

Lau Gar (C) [Style] *see* Lauh Ga

Lauh Faat Maahng (C) [Master] a prominent master of Ying Jaau

Lauh Ga (C) [Style] (*lit.* Lauh Family) A style founded by Lauh Sam Ngahn that has its origins at the Shaolin Temple and was prevalent in the late Qing dynasty. It uses a variety of mid-range techniques and is one of the five family styles of Guangdong Province.

Lauh Ga Gwan (C) [Lauh Ga, Huhng Ga] (*lit.* Lauh Family Staff) a weapons form using the staff

Lauh Ga Kyuhn (C) [Huhng Ga, Lauh Ga] a hand form

lau ma bo (M) [Common Usage] (*lit.* Crossing Horse Stance) a stance with the legs crossed at the knees

Lauh Sam Ngahn (C) [Master] the founder of the Lauh Ga

lau sau (C) [Wihng Cheun] scooping arm

la zhu (M) [Common Usage] *see* laahp juk

Lee Gar (C) [Style] *see* Leih Ga

leih (C) [Common Usage] sharp

Leih Ga (C) [Style] (*lit.* Leih Family) A style founded by Leih Yau Sahn, who was one of the Guangdong Sahp Fu. This fighting style uses a variety of short-range fighting techniques and is one of the five family styles of Guangdong Province.

Leih Jan Ching (C) [Master] *see* Li Zhen Qing

Leih Saam Jihn (C) [Master] a third-generation disciple of Chat Sing Tohng Lohng

leih yauh (C) [Common Usage] reason

Leih Yih Goui (C) [Master] a third-generation disciple of Chat Sing Tohng Lohng

lei si (M) [Common Usage] to resemble

leuhng (C) [Common Usage] (*lit.* two, ounce) a unit of weight for herbal medicines

leuhng (C) [Common Usage] food

Leuhng Bihk (C) [Master] a prominent master of Wihng Cheun

Leuhng Jahn (C) [Master] a prominent master of Wihng Cheun

leuhng sihk (C) [Common Usage] food

leuih chih (C) [Common Usage] *see* lei si

leuih toih (C) [Common Usage] arena, stage

leung (C) [Common Usage] strength

leung jit gwan (C) [Weapon] two-sectional staff

li (M) [Common Usage] strength

lian (M) [Common Usage] 1 face 2 to train or practice

lian chi (M) [Common Usage] *see* lian qi

liang (M) [Common Usage] 1 food 2 traditional Chinese unit of weight

liang (M) [Common Usage] *see* leuhng

liang gu lie cha (M) [Weapon] A short spear with a two-pronged, fork-shaped tip with tassels at the base of the fork. The opposite end of the shaft has a small metal spear point.

liang shi (M) [Common Usage] food

lian qi (M) [Common Usage] a Taoist internal training method that enables one's *qi* to be more abundant and stronger

lian quan (M) [Acupressure] a point that is located on the suprasternal notch

lian xu (M) [Medicine] a plant used in Chinese herbal medicine

liao (M) [Common Usage] to heal, to cure

Liao Chao Dai (M) [Common Usage] Liao Imperial dynasty, which ruled China from 916 to 1125 A.D.

liao shang (M) [Common Usage] to heal a wound

Lieh Lohk Nahng (C) [Master] the founder of the Hoh Bak style of xingyiquan

Li Er (M) [Common Usage] *see* Lao Zi

Li Fan Feng (M) [Master] a prominent master of Nan Quan from Guangdong Province

lihk (C) [Common Usage] bodily strength

lihk leuhng (C) [Common Usage] strength or power

lihn (C) [Common Usage] to practice

lihn fa (C) [Common Usage] lotus flower, water lily

lihng (C) [Common Usage] **1** soul, spirit **2** bell

lihng ging (C) [Common Usage] to chant prayers

lihng leih (C) [Common Usage] *see* ling li

lihn gung (C) [Common Usage] to practice martial arts

lihng wahn (C) [Common Usage] spirit

lihn jaahp (C) [Common Usage] to train or to practice

Lihn Kyuhn (C) [Ying Jaau] (*lit.* Linking Fist) a hand form

lihn wan kyuhn (C) [Common Usage] (*lit.* Chain Punches) alternating left and right punches in succession

Li Jia (M) [Style] *see* Leih Ga

Li Jia Duan Qiang (M) [Li Jia] (*lit.* Li Family Spear) a weapons form using the spear

li lian (M) [Common Usage] strength or power

Lin Ah Long (M) [Master] a prominent master of xingyiquan

Lin Fu Sheng (M) [Master] *see* Lahm Fuk Sang

ling (M) [Common Usage] soul, spirit

ling li (M) [Common Usage] smart, clever

ling mao pu shu (M) [Yang Taijiquan] (*lit.* The Spirited Cat Catches the Mouse) a movement in the Taiji Sword form

Lin Guo Ji (M) [Master] *see* Lahm Gwok Gei

Lin Zai Pei (M) [Master] a prominent master of Gau Quan

Li Shi taijiquan (M) [Style] (*lit.* Li Family Great Ultimate Fist) a taijiquan style

li tuo qian jin (M) [Common Usage] (*lit.* Raise Up Half a Ton) a breathing exercise in Shi San Tai Bao Gong

liu (M) [Common Usage] six

liu da kai (M) [Bajiquan] a hand form or routine in this northern style

Liu Guo Shi (M) [Hong Quan] (*lit.* Six Country Style) a hand form

liuh (C) [Common Usage] to heal

Liu He (M) [Style] (*lit.* Six Combinations) a Shaolin system that originated from the Wei Tuo style and combines external and internal training

liuh gaai (C) [Common Usage] to comprehend

liuh seung (C) [Common Usage] *see* liuh

Liu Jia (M) [Style] *see* Lauh Ga

Liu Jin Bian (M) [Bamenquan] *see* Luhk Jeun Bin

liu ye dao (M) [Weapon] a steel broadsword

li wu (M) [Common Usage] *see* laih sih

li you (M) [Common Usage] reason

Li Zhen Qing (M) [Master] a prominent master of baguazhang and a second-generation disciple

loa fua shih (M) [Yang Taijiquan] *see* luo hua shi

Lo Han Fuhk Fu Kyuhn (C) [Choy Leih Faht] (*lit.* Buddha Tames The Tiger Fist Form) a hand form

Lohhan Kyuhn (C) [Sai Chong Baahk Hok Kyuhn] (*lit.* Arhat Fist) a hand form

Lohhan Yi Sahp Say Gai Kyuhn (C) [Sai Chong Baahk Hok Kyuhn] (*lit.* Arhat Twenty-Four Fist Form) a hand form

lohk gwaih ma (C) [Common Usage] kneeling horse stance

Lohk Yiuh (C) [Master] a prominent master of Wihng Cheun

loi yam cheuih (C) [Common Usage] corkscrew punch

lok (C) [Common Usage] blood vessels

Lok Dim Boon Gwun (C) [Wihng Cheun] *see* Luhk Dim Buhn Gwan

lok kiuh (C) [Common Usage] grinding wheel grab

lok sau (C) [Wihng Cheun] a grabbing technique applied on the wrist or arm to pull an opponent off balance

long (C) [Common Usage] *see* luhng

long (M) [Common Usage] dragon

long chuan (M) [Common Usage] *see* luhng syuhn

long hu chu xian (M) [Hong Jia] *see* luhng fu cheut yihn

long lin bao dao (M) [Weapon] a specialized broadsword that has the appearance of dragon scales on the blade

Long Xing Baguazhang (M) [Style] (*lit.* Dragon Shape Eight Trigram Palm) a style of baguazhang

Long Xing Quan (M) [Style] *see* Luhng Yihng Kyuhn

loohng (C) [Common Usage] *see* luhng

louh (C) [Common Usage] old

louh fu (C) [Common Usage] tiger

Louh Ga Kyuhn (C) [Huhng Kyuhn] *see* Lao Jia Quan

lu (M) [Common Usage] **1** a routine **2** rules, regulations **3** rolling back; a defensive technique in taijiquan used to yield to an opponent's force by moving the hands and upper body in a circular motion

luhk (C) [Common Usage] six

Luhk Ah Choi (C) [Master] a prominent master of Huhng Ga from Guangdong Province; a student of Huhng Hei Gun, the founder of Huhng Ga

Luhk Dim Buhn Gwan (C) [Wihng Cheun] (*lit.* Six-and-a-Half Point Long Staff) a weapons form using an eight-foot staff; used to teach how to fight multiple attackers

luhk gan (C) [Medicine] deer tendon; a plant used in Chinese medicine to strengthen the tendons

Luhk Gwok Sik (C) [Huhng Kyuhn] *see* Liu Guo Shi

Luhk Hahp (C) [Style] *see* Liu He

Luhk Hahp Daaih Cheung (C) [Baat Gihk Kyuhn] (*lit.* Six Combination Big Spear) a weapons form using a spear

Luhk Hahp Fa Cheung (C) [Baat Gihk Kyuhn] (*lit.* Six Combination Blossom Spear) a weapons form using a spear

Luhk Hahp Kyuhn (C) [Style] (*lit.* Six Combination Fist) a northern style of Chinese martial arts

Luhk Hahp Seung Dou (C) [Chat Sing Tohng Lohng] (*lit.* Six Combination Double Swords) a weapons form using two broadswords

Luhk Hahp Tohng Lohng Kyuhn (C) [Style] (*lit.* Six Combination Praying Mantis) a northern style of Chinese martial arts

Luhk Heung Dou (C) [Ying Jaau] (*lit.* Six Direction Broadsword) a weapons form

Luhk Jeun Bin (C) [Baat Muhn Kyuhn] (*lit.* Six Proceeding Whip) a weapons form using a steel whip

Luhk Lihk Kyuhn (C) [Sai Chong Baahk Hok Kyuhn] a hand form

luhk sik (C) [Common Usage] green

Luhm Joh (C) [Master] a prominent master of Huhng Ga who was the nephew and a student of Lahm Sai Wihng

luhng (C) [Common Usage] dragon

luhng fu cheut yihn (C) [Huhng Ga] (*lit.* Dragon and Tiger Emerging) A salute that denotes the style practiced. The practitioner of this salute stands in a cat stance and extends both hands in front of the body. The right hand forms a fist and the left hand remains in an open position.

Luhng Fu Kyuhn (C) [Choy Leih Faht] (*lit.* Dragon and Tiger Fist Form) a hand form

Luhng Hahng Gwan (C) [Chat Sing Tohng Lohng] (*lit.* Dragon Walking Staff) a weapons form using the staff

Luhng Seung Tauh Gwan (C) [Choy Leih Faht] (*lit.* Coiling Dragon Double-Ended Staff Form) a weapons form using the staff

luhng syuhn (C) [Common Usage] (*lit.* Dragon Boat) a long and wide canoe-like boat decorated with carvings of dragons and used for racing

Luhng Yihng Kyuhn (C) [Style] (*lit.* Dragon Shape Fist) A southern style taught at the Woh Soh Toi temple in Guangdong Province by Daaih Yuhk, a monk who had taught Lahm Yiu Kwaih in the late nineteenth century. It is a short-range fighting style that generates power from low rooted stances, and uses explosive techniques using the palms, elbows, and dragon claw strikes.

Luhng Ying Kyuhn (C) [Choy Leih Faht] (*lit.* Dragon Hand Form) a hand form

Luhng Ying Kyuhn Deui Chuk Fu Ying Kyuhn (C) [Choy

Leih Faht] (*lit.* Dragon Versus Tiger) a two-man fighting
form

lu jiao (M) [Medicine] the horn of a male deer; used for re-
ducing swelling of the tendons and strengthening the bones

luk (C) [Common Usage] to roll

Luk Dim Boon Gwun (C) [Wihng Cheun] *see* Luhk Dim
Buhn Gwan

luk gan (C) [Medicine] *see* luhk gan

luk sau (C) [Wihng Cheun] *see* lok sau

Lung Ying Kune (C) [Style] *see* Luhng Yihng Kyuhn

lun wu shi jue (M) [Qigong] (*lit.* Wield a Weapon and Split a
Stone) a breathing exercise in Shi San Tai Bao Gong

luo (M) [Common Usage] *see* lok

luo hua shi (M) [Yang Taijiquan] (*lit.* Falling Flower Posture)
a movement in the Taiji Sword form

lu rong (M) [Medicine] horn of a deer used in Chinese herbal
medicine

lu se (M) [Common Usage] *see* luhk sik

lu zhu jin zhui (M) [Weapon] a weapon resembling a large
ice pick with a wooden handle and a long metal point

Lu Zi Ming (M) [Master] a prominent master of baguazhang

— M —

ma (J) [Common Usage] interval, space, or distance

ma (M, K) [Common Usage] horse

Maahng Fu Cheut Lahm Pah (C) [Ngh Jou Kyuhn] (*lit.* Brave
Tiger Comes Out of the Woods Fork) a weapons form using
a trident

maahng fu faan san (C) [Baahk Meih] A movement in the
Baahk Meih Pah form to counter an attack to the left side.
While the feet form a left triangular stance, the point of the
trident is swung toward the left front corner.

Maahn Tou (C) [Pek Gwa Kyuhn] (*lit.* Slow Set) a hand form

maai (J) [Common Usage] a concept that combines the motions of space, distance, timing, and opportunity

maan faahn (C) [Common Usage] dinner

maau (C) [Common Usage] cat

ma bu (M) [Common Usage] horse stance

Mabuni Kenwa (O) [Master] founder of the Shito-ryu system and student of Itosu Yasutsune and Higashionna Kanryo; one of the first Okinawans to teach karate in mainland Japan in the early 1920s

machi (J) [Weapon] a small notch that separates the tang from the blade; notches on the cutting edge of the blade are called *ha machi*, whereas the ones on the back are called *mune machi*

machi da (K) [Common Usage] to hit

machi dojo (J) [Common Usage] a private dojo

machiwara (O) [Karate] *see* makiwara

madake (J) [Iaido] a bamboo pole used in iaido as a cutting target when practicing *tameshi giri*

madang (K) [Tae Kyon] term denoting the individual sections of the first form, usually learned separately and later combined into a single, non-stop form when the student becomes more advanced; numbered Han Madang (first form) through Yeoseot Madang (eighth form), it comprises a total of 120 techniques

mae (J) [Common Usage] front, forward

Mae (J) [Iaido] the first *kata* done from *tatehiza* in the Seiza no Bu of the Zen Nihon Kendo Renmei Seitei Iai

maeba (J) [Karate] a ready position used for kumite

mae da (K) [Common Usage] to tie

maedeup (K) [Common Usage] square knot used to tie a uniform belt

mae empi uchi (J) [Karate] forward elbow strike

Maegashira (J) [Sumo] the sixteen members of the Makuno-uchi division of sumo who are not Sanyaku rank

mae geri (J) [Karate] front kick

mae geri keage (J) [Karate] front snap kick

mae geri kekomi (J) [Karate] front thrust kick

mae hiji ate (J) [Judo] forward elbow strike

maek (K) [Common Usage] vital point, pressure point

maek chagi (K) [Kuk Sool] vital-point kicking techniques

maek chigi (K) [Kuk Sool] vital-point striking techniques

maen bal (K) [Common Usage] barefoot

maen son (K) [Common Usage] barehanded, empty hand

maen son gisul (K) [Common Usage] empty-hand technique

Maen Son Muye (K) [Style] (*lit.* Empty Hand Martial Art) often used to refer to Tae Kyon

maeteu (K) [Common Usage] Korean pronunciation of floor mat

mae tobi geri (J) [Karate] jumping front kick

mae tsugi ashi (J) [Kendo] a forward sliding step

mae ude deai osae uke (J) [Karate] forearm pressing block

mae ude hineri uke (J) [Karate] forearm twisting block

mae ukemi (J) [Judo, Ju-jutsu] a forward breakfall

mae zumo (J) [Sumo] matches at a sumo tournament of novice *rikishi* who are not listed on the program

Magaki (J) [Sumo] a sumo *beya* located in Sumida Ward, Tokyo

magatsubi (J) [Shinto] an evil spirit

mah (C) [Common Usage] horse

mahanmi no neko ashi dachi (J) [Karate] a cat stance with the body angled forty-five degrees

mah bou (C) [Common Usage] horse stance; used for building a solid foundation by strengthening the legs

mah bouh (C) [Common Usage] *see* mah bou

mah dihk jong (C) [Choy Leih Faht] (*lit.* Horse Power Dummy) a training tool

maheun (K) [Common Usage] forty

Mah Hohk Lai (C) [Master] the founder of the Hoh Nanhm style of xingyiquan

mahk (C) [Common Usage] pulse

mahk (C) [Common Usage] vein, channel

mahn (C) [Common Usage] to ask

mahn taih (C) [Common Usage] question, problem

ma hsing huan shih (M) [Xingyiquan] *see* ma xing huan xi

maht (C) [Common Usage] socks

mai (C) [Common Usage] rice, grains

mai (M) [Common Usage] pulse, veins

maih jan (C) [Common Usage] maze, labyrinth

maitta (J) [Judo] "I quit! I give up!" This is signaled by tapping the floor, one's opponent, or oneself.

majimak (K) [Common Usage] final, last

majimak dongjak (K) [Common Usage] final movement of a form

maju megigi (K) [Tae Kyon] second level of training, which involves a partner

mak da (K) [Common Usage] to block

make (J) [Common Usage] *see* makeru

makekoshi (J) [Sumo] a losing record at a tournament

makeru (J) [Common Usage] to lose, to be beaten

makeum dari (K) [Tae Kyon] bent-leg block

makeum jil (K) [Tae Kyon] collective term for blocking techniques

makgi (K) [Common Usage] block

makgi beop (K) [Tang Soo Do] blocking method

maki (J) [Common Usage] wrap; the wrap used on the hilt of a *katana* or shaft of a *naginata*

maki (J) [Kobudo] the act of wrapping the chain of a *kusarigama* or *suruchin* around the arm or weapon of the opponent

makiwara (O) [Karate] a striking board; a post usually bolted or cemented into the ground, used for striking with the hands and feet

makneun beop (K) [Common Usage] blocking method

makoto (J) [Common Usage] sincerity; honesty; devotion; the pure or unstained mind, undisturbed by external nonessentials

Makunouchi (J) [Sumo] the top of six divisions in professional sumo

Makushita (J) [Sumo] the third-highest division of sumo

mal (K) [Common Usage] horse

ma lau (C) [Common Usage] monkey

mamori (J) [Common Usage] protection, defense

mamori kama (J) [Weapon] *see* kama

mamoru (J) [Common Usage] to defend, to protect

man (J) [Common Usage] ten thousand

manabu (J) [Common Usage] to learn, to study

mangchi (K) [Common Usage] **1** hammer **2** a Hapkido hammerfist

mangchi sul (K) [Common Usage] hammer technique

mang geng sau (C) [Wihng Cheun] neck-pulling hand

Maniwa Nen-ryu (J) [Style] a school of ken-jutsu, so-jutsu, yadome-jutsu, and naginata-jutsu founded in the seventeenth century; one of the earliest schools to train using protective equipment and *fukuro shinai*

mannaka (J) [Common Usage] center, midpoint

manriki gusari (J) [Weapon] *see* kusari fundo

man sau (C) [Wihng Cheun] curious arm

Manseikan (J) [Style] a style of aikido founded by Sunadomari Kanshu, an early student of Ueshiba Morihei

Man Tao (M) [Pi Gua Quan] *see* Maahn Tou

mao (M) [Common Usage] cat

mao gen (M) [Medicine] the root and stem of this plant are used in Chinese herbal medicine

marui (J) [Common Usage] circular

maru mimi (J) [Weapon] a *tsuba* with rounded edges

Masamune (J) [Master] a famous sword smith of the Kamakura period

Masatoshi Nakayama (J) [Master] *see* Nakayama Masatoshi

ma sul (K) [Common Usage] **1** horsemanship **2** magic

masutemi waza (J) [Judo] throwing techniques that involve sacrificing one's own balance to the rear

matawari (J) [Sumo] sumo-style splits; a basic stretching exercise

Matayoshi Shinko (O) [Master] founder of Okinawa Kobudo and a student of Chinese White Crane boxing; his lineage of *kobudo* was inherited by his son Shimpo

mat baejigi (K) [Ssi Rum] counter-technique in which a failed *baejigi* leads to the opponent's *baejigi* counter

matchweo gyeorugi (K) [Taekwondo] pre-arranged sparring

Matsubayashi-ryu (O) [Karate] (*lit.* Pine Forest Style) a style founded by Nagamine Shoshin; this combination of Shuri-te and Tomari-te has a large following outside of Okinawa, especially in the United States of America

Matsugane (J) [Sumo] a sumo *beya* located in Funabashi City, Chiba Prefecture

Matsukaze (J) [Karate] *see* Wankan

Matsumura Sokon (O) [Master] a master of Okinawan Shuri-te and kobudo; often referred to as "Bushi" Matsumura, he was a student of Sakugawa Kanga and also learned Jigen-ryu ken-jutsu and Chinese *quan fa;* he was the teacher of Itosu Yasutsune

Matsu Sanchin (O) [Karate] a *kata* practiced in the Bugeikan school

mauh (C) [Common Usage] to plot, to scheme

mauh saat (C) [Common Usage] to murder, to kill, to assassinate

ma ushiro (J) [Common Usage] directly to the back

mawaru (J) [Common Usage] to turn, rotate, spin

mawashi (J) [Common Usage] circular, round

mawashi empi uchi (J) [Karate] roundhouse elbow strike

mawashi geri (J) [Karate] roundhouse kick

mawashi tsuki (J) [Karate] roundhouse punch

mawashi uchi (J) [Karate] roundhouse strike

mawashi uke (J) [Karate] roundhouse block; windmill parry

ma xing huan xi (M) [Xingyiquan] (*lit.* Horse Form Changes the Posture) a movement or exercise that consists of a yielding blocking technique followed by an attack

Ma Yueh Liang (M) [Master] a prominent master of Wu taijiquan

me (J) [Common Usage] eyes

me (O) [Common Usage] front, forward

mehng (C) [Common Usage] life

mei (J) [Weapon] the inscribed signature of a sword smith on a *katana, tanto,* or *naginata*

Meibukan (O) [Karate] (*lit.* Bright/Enlightened Martial Hall) the style of Goju-ryu founded by Yagi Meitoku, who was one of Miyagi Chojun's senior students

Meibuken (O) [Karate] (*lit.* Bright/Enlightened Martial Fist) the name used by Yagi Meitoku to refer to the fighting applications taught at his Meibukan school

meih (C) [Common Usage] tail

Mei Hua (M) [Style] (*lit.* Plum Flower Fist) a northern style that emphasizes the training of footwork patterns on a series of stumps or posts buried into the ground in the pattern of a plum flower

Mei Hua Ji (M) [Gou Quan] (*lit.* Plum Blossom Season) a hand form

Mei Hua Tang Lang Quan (M) [Style] *see* Muih Fa Tohng Lohng Kyuhn

mei hua zhuang (M) [Common Usage] *see* muih fa jong

meih yahn jiu geng (C) [Huhng Ga] (*lit.* Beauty Looking into Mirror) an inside-outside open-hand block with the palm facing toward the practitioner like a mirror

Meiji jidai (J) [Common Usage] A historic era from 1863 to 1912, during which Japan went through enormous social change—the feudal system was abolished, the Shogun was stripped of his power, the samurai lost their swords, and the emperor was empowered like never before in Japanese history. This period also saw Japan open up to the Western world after two and a half centuries of self-imposed isolation under the Tokugawa *bakufu*.

meijin (J) [Common Usage] someone who has achieved mental, spiritual, and physical perfection in their art

Meikyo (J) [Karate] an advanced *kata* also referred to as Rohai

mei ren zhao jing (M) [Hong Jia] *see* meih yahn jiu geng

meiyo (J) [Common Usage] honor and reputation

mejumeok (K) [Taekwondo] hammerfist

mejumeok bakkat chigi (K) [Taekwondo] outward hammerfist strike

mejumeok jil ha da (K) [Taekwondo] to strike with a hammerfist

mekugi (J) [Weapon] a peg, usually made of bamboo, used to fasten the sword blade to the hilt

men (J) [Kendo, Naginata] **1** a blow that strikes the head **2** helmet; the part of the *bogu* that protects the head of the trainee

Meng Hu Chu Lin Pa (M) [Wu Zu Quan] *see* Maahng Fu Cheut Lahm Pah

meng hu fan shen (M) [Bai Mei] *see* maahng fu faan san

menkyo kaiden (J) [Common Usage] (*lit.* License of Complete Transmission) certificate of full proficiency in an art

men sheng (M) [Common Usage] *see* muhn sang

menuki (J) [Weapon] decorative object set into the hilt of a *katana;* today, it can be worth as much as the sword itself

meong (K) [Common Usage] bruise

meong deul da (K) [Common Usage] to bruise

meori (K) [Common Usage] head

meori deulgo (K) [Common Usage] head upright

meori karak (K) [Common Usage] (scalp) hair

metsubushi (J) [Nin-jutsu, Ju-jutsu] **1** a powder used by ninja to momentarily blind the opponent in order to escape **2** in ju-jutsu, a distraction technique performed by striking at the opponent's eyes

metsuke (J) [Common Usage] the point where one's vision is focused

Mh Dim Muih Fa Gwan (C) [Choy Leih Faht] (*lit.* Star Pattern Plum Blossom Staff Form) a weapons form using a staff

mh gung pihng (C) [Common Usage] unfair

mh jung sam (C) [Common Usage] to be disloyal

mh jyun juhng (C) [Common Usage] disrespectful, disobedient

mh leih (C) [Common Usage] dull, not sharp

Mh Luhn Cheuih (C) [Choy Leih Faht] (*lit.* Five Wheel Fist Form) an unarmed form that teaches basic hand techniques

Mh Luhn Ma (C) [Choy Leih Faht] (*lit.* Five Wheel Stance Form) a hand form that teaches the basic footwork and stances

Mh Ying Kyuhn (C) [Choy Leih Faht] (*lit.* Five Animals Hand Form) a hand form

mi (M) [Common Usage] rice, grains

mi (O) [Common Usage] eyes

Mi An Quan (M) [Style] (*lit.* Silk Floss Fist) a northern style of Chinese martial arts

miao (M) [Common Usage] *see* miu

miao jin ji (M) [Weapon] A spear with a double-edged halberd at the tip and tassels at the base of the blade. The opposite end of the spear is tipped with a small spear point.

michi (J) [Common Usage] (*lit.* Way, Path, Road) an alternate reading for the character read "-do" in karate-do, kendo, and judo

Michinoku (J) [Sumo] a sumo *beya* located in Chiba City

michi o osameru (J) [Common Usage] to attain the way, attain complete mastery

mideul geup (K) [Taekwondo] middleweight class in sparring competition

mienai (J) [Common Usage] (*lit.* Could Not See) term used by a referee when the technique was not visible

Mifune Kyuzo (J) [Master] a prominent 10th Dan master of Kodokan judo, noted for his *kuki nage*

miggeureum bal (K) [Taekwondo] sliding step

migi (J) [Common Usage] right

migi ashi (J) [Common Usage] right leg

migi kokutsu dachi (J) [Karate] back stance with the right leg in front

migi neko ashi dachi (J) [Karate] cat stance with the right leg in front

migi shizentai (J) [Common Usage] a natural stance with the right leg forward

migi sumi (J) [Common Usage] right corner

migi te (J) [Common Usage] right hand

migi tsuki (J) [Karate] right punch

migi yoko men (J) [Kendo, Naginata] strike to the right side of the head *(men)*

migi zenkutsu dachi (J) [Karate] front stance with the right leg in front

Miguk (K) [Common Usage] America

mihn (C) [Common Usage] face

Mihng Hok (C) [Style] *see* Ming He

mihng wahn (C) [Common Usage] destiny

mihng yuh (C) [Common Usage] fame, reputation

Mihn Kyuhn (C) [Style] (*lit.* Cotton Fist) a northern style of Chinese martial arts

Mihogaseki (J) [Sumo] a sumo *beya* located in Sumida Ward, Tokyo

mih tzong shen kung (M) [Common Usage] *see* mi zong shen gong

Mih Yihng Kyuhn (C) [Sai Chong Baahk Hok Kyuhn] a hand form that is performed slowly, and sometimes practiced on the *muih fa jong,* to develop *hei* in the body

mijeobu (K) [Taekwondo] small of the back

mikazuki geri (J) [Karate] crescent kick

mil da (K) [Common Usage] to push

mimi (J) [Common Usage] **1** ear **2** the edge of the *tsuba*

min (M) [Common Usage] reputation

minami (J) [Common Usage] south

Minato (J) [Sumo] a sumo *beya* located in Kawaguchi City, Saitama Prefecture

Minezaki (J) [Sumo] a sumo *beya* located in Nerima Ward, Tokyo

ming (M) [Common Usage] life

Ming Dai (M) [Common Usage] Ming Imperial dynasty, which ruled China from A.D. 1368 to 1644

Ming He (M) [Style] (*lit.* Crying Crane) one of the branches of the Bai He style, which mimics the crying sounds of a fighting crane to emphasize and promote *qi* development

ming yin (M) [Common Usage] destiny

ming yu (M) [Common Usage] fame, reputation

mireo chagi (K) [Taekwondo] push kick, thrust kick

mireo deonjigi (K) [Ssi Rum] pushing-and-throwing technique

mireo makgi (K) [Taekwondo] pushing block

misogi (J) [Common Usage] purification of mind and body

mitama (J) [Shinto] spirit, god

mit eobeo deonjigi (K) [Hapkido] low piggy-back throwing technique

mitokoro mono (J) [Weapon] a set of *kozuka, kogai,* and *menuki* made by the same artist

mit palmok (K) [Common Usage] underside of the wrist

mitsu dogu (J) [Common Usage] the three weapons commonly used by the *bushi* during the Edo period: *sasumata, sodegarami,* and *tsukibo;* at some times, the *jutte* and *kusarigama* were included in this list

Mi Tsung Yi (M) [Style] *see* Mi Zong Yi

miu (C) [Common Usage] temple

Miura-ryu (J) [Style] an empty-handed fighting art, developed by Miura Yoshitatsu, that was heavily influenced by sumo

Miura Yoshitatsu (J) [Master] a master of an ancient grappling art; he is credited with systematizing many moves that would later become goshin-jutsu

miyabi (J) [Bushido] courtesy, refinement; the ideal behavior of a samurai

Miyagi Chojun (O) [Master] A master of Naha-te, he was the most successful of Higashionna's students. After structuring and systematizing his master's teachings, he studied in southern China for several months before returning to Okinawa and starting the Goju-ryu lineage. His students, Yagi Meitoku, Miyazato Eiichi, Yamaguchi Gogen, Higa Seiko, and Toguchi Seikichi have become some of the most respected masters of this century.

Miyagino (J) [Sumo] a sumo *beya* located in Sumida Ward, Tokyo

Miyamoto Musashi (J) [Master] Considered by many to be the greatest swordsman ever, he was the founder of the Emmei-ryu and Niten Ichi-ryu schools of ken-jutsu. He was renowned not only for his fighting ability, but also for his wisdom on the art of strategy. His book *Gorin No Sho (The Book of Five Rings),* written in the sixteenth century, is still considered one of the authorities on military strategy.

Miyazato Eiichi (O) [Master] a long-time student of Miyagi Chojun and founder of the Jundokan, among his top students are Higaonna Morio and Chinen Teruo

mi zong shen gong (M) [Common Usage] a special, secretive Tibetan *qigong* exercise

Mi Zong Yi (M) [Style] Labyrinthine Boxing; a northern style utilizing both soft and hard postures; also known as Lost Path Style

mizu iri (J) [Sumo] a stop or break in a bout; it gives the *rikishi* an opportunity to catch their breath

mizukaki (J) [Nin-jutsu] **1** flippers tied to a ninja's feet to assist them in swimming **2** a paddle used with the *mizugamo*

mizu no kokoro (J) [Common Usage] (*lit.* A Heart Like Water) this concept denotes absolute tranquillity and lack of emotional distraction or turmoil

Mizuno Shinto-ryu (J) [Style] a school of iai-jutsu and ju-jutsu founded by Kobayashi Koemon Toshinari

mizu taimatsu (J) [Nin-jutsu] a torch used by ninja that would remain lit even in the rain

mo (M) [Common Usage] to touch

moa seogi (K) [Taekwondo] close stance

mochi (J) [Common Usage] grip

Mochizuki Minoru (J) [Master] founder of Yoseikan Aikido; a student of Ueshiba Morihei, Kano Jigoro, Hisataka Masa-yoshi, and Mifune Kyuzo

modeumbal (K) [Taekwondo] bringing the feet together

modeumbal chagi (K) [Taekwondo] feet-together kick

modum ap mureup chagi (K) [Ssi Rum] technique in which the opponent's front knee is grasped and his leg is swept

Mohk Ga (C) [Style] (*lit.* Mohk Family) A style founded by Mohk Ching Giuh, who was famous for his powerful kicks. It has its origins at the Shaolin Temple and uses a variety of short-range fighting techniques. It is one of the five family styles of martial arts in Guangdong Province.

Mohk Ga Gwan (C) [Mohk Ga] (*lit.* Mohk Family Staff) a weapons form using the staff

mohk yahn jong (C) [Common Usage] (*lit.* Wood Man Dummy) A training device used in many southern styles consisting of a wooden log with wooden appendages placed at various locations that represent the arms and legs of an opponent. The log is placed vertically and often is solidly secured into the ground, or suspended by wood giving it a springing action.

mohk yan jong faat (C) [Wihng Cheun] (*lit.* Wood Man Dummy Method) application of techniques on a wooden dummy

mohng gei (C) [Common Usage] to forget

Mo Jia (M) [Style] *see* Mohk Ga

moji batang (K) [Taekwondo] thumb ridge

mojiggeut (K) [Hapkido] fingertips

mojiggeut chigi (K) [Hapkido] fingertip strike

moji gweon (K) [Taekwondo] thumb fist

mo juchum seogi (K) [Taekwondo] close attention stance

mok (K) [Common Usage] throat, neck

mok deolmi (K) [Tae Kyon] back of the neck

mok geom (K) [Kum Do] wooden sword, *bokken* in Japanese

mok joreugi (K) [Kuk Sool] choke

mok jul ddi (K) [Tae Kyon] vital point on the suprasternal notch

moksori (K) [Common Usage] voice

moktong maek (K) [Common Usage] vital point on the side of the neck

mokuju (J) [Common Usage] a wooden bayonet used in jukendo

mom (K) [Common Usage] body

mom dollyeo chagi (K) [Taekwondo] body-turn kick

mom eul dolli da (K) [Common Usage] to turn the body

mom gwa maeum eui tongil (K) [Common Usage] body-mind unification

Mo Mian Quan (M) [Pi Gua Quan] *see* Mut Mihn Kyuhn

momi sujik (K) [Common Usage] body perpendicular to the floor

mom natchugi (K) [Taekwondo] body drop

mom natchweo ap chagi (K) [Taekwondo] body-dropping front kick

momtong (K) [Common Usage] trunk of the body

momtong bakkat makgi (K) [Taekwondo] outward middle block

momtong bandae jireugi (K) [Taekwondo] reverse punch to the body

momtong baro jireugi (K) [Taekwondo] straight punch to the body

momtong makgi (K) [Taekwondo] body-area block, middle block

mom umjigigi (K) [Taekwondo] movement of the body

mon (J) [Common Usage] a crest or emblem for a family, clan, or regent; usually worn on the *haori* or a flag

mondo (J) [Zen] A conversation between a master and a pupil, usually as a test of the student's understanding. The *sensei* will usually ask a short and simple question, and wait for the reply, often waiting weeks or months.

mong dung i (K) [Common Usage] club

monjin (J) [Common Usage] a disciple or student of a traditional martial art

monme (J) [Common Usage] a unit of weight equivalent to 3.75 grams

mono ii (J) [Sumo] a meeting of judges and the referee to discuss a disputed decision

monouchi (J) [Weapon] the striking area of the blade, located approximately one-fourth of a blade-length away from the tip

montei (J) [Common Usage] *see* monjin

Moo Duk Kwan (K) [Style] A school founded by Hwang Kee in 1945; it split into two distinct branches in 1960, the Tang Soo Do Moo Duk Kwan and the Taekwondo Moo Duk Kwan. The Taekwondo Moo Duk Kwan remained separated from the other *kwan* until the founding of the World Taekwondo Federation in 1973.

mook yan jong (C) [Common Usage] *see* mohk yahn jong

mook yan jong fa (C) [Wihng Cheun] *see* mohk yan jong faat

moon yan (C) [Common Usage] *see* muhn yan

moot yeuk (C) [Medicine] *see* muht yeuk

morae tong (K) [Taekwondo] sandbox into which the fingers are thrust for fingertip conditioning

Morikawa Kozan (J) [Master] a master of kyu-jutsu, who established the first structured teaching methods for this art in 1644; also credited with being the first person to use the term kyudo

moroha (J) [Weapon] a double-edged sword

moro ha zukuri (J) [Weapon] a type of blade found on Japanese short swords

morote (J) [Common Usage] two-handed, both hands, augmented hand technique

morote gari (J) [Judo] double-leg reap; similar to a double-leg takedown in wrestling

morote jime (J) [Judo] two-handed choke hold or strangulation

morote jodan uke (J) [Karate] two-handed upper block

morote naka uke (J) [Karate] two-handed inside block

morote seoi nage (J) [Judo] two-handed shoulder throw

morote sukui uke (J) [Karate] two-handed scooping block

morote tsuki (J) [Iaido, Kendo] a two-handed thrust or strike with either the *shinai* or a *katana*

morote uchi (J) [Karate] a two-handed strike

morote uke (J) [Karate] augmented forearm block

Morote Zuki (J) [Iaido] the second *kata* done from *iaihiza* in the Tachiai no Bu of the Zen Nihon Kendo Renmei Seitei Iai

moshiai geiko (J) [Sumo] a practice competition in which a winner takes on all challengers until he is defeated

mot matchu da (K) [Common Usage] to miss (a strike)

Motobu Choki (O) [Master] A master of Okinawan karate, best known for his Naihanchi *kata* and fighting abilities. His quick movements earned him the nickname *Saru,* or "Monkey."

Motobu-ryu (O) [Style] A small style, it was taught solely to Motobu family members until recently. The style is now headed by Uehara Sekichi, who has opened it to non-family members. The style is not karate-like in nature or appearance, utilizing a variety of Chinese weapons, aikido-like throws, and joint-locking techniques.

Motode (O) [Karate] a *kata* practiced in Motobu-ryu

moto no ichi (J) [Competitive Budo] starting position; the fighters face each other with the referee between them

Motote (O) [Karate] a series of six *kata* practiced in Motobu-
ryu

mou (M) [Common Usage] to plot, to scheme

Mou Dong (C) [Common Usage] Mou Dong mountain

mou douh (C) [Common Usage] martial arts

mou gun (C) [Common Usage] martial arts school

mou gung (C) [Common Usage] martial arts

mouh (C) [Common Usage] responsibility, duty

mouh chi (C) [Common Usage] shameless

mouh dak (C) [Common Usage] *see* wu de

Mouh Ga Daan Dou (C) [Mouh Ga Kyuhn] *see* Wu Jia Dan
Dao

Mouh Ga Kyuhn (C) [Style] *see* Wu Jia Quan

Mouh Ga Luhk Hahp Pah (C) [Mouh Ga Kyuhn] *see* Wu Jia
Liu He Pa

mouh min (C) [Common Usage] no face, shameful

Mouh Taai Gihk Kyuhn (C) [Style] *see* Wu taijiquan

mouh ying (C) [Common Usage] formless pattern

mouh ying geuk (C) [Huhng Ga] shadowless kick or leg

mouh yuhk (C) [Common Usage] to insult, an insult

mou kap (C) [Common Usage] martial arts book

mou seuht (C) [Common Usage] martial arts; martial technique or style

mou sha (M) [Common Usage] to murder, to kill, to assassinate

mou si (C) [Common Usage] lion dance; a performance using
a life-size lion costume worn by two dancers

mou si tauh (C) [Common Usage] to do the lion dance; a
ceremony performed to music using a lion costume

mo yao (M) [Medicine] myrrh; a yellowish-brown resin that
is used to improve circulation, reduce aches and pains, and
invigorate the blood

mu (J) [Common Usage] **1** nothingness, emptiness; often used
to refer to the concept of clearing the mind of any desire or

specific intention **2** an alternative reading for the character for *bu,* which means martial

mu (M) [Common Usage] **1** eyes **2** wood; one of the five elements of Chinese cosmology

mubobi chui (J) [Competitive Budo] a warning for passivity or lack of spirit

mudansha (J) [Common Usage] a student who holds only a *kyu* rank

mu di (M) [Common Usage] purpose, aim, goal, motive

mudo (K) [Common Usage] (*lit.* Martial Way) a collective term often used to mean martial art

Mugai-ryu Hyodo (J) [Style] a school of ken-jutsu founded in 1695 by Tsuji Getten Sakemochi, based on the Chinese concept of *yin-yang*

muge (K) [Common Usage] weight

mugi (K) [Common Usage] weapon

mugi gong (K) [Common Usage] weapon training

mugi hyeong (K) [Common Usage] weapon routine/form

mugisul (K) [Common Usage] weapon skill or technique

mu hak (K) [Common Usage] martial studies

muhk dang (C) [Weapon] (*lit.* Horse Bench) a wooden bench used as a weapon is many southern styles; also called *muhk mah*

muhk dik (C) [Common Usage] purpose, aim, goal, motive

muhk mah (C) [Weapon] *see* muhk dang

muhk yahn (C) [Common Usage] *see* mohk yahn jong

muhk yahn jong (C) [Common Usage] *see* mohk yahn jong

muhk yahn jong faat (C) [Wihng Cheun] *see* mohk yahn jong faaht

muhn kwai (C) [Common Usage] (*lit.* Door Rules) the rules and regulations one must follow in a home or school

muhn sang (C) [Common Usage] disciple, student

muhn yan (C) [Common Usage] disciples, followers, or brotherhood

muht yeuk (C) [Medicine] a sap or resin used in Chinese medicine to stop bleeding, heal cuts, speed healing, and reduce pain

mui fa jeong (C) [Common Usage] *see* muih fa jong

muih fa (C) [Common Usage] (*lit.* Plum Blossom) a flower from the southern region of China used to make wine; also the insignia for the Choy Leih Faht style

Muih Fa Baatgwa (C) [Choy Leih Faht] (*lit.* Plum Blossom Eight Trigram Hand Form) a hand form

Muih Fa Cheung (C) [Chat Sing Tohng Lohng, Choy Leih Faht, Huhng Ga] (*lit.* Plum Blossom Spear) a weapons form using a spear

Muih Fa Cheung Gwan (C) [Choy Leih Faht] (*lit.* Plum Blossom Staff Spear) a long staff that is tapered on one end

Muih Fa Daahn Dou (C) [Choy Leih Faht] (*lit.* Plum Blossom Single Sword Form) a weapons form using the sword

Muih Fa Dou (C) [Huhng Ga] (*lit.* Plum Blossom Sword) a weapons form using a broadsword

Muih Fa Gwai (C) [Gau Kyuhn] *see* Mei Hua Ji

muih fa jau (C) [Common Usage] plum blossom wine

muih fa jong (C) [Common Usage] (*lit.* Plum Blossom Stumps) a series of raised stumps placed in the ground in the shape of a plum blossom, used for stance training

Muih Fa Kyuhn (C) [Style] (*lit.* Plum Blossom Fist) a northern style

Muih Fa Kyuhn (C) [Huhng Ga] (*lit.* Plum Blossom Fist) a hand form

Muih Fa Seung Dou (C) [Chat Sing Tohng Lohng] (*lit.* Plum Blossom Double Swords) a weapons form using two broadswords

Muih Fa Siu Touh Kyuhn (C) [Huhng Ga] (*lit.* Plum Blossom Small Peach Fist) a hand form

Muih Fa Tohng Lohng Kyuhn (C) [Style] (*lit.* Plum Blossom Praying Mantis) a northern style

mu in (K) [Common Usage] warrior

muken (J) [Kendo] no contact between the two competitor's *shinai*

muko (O) [Common Usage] forehead

mukyu (J) [Common Usage] without rank; a beginner who has not yet attained any rank

mulgunamu (K) [Common Usage] handstand

mulgunamu ssangbal chigi (K) [Tae Kyon] two-foot handstand kick

mullebanga (K) [Common Usage] cartwheel

mumei (J) [Weapon] a blade that does not bear the smith's signature or mark

mumi (O) [Common Usage] kidney

muna dori (J) [Aikido] single-handed lapel grab

mune (J) [Common Usage] chest

mune ate (J) [Kendo] the original name for the armor breastplate now called *do* in kendo

mune chi kawa (J) [Kendo] the loops through which the cords of the kendo breast-plate are inserted in order to fasten it securely

munen mushin (J) [Common Usage] an empty or clear mind

munen muso (J) [Common Usage] a state of no-thought; emptiness of mind; clear-headed

mune oshi (J) [Judo] a push to the chest

mu ren (M) [Common Usage] *see* mohk yahn jong

mu ren zhuang (M) [Common Usage] *see* mohk yahn jong

mu ren zhuang fa (M) [Yong Chun] *see* mohk yahn jong faat

mureup (K) [Common Usage] knee

mureup chagi (K) [Tang Soo Do] knee thrust

mureup cha olligi (K) [Hapkido] upward knee thrust

mureup dae eo dolligi (K) [Ssi Rum] technique in which the foot touches the outside of the opponent's knee and the opponent's body is then turned

mureup dolligi undong (K) [Ssi Rum] knee-circling exercise

mureup geori (K) [Tae Kyon] jamming technique in which the foot strikes the knee area of the opponent's kicking leg

mureup ggeokgi (K) [Common Usage] knee-lock

mureup ggul dda (K) [Common Usage] to kneel

mureup jaegi (K) [Tae Kyon] knee-lift exercise

mureup ollyeo chagi (K) [Common Usage] upward knee thrust

mureup ollyeo jaegi (K) [Tae Kyon] upward knee thrust

mureup pyeogi (K) [Taekwondo] knee stretch

mureup teulgi (K) [Ssi Rum] knee-twisting technique

Musashigawa (J) [Sumo] a sumo *beya* located in Arakawa Ward, Tokyo

musha shugyo (J) [Common Usage] touring the entire length of the country in order to seek out masters to study under

mushin (J) [Common Usage] an empty or clear mind; a mind not fixed on anything and open to everything

Mushin-ryu (J) [Style] a style of ken-jutsu

musho go (J) [Zen] the principle of not looking for what one seeks

mushotoku (J) [Zen] the non-desire of achieving a goal or receiving a reward

mu sim (K) [Common Usage] condition of "no mind" or "empty mind"

muso (J) [Zen] the act of not thinking

Muso Jikiden Eishin-ryu (J) [Style] an eighteenth-century school of iaido from which the Muso Shinden-ryu was derived

Muso Jikiden-ryu (J) [Style] a school of ken-jutsu specializing in armored combat

Muso Shinden-ryu (J) [Style] the most famous and influential iaido school, founded by Nakayama Hakudo in the early twentieth century

musubi (J) [Common Usage] a state of perfection

musubi dachi (J) [Common Usage] open-foot stance

musubinawa (J) [Nin-jutsu] a climbing rope made of horse-hair, used by ninja

musul (K) [Common Usage] (*lit.* Martial Skill) martial art

musul in (K) [Common Usage] (*lit.* Martial Skill Person) martial artist

musul sajeon (K) [Common Usage] martial arts dictionary

muteiko (J) [Common Usage] no resistance

mutekatsu (J) [Common Usage] to vanquish one's opponent without combat

Mut Mihn Kyuhn (C) [Pek Gwa Kyuhn] (*lit.* Spread Surface Fist) a hand form

muto (J) [Common Usage] without a sword; unarmed

Muto-ryu (J) [Style] a school of ken-jutsu; its full name is Itto Shoden Muto-ryu

Mutudi Sanchin (O) [Karate] a *kata* practiced in both the Motobu-ryu and the Bugeikan styles

mu xiang (M) [Medicine] the root of this is used to control pain

muye (K) [Common Usage] (*lit.* Martial Art) used to emphasize the more artistic martial arts styles such as Tae Kyon

Mu Yong Chong (K) [Common Usage] tomb in Manchuria that contains ancient wall paintings of martial poses, created by Koreans when the Koguryo dynasty ruled the area

myeongchi (K) [Common Usage] solar plexus

myeongsang (K) [Common Usage] meditation

myeongsang ha da (K) [Common Usage] to meditate

myeon ha da (K) [Common Usage] to escape (from a hold, choke, etc.)

myojo (J) [Acupressure] a vital point located five centimeters below the navel

— N —

naahm (C) [Common Usage] south

nae (K) [Common Usage] internal

nae chagi (K) [Tae Kyon] axe kick

naegong (K) [Common Usage] internal power

naegong musul (K) [Common Usage] internal-energy martial art

nae jeonhwan (K) [Hapkido] turning to the inside

naerichyeo be da (K) [Common Usage] to slash

naeryeo chagi (K) [Taekwondo] downward kick

naeryeo ddaerlgi (K) [Taekwondo] downward strike

naeryeo jireugi (K) [Taekwondo] downward punch

naeryeo makgi (K) [Taekwondo] downward block

naeswi da (K) [Common Usage] to exhale

naeswigi (K) [Common Usage] exhalation

nafuda kake (J) [Common Usage] the name and rank board

on the wall of a dojo that indicates the hierarchy of people there

nagamaki (J) [Common Usage] a long-bladed glaive with a blade that is equal in length to the haft; it is somewhat heavier and more cumbersome than most *naginata*

Nagamine Shoshin (O) [Master] a master of Matsubayashi-ryu Shorin-ryu; a student of Motobu Choki, Kyan Chotoku, and Arakaki Ankichi

Nagao Kemmotsu (J) [Master] a master of Itto-ryu and Yagyu Shinkage-ryu, he founded Nagao-ryu tai-jutsu in the seventeenth century

nagareru (J) [Common Usage] to flow, to run (as in running water)

nagashi (J) [Common Usage] to avoid or side-step an attack

nagashi uke (J) [Karate] sweeping block

naga surujin (O) [Kobudo] a thick and heavily weighted chain, usually over 2.75 meters in length

nagatachi (J) [Naginata] an ancient name for the *naginata*

nage (J) [Common Usage] throw one's opponent down

nage ashi (J) [Karate] a leg sweep resulting in a throw

Nage no Kata (J) [Judo] (*lit.* Forms of Throwing) A *kata* comprised of fifteen techniques made up of five groups of three, each of which are done to the right and left sides. The groups consist of representative throws from each of the major categories of technique (*i.e.,* hand, leg, hip, backward- and sideward-sacrifice throws).

Nagete (O) [Karate] a *kata* practiced in Motobu-ryu

nage teppo (J) [Nin-jutsu] a crude hand grenade made and used by ninja

nage waza (J) [Common Usage] throwing techniques

naginata (J) [Weapon] A long weapon resembling a glaive. The blade resembles a sword and is often used in wide, sweeping movements together with the butt end, which is used for striking

naginata-do (J) [Style] (*lit.* The Way of the Naginata) the pre-World War II name for Atarashii Naginata

Naha (J) [Common Usage] the present capital of Okinawa

Prefecture; an ancient port and merchant city that linked Japan, Korea, China, and Southeast Asia

Naha-te (O) [Karate] one of two traditional categories of Okinawan karate, later the style was systematized and became known as Goju-ryu

nahng lihk (C) [Common Usage] ability

Naifanchi (O) [Karate] A series of *kata* in Shuri-te; a family of three *kata:* Naifanchi Shodan, Nidan, and Sandan. They are unique in that they are the only *kata* using only lateral movements. These *kata* were the main forms practiced by Motobu Choki.

Naihanji (O) [Karate] *see* Naifanchi

Naihanjji hyeong (K) [Tang Soo Do] a series of three forms named after the karate Naifanchi forms

nai wan (J) [Common Usage] inner arm, the inner forearm

nakabi (J) [Sumo] the middle day of a sumo tournament

nakadaka ippon ken tsuki (J) [Karate] middle finger, single-knuckle strike; the extended middle knuckle of the middle finger is the striking surface

nakadaka ken (J) [Karate] a fist with the middle knuckle protruding and used as a striking surface

Nakamura (J) [Sumo] a sumo *beya* located in Edogawa Ward, Tokyo

Nakamura-ryu (J) [Style] a school of batto-jutsu founded by Nakamura Taisaburo

Nakamura Shigeru (O) [Master] the founder of Okinawan Kempo, and a student of Motobu Choki, Yabu Kentsu, and Hanashiro Chomo; he is best known for developing a full-contact system of competitive *kumite* in which body armor is used

Nakano Michiomi (J) [Master] a student of the Hakko-ryu school, he later changed his name to So Doshin and is best known as the creator and spiritual leader of Shorinji Kempo

Nakasone Seiyu (O) [Master] the last master of pure Tomari-te and a student of Matsumora Kosaku; he passed on his lineage to Tokashiki Iken

Nakayama Hiromichi (J) [Master] the founder of Muso Shinden-ryu

Nakayama Masatoshi (J) [Master] the founder of the Japan Karate Federation (JKF); one of the most important exponents of tournament karate

Nakayama-ryu (J) [Style] a name sometimes used in reference to Muso Shinden-ryu

nakayawai (J) [Kendo] the part of the *shinai* one third of the way down the shaft from the tip; the area most often used as the striking surface

nakayubi (J) [Common Usage] middle finger

nakayubi ippon ken (J) [Karate] middle finger-fist; often referred to as middle-finger spearhand

nakbeop (K) [Common Usage] falling method

nakha (K) [Common Usage] fall

nakha ha da (K) [Common Usage] to fall

nakham (K) [Tae Kyon] open-handed strike with the lower part of the palm

nakksi geori (K) [Ssi Rum] fish-hooking technique in which the forward leg is swept to the inside

nakksi geori (K) [Tae Kyon] mid-level outside hooking kick

namban tetsu (J) [Common Usage] imported steel used in sword production

Nam Han (K) [Common Usage] South Korean name for South Korea

Nami Gaeshi (J) [Iaido] the eighth *kata* in the Muso Shinden-ryu Hasegawa Eishin-ryu Chuden series, which is done from *tatehiza*

nami gaeshi (J) [Judo] avoiding a leg sweep by raising the leg

namja (K) [Common Usage] man

Nam Joseon (K) [Common Usage] North Korean name for South Korea

nan (M) [Common Usage] south

nanadan (J) [Common Usage] seventh-grade, seventh-degree black belt; also called *shichidan*

naname (J) [Common Usage] oblique, diagonal (direction)

naname uchi (J) [Judo] a diagonal strike

nanbei (O) [Common Usage] oblique, slant

Nan Bei He (M) [Style] Southern White Crane; a style based on the movements of a crane

Nan Chao Dai (M) [Common Usage] (*lit.* Southern Imperial dynasties) consisting of the Song, Qi, Liang, and Chen, these dynasties ruled China from A.D. 420 to 589

nangsim (K) [Common Usage] groin

nangsim bohodae (K) [Common Usage] groin protection cup

Nan Quan (M) [Common Usage] (*lit.* Southern Boxing Style) a generic term used to describe Chinese martial art styles developed south of the Yangtze river

nan shan fu hu (M) [Qigong] (*lit.* Sleeping in the Nanshan Peaks) a breathing exercise in Shi San Tai Bao Gong

nao (M) [Common Usage] brain

naore (J) [Competitive Budo] a command to return to one's original starting position

naotte (J) [Common Usage] a command to stand at ease

nara (K) [Common Usage] country

narabi juji jime (J) [Judo] a choke hold with the hands in a cross pattern

narabu (J) [Common Usage] to arrange oneself in a row with other trainees

naranhi seogi (K) [Taekwondo] parallel stance

Naruto (J) [Sumo] a sumo *beya* located in Matsudo City, Chiba Prefecture

natchugi (K) [Common Usage] ducking technique

natchweo seogi (K) [Taekwondo] low stance

natsu gasshuku (J) [Common Usage] a summer training camp

nau (C) [Common Usage] angry, to be angry

nau (C) [Common Usage] *see* niu

nau ma (C) [Common Usage] twist horse stance

nawa (J) [Hojo-jutsu] rope; tying cord

nayashi (J) [Kendo, Ken-jutsu] defending against an opponent's attack by absorbing and weakening his technique

Negishi-ryu (J) [Style] a martial tradition specializing in shuriken-jutsu

nehan mon (J) [Common Usage] (*lit.* Gateway to Nirvana) the entrance by which the assistant in *seppuku* (ritual suicide) enters

nei (M) [Common Usage] inside, within

Nei Dan (M) [Style] an internal style of *qigong* in which *qi* is built up in the body and is distributed to the extremities of the body

nei gong (M) [Style] an internal practice that emphasizes internal training and development of *qi*

nei guan (M) [Acupressure] a point located on the inside of the wrist

nei wai he yi (M) [Common Usage] unity of the inside and outside elements

neko ashi dachi (J) [Karate] cat stance

neko de (J) [Nin-jutsu] claws worn on the hands to assist in climbing as well as in fighting

neng li (M) [Common Usage] ability

Nen-ryu (J) [Style] a school of ken-jutsu founded in the fifteenth century by a monk named Nen Ami Jion

neoul geori (K) [Tae Kyon] raised-knee block

nerai (J) [Common Usage] aim

net (K) [Common Usage] four

neu (M) [Bai He] *see* niu

neuk gol (K) [Common Usage] ribs

neun jilleo chagi (K) [Tae Kyon] front kick that strikes with the heel

neurin dongjak (K) [Common Usage] slow-motion movement

ne waza (J) [Judo] groundwork or grappling techniques

ngaahn (C) [Common Usage] eye

ngaahng geng (C) [Common Usage] stubborn

ngaahng gung (C) [Common Usage] *see* ying gong

ngaahn sik (C) [Common Usage] color

ngaak (C) [Common Usage] to lie

ngaak (C) [Kahm Na] *see* wo

ngaat (C) [Kahm Na] to crush

Ngaauh Ba Sehn Kyuhn (C) [Sai Chong Baahk Hok Kyuhn] a hand form

ngahn (C) [Common Usage] silver

ngah sau (C) [Taai Gihk Kyuhn] *see* wa shou

ngai (C) [Common Usage] short in height

ngau (C) [Common Usage] to hook

ngau daaih lihk (C) [Medicine] the root of this plant is used in Chinese medicine to strengthen tendons and increase blood circulation

ngau dai lik (C) [Medicine] *see* ngau daaih lihk

Ngauh Kyuhn (C) [Style] *see* Niu Quan

ng ga pei (C) [Medicine] *see* ngh gwo peih

ngh (C) [Common Usage] five

Ngh Fa Paau Kyuhn (C) [Ying Jaau] (*lit.* Five Blossom Leopard Fist) a hand form

Ngh Fu Cheung (C) [Ying Jaau] (*lit.* Five Tiger Spear) a weapons form using the spear

Ngh Fu Jin Kyuhn (C) [Ngh Jou Kyuhn] (*lit.* Five Tiger Battle Fist) a hand form

ngh gwo peih (C) [Medicine] a fruit peel commonly used in Chinese medicine to strengthen bones and tendons

Ngh Hahng Daan Dou (C) [Chat Sing Tohng Lohng] (*lit.* Five Walking Single Sword) a weapons form using a broadsword

Ngh Hahng Kyuhn (C) [Huhng Ga] (*lit.* Five Element Fist) a hand form

Ngh Jou Kyuhn (C) [Style] (*lit.* Five Ancestor Fist) a southern Shaolin-related style founded by Choy Yuhk Mihng that originated in Fujian Province

Ngh Lohng Baatgwa Gwan (C) [Huhng Ga] (*lit.* Fifth Son Eight Trigram Staff) a weapons form using a long staff

Ngh Lohng Gwan (C) [Chat Sing Tohng Lohng] (*lit.* Fifth Son Staff) a weapons form using a staff

Ngh Muih (C) [Master] a Shaolin nun who had trained in Muih Fa Kyuhn; she taught the art to Yihm Wihng Cheun who perpetuated the style that would later be known as Wihng Cheun

Ngh Siu Chung (C) [Master] the founder of Tibet White Crane

Ngh Siu Chung Kyuhn Gihng (C) [Sai Chong Baahk Hok Kyuhn] a book written by Ngh Siu Chung that contains the theory, philosophy, and fighting applications of Tibetan White Crane

Ngh Yihng Kyuhn (C) [Huhng Ga, Sai Chong Baahk Hok, Baahk Meih] a form containing fighting movements of the dragon, snake, leopard, tiger, and crane

Ngh Yiuh (C) [Master] a prominent master of Baahk Meih

Ngoh Meih Daai Pung Kung (C) [Style] a Chinese bird style developed at Ngoh Meih Saan

Ngoh Meih Saan (C) [Common Usage] a mountain located in Sichuan Province, China where a variety of internal styles of martial arts originated

ngoih gung (C) [Common Usage] *see* wai gong

ngoih muhn (C) [Common Usage] (*lit.* Outdoor Area) the outer area of the body

nguk kei (C) [Common Usage] home

Nhg Fu Cheung (C) [Ying Jaau] (*lit.* Five Tiger Spear) a weapons form using the spear

ni (J) [Common Usage] two

ni (M) [Qin Na] to oppose

nian (M) [Common Usage] *see* nian qin

nian qin (M) [Common Usage] young

Nian Si Shi (M) [Hong Quan] (*lit.* Twenty-Four Style) a hand form

Nichiren-shu (J) [Common Usage] Lotus Sect; a Buddhist group that has over 5800 temples in Japan

nicho gama (O) [Kobudo] farming *kama* used in pairs

nidan (J) [Common Usage] second-degree black belt; 2nd Dan

Nidanbu-Dai (O) [Karate] a *kata* practiced in the Bugeikan style

nidan geri (J) [Karate] double jumping kick

nidan waza (J) [Kendo, Naginata] the second technique in a series of attacks

nie (M) [Qin Na] to hold with two fingers

nihn heng (C) [Common Usage] young

Nihon (J) [Common Usage] Japan

Nihon Kendo Kata (J) [Kendo] a *kata* developed in 1912 and originally called Dai Nippon Teikoku Kendo Kata, it consists of ten techniques, seven with *odachi* and three with *kodachi*

nihon nukite (J) [Karate] a two-finger spearhand

Nihon-ryu (J) [Style] the first school of kyu-jutsu, founded in the fifteenth century

nihon shobu (J) [Common Usage] fighting to two points

Nihon Sumo Kyokai (J) [Sumo] Japan Sumo Association

nijiri (O) [Common Usage] right

Nijushiho (J) [Karate] *see* Niseishi

nikajo (J) [Aikido] the second immobilization technique, also called *nikyo* or *kote mawashi*

nikyo (J) [Aikido] *see* nikajo

ninja (J) [Common Usage] trained spies, infiltraters, and assassins

ninja to (J) [Weapon] a short sword without curvature, used by ninja

nin-jutsu (J) [Style] (*lit.* The Art of Stealth) a general term used for all the arts taught to the ninja, which included: espionage, camouflage, military strategy, hand-to-hand combat, a variety of bladed weapons, as well as firearms and explosives; also called *shinobi*

ninpo (J) [Style] (*lit.* Methods of Stealth) another term for nin-jutsu

nip (C) [Kahm Na] *see* nie

Nipaipo (J) [Karate] a *kata* practiced by Shito-ryu

Nippon (J) [Common Usage] Japan

Nippon Den Kodokan Judo (J) [Judo] the formal, though seldom used, name for Kano Jigoro's judo

Nippon Den Seito Shorinji Kempo (J) [Style] *see* Shorinji Kempo

Nippon Shorinji Kempo (J) [Style] *see* Shorinji Kempo

Nippon to (J) [Common Usage] (*lit.* Japanese Sword) only used when referring to the classic Japanese sword made by traditional methods

niramiai (J) [Sumo] the pre-fight staring match; a face-off often done by *rikishi*

nise (J) [Common Usage] fake, counterfeit; a sword not made by a particular sword smith

Niseishi (O) [Karate] a *kata* practiced in Ryuei-ryu, Okinawan Kempo, Kobayashi-ryu, and the Bugeikan styles

nise mei (J) [Common Usage] a counterfeit signature on a *katana*

nise mono (J) [Common Usage] *see* nise

nishi (J) [Common Usage] west

Nishonoseki (J) [Sumo] a sumo *beya* located in Sumida Ward, Tokyo

Niten Ichi-ryu (J) [Style] a sixteenth-century ken-jutsu tradition founded by the legendary Miyamoto Musashi notable for its double-sword techniques in which a sword is held in each hand

nito (J) [Ken-jutsu] (*lit.* Two Swords) fighting with a sword in each hand; most often a long sword and a short sword are used, although occasionally two short swords are used; also called *ryoto*

nito kin (J) [Common Usage] biceps

niu (M) [Common Usage] **1** ox, cow **2** twist; a key movement in Zhang He

niu jiao guai (M) [Weapon] a walking cane with a hammer-shaped handle and a spear point at the opposite end

Niu Quan (M) [Style] (*lit.* Ox fist; Cow fist) a style developed in Fujian Province

niu xi (M) [Medicine] ox knee; a herb used to invigorate the flow of blood through joints and tendons to reduce inflammation

nobasu (J) [Common Usage] to reach out, lengthen, stretch

nodachi (J) [Weapon] an especially long Japanese sword; most often carried on one's back

nogareru (J) [Common Usage] to escape

noih (C) [Common Usage] *see* nei

noih gung (C) [Common Usage] *see* nei gong

noih muhn (C) [Common Usage] (*lit.* Indoor Area) a term used to describe the inside area of the body

noi moon (C) [Common Usage] *see* noih muhn

nok (K) [Common Usage] green

no Kami (J) [Common Usage] a title given to a *kaji* or *bushi* by the emperor for exceptional craftsmanship or services to the government

nok ddi (K) [Common Usage] green belt

nok saek (K) [Common Usage] green color

nop da (K) [Common Usage] high; to a high area

nopi (K) [Common Usage] height

nopi ddwigi (K) [Common Usage] high jump

noran (K) [Common Usage] yellow

noran ddi (K) [Common Usage] yellow belt

noran saek (K) [Common Usage] yellow color

norikata (J) [Ba-jutsu] horse-mounting and riding techniques taught in ba-jutsu

noto (J) [Iaido] to return the sword to its sheath

nouh (C) [Common Usage] brain

nuhk sau (C) [Wihng Cheun] (*lit.* Free-Hand Fighting) a term used to describe the practice of free-hand sparring

nukazu ni sumu (J) [Bushido] the act of not drawing the sword; this idea stems from the tradition that the sword was a means of creating and preserving peace rather than making war

nuki ai (J) [Iaido] another name for iaido

nukite (J) [Karate] spearhand

nuki tsuke (J) [Iaido] drawing the sword in a single motion

nuki uchi (J) [Iaido] drawing and striking with the sword in a continuous movement

Nuki Uchi (J) [Iaido] **1** the tenth *kata* in the Muso Shinden-ryu Hasegawa Eishin-ryu Chuden series done from *tatehiza* **2** the twelfth iaido *kata* in the Muso Shinden-ryu Omori-ryu Shoden series, which is done from *seiza*

nuki waza (J) [Kendo] side-stepping or retreating as a means to stay just beyond the opponent's attack

nuku (J) [Iaido, Kendo] to draw the *shinai* or *katana*

nulleo makgi (K) [Taekwondo] pressing block

nun (K) [Common Usage] eye

nunchaku (O) [Weapon] a weapon made of two short rods joined by a short chain or rope, derived from a flail used to thresh grain

nunchaku kun (O) [Weapon] *see* nunchaku

nun chigi (K) [Common Usage] eye strike

nun ggeopul (K) [Common Usage] eyelid

nun sseop (K) [Common Usage] eyebrow

nunte (O) [Weapon] a metal trident with the projecting tines facing opposite directions

nuntei (O) [Weapon] a two-meter long staff with a metal trident at the tip

nuoi (J) [Shorinji Kempo] a short stick

nyuhn (C) [Common Usage] young

nyumonsha (J) [Common Usage] a student accepted by a traditional school of martial arts

nyunan shin (J) [Common Usage] the willingness or ability to receive knowledge

— O —

o (J) [Common Usage] big, large, great; used as a prefix to indicate that the object or person that is being referred to is held in great esteem

o (K) [Common Usage] five

Obaku-shu (J) [Zen] a Zen school founded in China in the ninth century and introduced to Japan in 1654

obi (J) [Common Usage] belt; this term also applies to the sash worn with a kimono

obi tori (J) [Common Usage] **1** to grab the belt **2** a small loop attached to the belt in order to hang a *tachi* from the *obi*

odachi (J) [Weapon] the larger of the two swords worn by a samurai; can be a *katana* or a *tachi*

odan (K) [Common Usage] fifth-degree black belt; 5th Dan

Odo Seikichi (O) [Master] a master of both Nakamura Shigeru's Okinawa Kempo and Matayoshi Shinko's Okinawa Kobudo

Ogamite (O) [Karate] a *kata* practiced in Motobu-ryu

Ogasawara-ryu (J) [Style] the most popular school of kyudo in Japan, noted for its formal etiquette

ogeum (K) [Common Usage] back of the knee

ogeum chigi (K) [Tae Kyon] back-of-the-knee striking exercise

ogeum danggigi (K) [Ssi Rum] back-of-the-knee pulling technique

ogeum geolgi (K) [Ssi Rum] back-of-the-knee hooking technique

ogeum hak dari seogi (K) [Taekwondo] crane back stance

o geup (K) [Common Usage] fifth rank under black belt

ogeuryeo seogi (K) [Taekwondo] crouching stance

ogoshi (J) [Judo] a type of hip throw that is not often seen in competition; used as a tool for teaching, to help develop full hip movement

Oguruma (J) [Judo, Sumo] **1** a pulling, twisting motion used to throw an opponent **2** a sumo *beya* located in Koto Ward, Tokyo

Ohtsuka Hironori (J) [Master] *see* Otsuka Hironori

o haeng (K) [Common Usage] the five elements (*i.e.,* metal, wood, water, fire, and earth)

Ohan (O) [Karate] a *kata* practiced in the Ryuei-ryu

oi (J) [Common Usage] lunge

oi bal seogi (K) [Taekwondo] one-leg stance

oi bu (K) [Common Usage] external

oichomage (J) [Sumo] an elaborate topknot worn mostly by *rikishi* ranked Juryo and above

oi geri (J) [Karate] a lunge kick

oigong (K) [Common Usage] external power

oigong musul (K) [Common Usage] external-energy martial art

oi jeonhwan (K) [Hapkido] turning to the outside

oi mae geri (J) [Karate] a front lunge kick

oi mawashigeri (J) [Karate] a roundhouse lunge kick

oi moon (C) [Common Usage] *see* ngoih muhn

oin (K) [Common Usage] left

oinjjok (K) [Common Usage] left side

oinjjokeuro giul da (K) [Common Usage] to lean to the left

Oin Ssi Rum (K) [Style] type of Ssi Rum practiced throughout Korea

oi palja seogi (K) [Taekwondo] outward open stance

Oishi Shinkage-ryu (J) [Style] a school of ken-jutsu founded by Oishi Susumu

Oishi Susumu (J) [Master] a kendo master who became very wealthy as a result of his teaching; his school was noted for training with a *shinai* of unusual length

oi zuki (J) [Karate] lunge punch

oji waza (J) [Kendo, Naginata] a technique of anticipating the opponent's attack and striking before the attacks are delivered

Okan (O) [Karate] *see* Wankan

okinaga no ho (J) [Shinto] a deep breathing exercise

Okinawa (J) [Common Usage] The main island of the Ryukyu archipelago and the birthplace of karate. Though part of Japan since the Edo period, its culture and language were quite different until the end of World War II. It was a center of the great sea-going commercial routes and hence became a melting pot of Asian culture and art. It has traditionally had very strong ties with China.

Okinawa Kobudo (O) [Style] a Matayoshi family style of weapons arts; some of the weapons used were brought from China, although the majority are native to the island of Okinawa

okitsu kagami (J) [Shinto] meditation with the intention to be able to see the soul of the gods

okuden (J) [Common Usage] **1** secret teachings **2** in Muso Shinden-ryu, an advanced level or techniques taught after *shoden* and *chuden;* it includes thirteen *tachi waza* and eight *suwari waza*

Okuden Suwariwaza (J) [Iaido] a series of eight *kata* in Muso Shinden-ryu done from a seated position

Okuden Tachiwaza (J) [Iaido] a series of thirteen *kata* in Muso Shinden-ryu done from a standing position

okuri ashi (J) [Common Usage] a short quick step used to cover large distances

okuri ashi harai (J) [Judo] ankle-sweeping throw; a lateral foot sweep usually done as the opponent is moving sideways

okuri dashi (J) [Sumo] to force the opponent out of the ring by pushing on his back with both hands

okuri taoshi (J) [Sumo] to force the opponent down to the *dohyo* floor by pushing him from behind

Okuyama Yoshiharu (J) [Master] a student of Daito-ryu who went on to create the Hakko-ryu system of ju-jutsu

ollyeo chagi (K) [Taekwondo] front rising kick

ollyeo jaegi (K) [Tae Kyon] lateral heel-raising exercise

ollyeo makgi (K) [Taekwondo] front rising block, upward block

omato (J) [Kyudo] a 162-centimeter target used in shooting practice

omgyeo didigi (K) [Taekwondo] stepping

omgyeo didimyeo dolgi (K) [Taekwondo] stepping turn

omote (J) [Aikido, Weapon] **1** the front; the obvious, visible part of something; the opposite of *ura* **2** A term used in reference to the basic aikido movements when executed in a forward entering direction *(ikkyo omote, ikka o omote)*. All the basic movements in aikido are done either in a forward direction *(omote)* when the initiative is taken by the person applying the technique, or in a turning movement *(ura)* when the technique is applied after the attacker begins his attack. **3** the side of a sword blade that faces outside or away from the bearer as the sword is worn in the scabbard at the person's side; when held in the normal fashion, this would be the left side of the blade

Omoto-kyo (J) [Shinto] A branch of Shinto faith that does not consider the emperor divine. Some styles of aikido are heavily influenced by this type of Shinto. Ueshiba Morihei was a very active follower of Omoto-kyo.

Onaga Yoshimitsu (O) [Master] a lifetime student of Higa Yuchoku and heir to the Kobayashi traditions of the Kyudokan, he founded the Shinjinbukan school of Shorin-ryu; he was appointed president of the All Okinawa Karate-Do Federation in 1993

onegai shimasu (J) [Common Usage] (*lit.* If You Please) often said before entering a dojo, as a way to ask for permission to come in, or when asking someone to practice

oni (J) [Common Usage] devil, demon

on kyuhn (C) [Gau Kyuhn] *see* an quan

on mo (C) [Common Usage] to manage

oreun (K) [Common Usage] right

oreun baejigi (K) [Ssi Rum] right-side stomach-lifting technique

oreunjjok (K) [Common Usage] left side

oreunjjokeuro giul da (K) [Common Usage] to lean to the right

Oreun Ssi Rum (K) [Style] type of Ssi Rum practiced in Kyonggi and Cholla Provinces

Oroshi (J) [Iaido] the fifth *kata* in the Muso Shinden-ryu Hasegawa Eishin-ryu Chuden series, which is done from *tatehiza*

oroshi (J) [Karate] a downward strike or block

osae (J) [Common Usage] to hold down, restrict, control

osae komi (J) [Judo] a statement from the referee that an immobilization technique is in effect and time counting should start

osae komi toketa (J) [Judo] the referee's statement that a competitor has escaped from or broken free of an immobilization technique

osae uke (J) [Karate] pressing block

O-Sensei (J) [Common Usage] (*lit.* Great Teacher) although this is a generic term that could be used in regard to any revered master, it is most often used in reference to Ueshiba Morihei, the founder of aikido

oshidachi (J) [Sumo] a push on the opponent's chest, to make him lose balance and move outside the ring

oshigata (J) [Weapon] an impression or rubbing of a sword blade or tang's engravings

oshikiuchi (J) [Style] an empty-handed fighting system reserved for upper-class samurai; said to be the forerunner of Daito-ryu

Oshima (J) [Sumo] a sumo *beya* located in Sumida Ward, Tokyo

Oshiogawa (J) [Sumo] a sumo *beya* located in Koto Ward, Tokyo

Oshiro Chodo (O) [Master] an early pioneer of kobudo as taught by Chinen Masaru in the Yamani-ryu lineage

osoto gari (J) [Judo] major outer reaping throw; a technique favored by larger men

osoto otoshi (J) [Judo] a variant of *osoto gari*

otagai (J) [Common Usage] together; as one

otagai ni rei (J) [Common Usage] (*lit.* Bow Together with the Others) often said by the *sensei* after class, instructing the students to bow and show respect to one another

o-tera (J) [Common Usage] Buddhist temple

otoshi (J) [Common Usage] **1** to sweep or drop **2** in kendo, to thrust the opponent's *shinai* toward the ground

otoshi empi uchi (J) [Karate] a downward elbow strike

otoshi uke (J) [Karate] a downward pushing block

Otsubo-ryu (J) [Style] a fifteenth-century school from which ba-jutsu originated

Otsuka Hironori (J) [Master] the founder of the Wado-ryu system of Japanese karate; he was a disciple of Funakoshi Gichin and a master of Shinto Yoshin-ryu ju-jutsu

ouchi gari (J) [Judo] major inner reaping throw

oyakata (J) [Sumo] stablemaster; a sumo coach

Oyama Masutatsu (J) [Master] The founder of the Kyokushin karate school. He was a student of Shotokan karate under Funakoshi Gichin and Okinawan Goju-ryu under So Neichu, a Korean student of Miyagi Chojun. He is famous for his powerful *tameshi wari* demonstrations.

oyayubi (J) [Common Usage] thumb

Ozeki (J) [Sumo] the top Sanyaku rank, the second-highest rank in sumo, just below Yokozuna

— P —

paai (C) [Common Usage] a group or faction of individuals that practice a particular style

paaih (C) [Common Usage] plaque, award

Paak On Kyuhn (C) [Chat Sing Tohng Lohng] (*lit.* Beating Record Fist) a hand form

paak sau (C) [Wihng Cheun] (*lit.* Slapping Hand) a horizontal slapping block

paau (C) [Common Usage] **1** leopard, panther **2** to run

paau cheuih (C) [Common Usage] uppercut

Paau Kyuhn (C) [Baat Muhn Kyuhn] (*lit.* Cannon Fist) a hand form

pa chau (C) [Common Usage] shy

pa chi tan (M) [Medicine] morinda; a grayish herb used to strengthen tendons and bones

Pachu (O) [Karate] a *kata* practiced in the Ryuei-ryu

Paekche sidae (K) [Common Usage] Paekche dynasty period (18 B.C.–A.D. 668)

Paekche wangjo (K) [Common Usage] Paekche dynasty, a political entity that ruled the south-western part of the Korean peninsula

pa hsien kuo hai (M) [Baguazhang] *see* ba xian guo hai

pai (M) [Common Usage] plaque, award

pai ba (M) [Weapon] A rake consisting of a series of short spikes on a rectangular surface supported by a long shaft. At the opposite end of the shaft there is a small spear point.

pai chaang (C) [Wihng Cheun] elbow hacking

pai fu chow wei (M) [Yang Taijiquan] *see* bai hu chao wei

pai hao liang chih (M) [Taijiquan] *see* bai he liang chi

Paiho (O) [Karate] *see* Paipo

pai pihng (C) [Common Usage] to criticize

Paipo (O) [Karate] a *kata* practiced in Ryuei-ryu

pai she tu shen (M) Baguazhang] *see* bai she tu xin

pai yuan ching tao (M) [Luohan Quan] *see* bai yuan jing tao

pai yuen hsien guoo (M) [Yang Taijiquan] *see* bai yuan xian guo

Pa Kua Chang (M) [Style] *see* baguazhang

pal (K) [Common Usage] arm, eight

paldan (K) [Common Usage] eighth-degree black belt

paldduk (K) [Common Usage] forearm

paldduk makgi (K) [Taekwondo] forearm block

paleul gotge ha da (K) [Common Usage] to straighten the arm

pal gama deonjigi (K) [Hapkido] arm-wrapping throwing technique

pal geup (K) [Common Usage] eighth rank under black belt

palggumchi (K) [Common Usage] elbow

palggumchi aneuro (K) [Common Usage] elbows in

palggumchi chigi (K) [Common Usage] elbow strike

palggumchi dollyeo chigi (K) [Common Usage] turning elbow strike

palggumchi naeryeo chigi (K) [Common Usage] downward elbow strike

palggumchi ollyeo chigi (K) [Common Usage] upward elbow strike

palggumchiro chi da (K) [Common Usage] to strike with the elbow

palgup (K) [Common Usage] elbow

palgup chigi (K) [Tang Soo Do] elbow strike

Palgwae Pumse (K) [Taekwondo] a series of nine forms

pal jaba dolligi (K) [Ssi Rum] arm-grasping turning technique

palja seogi (K) [Taekwondo] open stance

palmok (K) [Common Usage] wrist area

palmok arae makgi (K) [Taekwondo] low wrist block

palmok arae yeop makgi (K) [Taekwondo] low wrist side block

palmok bohodae (K) [Common Usage] forearm/wrist pad

palmok makgi (K) [Taekwondo] wrist block

palsip (K) [Common Usage] eighty

pao (M) [Common Usage] to run

pao chui (C) [Common Usage] *see* paau cheuih

Pao Chui (M) [Chen Taijiquan] (*lit.* Cannon Strike) the second form or routine in the Chen style of taijiquan, it emphasizes fast action, hardness, and jumping

pao jen kuai yuan (M) [Yang Taijiquan] *see* pao ren kuai yuan

Pao Quan (M) [Bamenquan] *see* Paau Kyuhn

pao ren kuai yuan (M) [Yang Taijiquan] (*lit.* Hold the Sword and Return to the Original Position) a movement in the Taiji Sword form that is used to end the routine

Pao Twi (M) [Chen Taijiquan] *see* Pao Chui

paran (K) [Common Usage] blue

paran ddi (K) [Common Usage] blue belt

paran saek (K) [Common Usage] blue color

Passai (O) [Karate] a Shuri-te *kata* divided into two parts, Passai no Dai and Passai no Sho; often called Bassai in Japanese karate

pa xiu (M) [Common Usage] shy

Pecchurin (O) [Karate] *see* Suparinpei

Peichurin (O) [Karate] *see* Suparinpei

peih (C) [Common Usage] skin

peih fu (C) [Common Usage] *see* peih

peih gyuhn (C) [Common Usage] exhausted, tired

peih hei (C) [Common Usage] temper; temperament

peih jaan (C) [Wihng Cheun] elbow hacking

pek (C) [Common Usage] a vertical downward movement

pek cheuih (C) [Common Usage] vertical hammerfist

Pek Gwa Kyuhn (C) [Style, Form] **1** (*lit.* Splitting and Hitching Fist) A northern style developed before the Ming dynasty that incorporates various long-range and circular arm movements. This style is known for its palm techniques and extensive use of high kicks. **2** (*lit.* Splitting the Trigram Fist) a hand form taught in Baat Gihk Kyuhn

peng (M) [Taijiquan] ward off; a posture in taijiquan that is used to redirect an opponent's force

peullai geup (K) [Taekwondo] flyweight class in sparring competition

pi (K) [Common Usage] blood

pi (M) [Common Usage] **1** spleen **2** to split open **3** splitting; a method of trapping and striking in xingyiquan that prevents an opponent from retreating and places him off balance

pibu (K) [Common Usage] skin

pie jarn (C) [Wihng Cheun] *see* pai chaang

pi fu (M) [Common Usage] skin

piga naneun (K) [Common Usage] bloody

Pi Gua Quan (M) [Style] *see* Pek Gwa Kyuhn

piha da (K) [Common Usage] to dodge, to evade

pihagi (K) [Taekwondo] dodging technique

pihng gwan (C) [Common Usage] equal; a tie or a draw in competition

Pihng Mah Jin Kyuhn (C) [Ngh Jou Kyuhn] (*lit.* Level Horse War Fist) a hand form

pihng pun yuhn (C) [Common Usage] referee, mediator

pilseung (K) [Common Usage] certain victory

Pinan (O) [Karate] a group of five basic *kata* in Shuri-te, they were developed in order to simplify and standardize the teaching of karate in the Okinawan school system; usually called Heian in mainland Japan

pin chaap (C) [Choy Leih Faht] a straight forward thrusting punch, resembling a leopard fist strike with the back of the hand facing up and the palm facing down; also called *jin cheuih*

Ping Fa (M) [Common Usage] *see* Sun Tzu Ping Fa

pin geup (K) [Taekwondo] finweight class in sparring competition

ping guan (M) [Common Usage] *see* pihng gwan

Ping Ma Zhan Quan (M) [Wu Zu Quan] *see* Pihng Mah Jin Kyuhn

ping pan yuan (M) [Common Usage] referee, mediator

Pinian (J) [Karate] *see* Pinan

pi ping (M) [Common Usage] to criticize

piu choi (C) [Common Usage] (*lit.* Floating Color) a cloth that is tied to the head of a broadsword

pi zhuan (M) [Common Usage] exhausted, tired

po (M) [Common Usage] to coerce, to force

Poa Twi (M) [Chen Taijiquan] *see* Pao Chui

pobak sul (K) [Kuk Sool] rope technique

poomsae (K) [Taekwondo] form

po pai cheung (C) [Common Usage] *see* po pai jeuhng

po pai jeuhng (C) [Wihng Cheun] Double palm; a technique utilizing the palms as striking surfaces; the fingers of one palm points toward the ground and the others toward the sky

pouh (C) [Common Usage] robe

Pouh Saat (C) [Common Usage] Buddha

Po Un hyung (K) [Taekwondo] form named after pseudonym of poet Chong Mong-Chu

pu dao (M) [Weapon] a small, curved broadsword mounted at the end of a staff

puhn gwat (C) [Common Usage] pelvis, hips

puhn kiuh (C) [Common Usage] inward and downward block

Puhn Mah Gim (C) [Sai Chong Baahk Hok Kyuhn] a straight sword form that is practiced in a slow manner

pum balggi (K) [Tae Kyon] rhythmical stepping movement

pum dobok (K) [Taekwondo] uniform with red and black collar for students fifteen years of age and older

pumse (K) [Taekwondo] *see* poomsae

pun touh (C) [Common Usage] a rebel

pun yik (C) [Common Usage] rebellious

pyeo da (K) [Common Usage] to stretch

pyeogi undong (K) [Common Usage] stretching exercise

Pyeongan hyeong (K) [Taekwondo] (*lit.* Peace/Tranquillity Form) a series of five forms named after the karate Heian or Pinan series

pyeong bal (K) [Common Usage] flat-footed

pyeong gwansu (K) [Taekwondo] flat spear-finger

pyeong gweon (K) [Taekwondo] flat fist

pyeong hwa (K) [Common Usage] peace

pyeong jase (K) [Hapkido] standing posture

pyeong jase ddwieo dora chagi (K) [Hapkido] jump turning kick executed from a standing posture

pyeongnip jase (K) [Tang Soo Do] vertical posture

pyeongnip teureo seogi jase (K) [Tang Soo Do] twisted vertical stance posture

pyeong su (K) [Kuk Sool] palm strike

pyeong weon pumse (K) [Taekwondo] a fourth-degree form

pyeonhi seogi (K) [Taekwondo] ease stance

pyeon jumeok (K) [Taekwondo] flat fist

pyeonson ggeut (K) [Taekwondo] spear-fingers

pyeonson ggeut seweo jireugi (K) [Taekwondo] spearhand thrust

pyojeok (K) [Common Usage] target

— Q —

qi (M) [Common Usage] **1** breath, energy; life energy that circulates throughout the body and can be harnessed for healing or to maximize the damage of one's attacks **2** seven **3** flag, banner **4** to deceive, to cheat **5** to dot; to paint

qian (M) [Common Usage] **1** humble, modest **2** to drag

qian (M) [Common Usage] *see* chihn

qiang (M) [Common Usage] **1** spear **2** strong

qian xu (M) [Common Usage] humility; a virtue taught to those who study martial arts

qiao (M) [Common Usage] (*lit.* Bridge) a reference to the arm techniques in Nan Quan

qiao shou (M) [Yong Chun] bridge arm

Qi Bu Lian Hua (M) [Su He Quan] (*lit.* Seven Walking Lotus Blossom) a hand form practiced in this southern style

qi cao (M) [Medicine] the larva of a June beetle; used in Chinese herbal medicine

qigong (M) [Common Usage] the study or practice of exercises related to *qi* development, inner energy, or strength

qi guan (M) [Common Usage] *see* hei gun

qi huo (M) [Qigong] *qi* fire; the accumulation of *qi* energy in the lower *dan tian*

Qi Jiguan (M) [Common Usage] a general who lived in the sixteenth century and wrote the *Jixiao Xinshu,* a massive treatise on military tactics that included illustrations of armed and unarmed combat techniques

qi ma shi (M) [Shandong Hei Hu Pai] riding horse stance

qi men (M) [Acupressure] a point located on the ribcage

Qin Chao Dai (M) [Common Usage] Qin Imperial dynasty, which ruled China from 221 to 207 B.C.

qing (M) [Common Usage] to offer politely

Qing Chao Dai (M) [Common Usage] Qing Imperial dynasty, which ruled China from 1644 to 1911

qing long chu shui shi (M) [Wu Taijiquan] (*lit.* Blue Dragon Flying Out from the Water) a push with one hand placed above the head with the other pushing forward with the fingers pointing up

qing long dan zhao (M) [Yang Taijiquan] (*lit.* Blue Dragon Waves Its Claws) a weapons form using the sword

qing long gai wei (M) [Bai Mei] *see* ching luhng gaai meih

qing long jian (M) [Weapon] a sword with a hand-guard shaped like the petals of a flower and a dragon design etched on the blade

qing ru (M) [Common Usage] *see* cham yahp

qing tong dian xue bi (M) [Weapon] a set of paint brushes

qing zhu (M) [Common Usage] to celebrate

qin li (M) [Common Usage] to be diligent

qin ma (M) [Zhu Jia] (*lit.* Forward Horse) an exercise for building a strong horse stance

Qin Na (M) [Style] (*lit.* Seizing and Capturing) a style that utilizes the grabbing of joints and muscles and attacking vital areas of the body to control an opponent

qi shi (M) [Common Usage] an opening movement in a form

qiu tian (M) [Common Usage] fall, autumn

Qi Xing (M) [Gou Quan] (*lit.* Seven Stars) a hand form

Qi Xing Chui Quan (M) [Bamenquan] *see* Chat Sing Cheuih

qi xing jian (M) [Weapon] a straight sword with a hand-guard shaped like the petals of a flower, and seven stars etched along the blade

Qi Xing Tang Lang Quan (M) [Style] *see* Chat Sing Tohng Lohng Kyuhn

qi zhi (M) [Common Usage] banner or flag

quan (M) [Common Usage] **1** fist **2** fist form; a fighting art or style **3** to save **4** to circle

quan fa (M) [Common Usage] fist technique; a method of fighting with the fists

quan pu (M) [Common Usage] a secret book that contains the history, forms, and techniques of a style that is passed down from generation to generation

quan tou (M) [Common Usage] fist

qu chi (M) [Acupressure] a point located just below the elbow joint on the outside of the arm

qui (M) [Common Usage] to beg, beseech, ask for

qu ze (M) [Acupressure] a point located on the top of the forearm

qu zhu (M) [Common Usage] to exile, expel, banish

— R —

randori (J) [Judo, Ju-jutsu] free exercise; it teaches a student how to make techniques flow smoothly

ran o toru (J) [Judo, Ju-jutsu] (*lit.* to Take Liberty) exercises in which the student is allowed to freely improvise

rao (M) [Qin Na] to surround

rao shu (M) [Common Usage] *see* syu

rei (J) [Common Usage] bow

reigi saho (J) [Common Usage] courtesy, manners; formal etiquette

ren (M) [Common Usage] **1** edge of a sword **2** person **3** to bear, to tolerate; patience

renkuwan (O) [Weapon] a *nunchaku*-like weapon with one side longer than the other

renmei (J) [Common Usage] league, federation

ren nai (M) [Common Usage] endurance; a virtue taught to those who study martial arts

renoji dachi (J) [Karate] a stance with the feet in an L-shape

rensa (J) [Weapon] a chain used as a weapon

renshi (J) [Common Usage] the first of three instructor ranks; usually a 6th Dan ranking is required, although this rank is technically independent of the *kyu-dan* ranking system

renshu (J) [Common Usage] exercise, practice

rentai-ho (J) [Common Usage] physical training; one of Kano Jigoro's three principles of culture along with *shushin-ho* and *shobu-ho*

ren tsuki (J) [Karate] continuous punches

renzoku geri (J) [Karate] continuous kicks

renzoku sayu men (J) [Kendo] a series of consecutive strikes alternating to the right and left side of the head *(men)*

ri (J) [Common Usage] principle; reason

Rigi Ittai (J) [Common Usage] Theory and Technique are One

riki (J) [Common Usage] strength; power

rikishi (J) [Sumo] *(lit.* Gentleman of Strength) a person who does sumo

Rinzai-shu (J) [Common Usage] a Zen Buddhist sect

ritsu rei (J) [Common Usage] standing bow

ri yue feng huo juan (M) [Weapon] hand-held weapons usually used in pairs consisting of a flat wheel-shaped blade with a crescent-shaped blade in the center and two rings on either side of the handle

rochin (O) [Weapon] a short spear used in combination with the *tinbe*

Rohai (O) [Karate] a *kata* from the Tomari-te lineage; in the Matsumura style of Shorin-ryu, three versions of it are taught: Rohai Ge, Rohai Chu, and Rohai Jo

roku (J) [Common Usage] six

rokudan (J) [Common Usage] sixth-degree black belt; 6th Dan

rokushaku bo (O) [Weapon] *see* bo

rokushaku kama (O) [Weapon] a 198-centimeter long staff with a sickle attached at the end

rong yi (M) [Common Usage] easy

ronin (J) [Common Usage] a samurai without any rank or master to serve

rozan gyo (J) [Zen] the austere exercise requiring a twelve-year internment in a Buddhist monastery or temple

ruan (M) [Common Usage] *see* yuhn

ru dong (M) [Acupressure] a point located between the spine and the shoulder blade

Rufua (O) [Karate] a form practiced in the Bugeikan style

ru jia (M) [Common Usage] Confucian family; one who follows the Confucian way of thinking

ruo (M) [Common Usage] weak

ru xiang (M) [Medicine] a resin of a tree used to control bleeding and pain

ru yi jin gou (M) [Weapon] a staff with an S-shaped hook at one end with the other end narrowing to a point

ru yi juan (M) [Weapon] hand-held weapons usually used in pairs consisting of solid metal rings with a handle on one side

ryo ashi (J) [Common Usage] both legs, both feet

ryoba (J) [Weapon] a double-edged blade

ryofundo (J) [Weapon] *see* kusari fundo

ryogan tsuki (J) [Judo] a thrust to both eyes

ryo kata oshi (J) [Judo] pressing on both shoulders

ryong (K) [Common Usage] dragon

ryo sode dori (J) [Ju-jutsu, Aikido] to grab both of the opponent's sleeves, one with each hand

ryote (J) [Common Usage] two-handed

ryote dori (J) [Aikido] to seize both hands or wrists of the opponent

ryoto (J) [Ken-jutsu] *see* nito

Ryozume (J) [Iaido] the seventh *kata* in the Muso Shinden-ryu Okuden Suwariwaza series, which is done from *tatehiza*

ryu (J) [Common Usage] style, lineage (as in Shorin-ryu, Goju-ryu, Muso Shinden-ryu)

ryubi (J) [Karate] dragon tail stance; a posture for *kumite*

Ryuei-ryu (O) [Style] A style founded by Nakaima Norisato, who studied the Chinese fighting traditions in China under

Ryu Ru Ko, the master who also taught Higashionna Kanryo. It is a relatively small style in Okinawa and is virtually unknown overseas.

ryuha (J) [Common Usage] school or system; martial tradition; bu-jutsu schools were founded on the *ryu* system and often split up into different branches *(ha)* as students developed special training methods and interpretations of techniques

Ryukyu (J) [Common Usage] the name of an archipelago of islands, the largest of which is Okinawa, situated halfway between Kyushu and Taiwan

Ryukyu Kobudo (O) [Style] One of the two major weapons styles in Okinawa. The majority of the weapons used are based on farming tools and implements of daily life. The most noted twentieth-century exponent of this art was Taira Shinken.

Ryu Ru Ko (O) [Master] a famous master of *quan fa* in Fujian Province, China, who taught Higashionna Kanryo and Nakaima Norisato

Ryuto (J) [Iaido] the sixth *kata* in the Muso Shinden-ryu Omori-ryu Shoden series, which is done from *seiza*

ryuto ken (J) [Karate] dragon's head fist

— S —

sa (C) [Common Usage] sand

sa (K) [Common Usage] four

saam (C) [Common Usage] three

saam baai faht (C) [Common Usage] praying three times to the Buddha

Saam Bouh Jin (C) [Chyu Ga] (*lit.* Three Step Arrow) the first form

saam choih (C) [Common Usage] *see* San Cai

saam fu (C) [Common Usage] shirts and pants; clothing or apparel

saam gok bouh (C) [Wihng Cheun] triangular stance stepping; a training exercise that develops the ability to retreat and advance on an opponent

Saam Hahp Cheung (C) [Chat Sing Tohng Lohng] (*lit.* Three Combination Spear) a weapons form using a spear

Saam Hok (C) [Fei Hok Kyuhn] *see* San He

Saam Jeun (C) [Shik Hok Kyuhn] *see* San Jin

Saam Jin (C) [Fei Hok Kyuhn, Gau Kyuhn] *see* San Zhan

Saam Jin Kyuhn (C) [Baahk Hok, Ngh Jou Kyuhn] (*lit.* Three Battles, Three Wars) a hand form taught in these styles

saam jit gwan (C) [Weapon] three-sectional staff

saam kok bouh (C) [Wihng Cheun] *see* saam gok bouh

Saam Muhn Baatgwa Jeung (C) [Baahk Meih] (*lit.* Three Gate Eight Trigram Palm) a hand form

Saam Sahp Luhk Bouh Kyuhn (C) [Gau Kyuhn] *see* San Shi Liu Bu Quan

Saam Sahp Luhk Gwan (C) [Sai Chong Baahk Hok Kyuhn] (*lit.* Thirty-Six Form) a weapons form using the staff

saam sing jong (C) [Common Usage] (*lit.* Three Star Dummy) a training device used to develop one's techniques

Saam Tuhng Kyuhn (C) [Luhng Yihng Kyuhn] a hand form

saan (C) [Common Usage] **1** mountain **2** umbrella

Saandung Haak Fu Paai (C) [Style] (*lit.* Black Tiger Style) A centuries-old style originally developed in the Shaolin Temple in northern China. This Shaolin style combines soft defensive movements that can redirect attacks with hard movements to intercept powerful blows.

Saandung Hak Fu Paai (C) [Style] *see* Shangdong Hei Hu Pai

saang choi (C) [Common Usage] lettuce; used as an offering during lion dances

saang yaht (C) [Common Usage] birthday

saat (C) [Common Usage] to kill

sa baau (C) [Common Usage] sandbag; a training device used to strengthen palms and arms

sa baau jong (C) [Common Usage] sandbag dummy; a training device used to strengthen the legs

sabaori (J) [Sumo] to thrust or push the opponent forward with one's own body

sabeom (K) [Common Usage] teacher, master, instructor

sa chahn (C) [Common Usage] arrogant, conceited

Sadagotake (J) [Sumo] a sumo *beya* located in Matsudo City, Chiba Prefecture

sadan (K) [Common Usage] fourth-degree black belt

saeggi songarak (K) [Common Usage] little finger

saenghwal (K) [Common Usage] life

sageo (J) [Weapon] the cord that hangs off the scabbard of a sword, and is used to fasten it to the *obi,* sometimes also used in hojo-jutsu

sage uchi (J) [Karate] a downward strike

sa geup (K) [Common Usage] fourth rank under black belt

sa gi (K) [Common Usage] martial spirit

sagi machiwara (O) [Karate] hanging *makiwara*

sagorip jase (K) [Tang Soo Do] horse posture

sagurite no kamae (J) [Karate] (*lit.* Searching Hands Ready Position) used in many Shuri-te *kata*

sa gweon (K) [Common Usage] death strike

sahn (C) [Common Usage] kidney

sahn (C) [Common Usage] *see* shen

sahn ging sin (C) [Common Usage] nerve

sahn toih (C) [Common Usage] altar

sahoi (K) [Common Usage] society

sahp (C) [Common Usage] ten

Sahp Baat Mohn Kiuh Gong (C) [Baahk Meih] (*lit.* Eighteen Gate Bridge Skill) a hand form

Sahp Jih Muih Fa Seung Gim (C) [Huhng Ga] (*lit.* Cross Pattern Plum Blossom Swords) a weapons form using two straight swords

Sahp Yihng Kyuhn (C) [Huhng Ga] (*lit.* Ten Shape Fist) An advanced hand form, it is commonly referred to as the Five Animals and Five Elements form. It contains the fighting movements of the dragon, snake, tiger, leopard, and crane, as well as the fist strikes of the five elements (gold, wood, water, fire, and earth).

---

sai (C) [Common Usage] west

Sai Chong Baahk Hok Kyuhn (C) [Style] (*lit.* Tibetan White Crane) Founded by Ngh Siu Chung who studied Lama Paai under Wohng Luhm Hoi. The style is a long-range system with high kicks, long arm attacks, and movements that mimic the crane.

sai daam (C) [Common Usage] to be cowardly or timid

Saifa (O) [Karate] a *kata* practiced in Goju-ryu

saigo (J) [Common Usage] last

sai lihk (C) [Common Usage] *see* shi li

Sai Muhn Cheung (C) [Chat Sing Tohng Lohng] (*lit.* Four Gate Spear) a weapons form using a spear

Sai Muhn Daaih Dou (C) [Ying Jaau] (*lit.* Four Gate Big Sword) a weapons form

Sai Sahn Hay Soi Kyuhn (C) [Baahk Hok] a hand form

sajeon (K) [Common Usage] dictionary

saju jireugi (K) [Taekwondo] four-direction punch

saju makgi (K) [Taekwondo] four-direction block

Sakagami Ryusho (J) [Master] founder of the Itosu-kai school of Shito-ryu and student of Mabuni Kenwa, Yabiku Moden, and Taira Shinken

sakaki (J) [Shinto] the sacred plant that adorns a Shinto altar

sake (J) [Common Usage] rice wine

sakeru (J) [Common Usage] to avoid

saki (J) [Weapon] the point of a spear, blade, or staff

sakigawa (J) [Kendo] the leather tip of the *shinai*

sakotsu (J) [Common Usage] collarbone, clavicle

Sakugawa Kanga (O) [Master] a master of Shuri-te and *kobudo;* Sakugawa is often referred to as "Tode" Sakugawa, he was a student of the fighting arts of Okinawa and Satsuma (Japan) as well as training in the Chinese fighting arts under the famous master Kusanku; his students include Chinen Masami and Matsumura Sokon

Sakugawa no Kon (O) [Kobudo] two staff *kata* practiced in Ryukyu Kobudo: Sakugawa no Kon Sho and Sakugawa no Kon Dai

sam (C) [Common Usage] heart

sam (K) [Common Usage] three

samagwi (K) [Common Usage] praying mantis

sambaek yuksip do dolgi (K) [Common Usage] 360-degree turn

sambo daeryeon (K) [Taekwondo] three-step sparring

sambo jayu daeryeon (K) [Taekwondo] three-step free sparring

sambo (J) [Common Usage] a white plate in which the *matsugo no misu i*s placed for the ritual of *seppuku*

samdan (K) [Common Usage] third-degree black belt

same gawa (J) [Common Usage] shark or ray skin; used for binding sword hilts

same zaya (J) [Weapon] a sword scabbard decorated with shark or ray skin

sam geup (K) [Common Usage] third rank under black belt

Sam Guk sidae (K) [Common Usage] Three Kingdoms period

Samil hyung (K) [Taekwondo] form named after March 1, start of Korean independence movement

samjeol gon (K) [Weapon] three-sectional staff; also known as *samjeol bong*

sampai (J) [Zen] a formal bow to a Zen master; the forehead touches the floor, with the palms of the hands on the side facing the sky

sam pai fut (C) [Common Usage] *see* saam baai faht

Sam Sil Chong (K) [Common Usage] one of three tombs in Manchuria, along with Gak Jeo Chong and Mu Yong Chong that contains ancient wall paintings of martial poses, built by Koreans when the Koguryo dynasty ruled the area

sam sing chong (C) [Common Usage] *see* saam sing jong

sam sing jong (C) [Common Usage] *see* saam sing jong

samsip (K) [Common Usage] thirty

samurai (J) [Common Usage] (*lit.* One Who Serves) A rank of *bushi*. A samurai serves his lord with absolute obedience. Of great importance to the samurai was the right to wear the *daisho* and to serve his lord.

san (C) [Common Usage] body

san (J) [Common Usage] three

san (M) [Common Usage] **1** three **2** umbrella

san bei (C) [Common Usage] arm

sanbon kumite (J) [Competitive Budo] sparring competition in which the objective is to attain three points

San Cai (M) [Common Usage] the Three Natural Powers: heaven, earth, and man

sanchaku kun (O) [Weapon] a three-sectional staff consisting of short thirty centimeter shafts connected by cord or chain

Sanchin (O) [Karate] a *kata* that emphasizes breathing and internal strength; it is practiced in Uechi-ryu and Goju-ryu

sanchin dachi (J) [Karate] hour-glass stance

sandan (J) [Common Usage] third-degree black belt; 3rd Dan

san fuan tao yueh (M) [Yang Taijiquan] *see* san huan tao yue

sang (C) [Common Usage] to live

Sang Bak (K) [Style] ancient form of wrestling similar to Ssi Rum

sangbansin (K) [Taekwondo] parts of the hand

sangche dolligi undong (K) [Ssi Rum] upper body-circling exercise

sangdan bal chagi (K) [Common Usage] high-level kick

sangdan bangeo (K) [Common Usage] high-level defense

sangdan jumeok (K) [Common Usage] high-level punch

sangdan makgi (K) [Tang Soo Do] high-level block

sang eui (K) [Common Usage] uniform top

sang hei (C) [Common Usage] angry; to be angry

sang mihng (C) [Common Usage] life

sangtu (K) [Common Usage] topknot

san gun chouh (C) [Medicine] the entire plant, except for the root, is used to strengthen and relax tendons

San Guo Chao Dai (M) [Common Usage] Three Kingdoms, consisting of the Wei, Shu Han, and Wu, collectively these dynasties ruled China from A.D 220 to 280.

San Guo Zhi Yan Yi (M) [Common Usage] *Romance of the Three Kingdoms;* a fourteenth-century historical novel that is 120 chapters in length

sang wuht (C) [Common Usage] life, lifestyle, the art of living

San He (M) [Fei He Quan] (*lit.* Three Crane) a hand form practiced in this southern style

san huan da dao (M) [Weapon] A large broadsword, with three rings on the back edge of the blade, mounted at the head of a staff. The opposite end of the staff is tipped with a small spear point.

san huan tao yue (M) [Yang Taijiquan] (*lit.* Three Rings Envelop the Moon) a movement in the Taiji Sword form

sanjaku bo (J) [Kobudo] a short staff that is *sanjaku* or about one meter in length

san jian liang ren dao (M) [Weapon] A three-pointed double-sided metal blade resembling a king's crown. This weapon is supported by a long shaft and has a spear tip at the opposite end.

San Jin (M) [Shi He Quan] (*lit.* Three Proceeding) a hand form practiced in this southern style

sankajo (J) [Aikido] the third immobilization technique of aikido; also called *sankyo* or *kote hineri*

sankaku (J) [Common Usage] triangle

sankaku no irimi (J) [Aikido] triangular entry; a technique in which one steps to the opponent's side and re-enters from behind, forming a triangular movement pattern

sankaku tenshin (J) [Karate] triangular movements; a footwork pattern

sanko (J) [Weapon] a short stick with three points, used to attack vital points

San Kuo Chih Yen I (M) [Common Usage] *see* San Guo Zhi Yan Yi

sankyo (J) [Aikido] *see* sankajo

san nen goroshi (J) [Karate] a secret technique said to kill with a delayed reaction, sometimes several years after the strike is delivered

san nihn (C) [Common Usage] New Year; Chinese New Year

Sanpabu (O) [Karate] two forms practiced in the Bugeikan style: Sanpabu Ichi and Sanpabu Ni

sanpo (J) [Common Usage] three directions

Sanpo Giri (J) [Iaido, Kendo] the third *kata* done from *iaihiza* in the Tachiai no Bu of the Zen Nihon Kendo Renmei Seitei Iai

Sanseru (O) [Karate] a *kata* practiced in Goju-ryu and Uechi-ryu

Sanseryu (O) [Karate] *see* Sanseru

sansetsu kun (O) [Weapon] a three-sectional staff

San Shi Liu Bu Quan (M) [Gou Quan] (*lit.* Thirty-Six Walking Fist) a hand form

San Sho (J) [Sumo] (*lit.* Three Prizes) three prizes awarded to *rikishi* below the rank of Ozeki for the Best Technique, Fighting Spirit, and Outstanding Performance

santeul makgi (K) [Taekwondo] mountain-shape block

San Tiao Xian (M) [Su He Quan] (*lit.* Three Twig Thread) a hand form practiced in this southern style

santo kin (J) [Common Usage] triceps

San Zhan (M) [Bai He, Gou Quan] (*lit.* Three Battles) a hand form practiced in these southern styles

San Zhan Quan (M) [Wu Zu Quan] *see* Saam Jin Kyuhn

sao (M) [Common Usage] broom

sasae (J) [Common Usage] to support, to prop

sasae tsurikomi ashi (J) [Judo] propping drawing ankle throw; a fast twisting and pulling motion is used to take the opponent down

saseon seogi (K) [Taekwondo] diagonal stance

sashi (O) [Karate] a stone and concrete blocks used for strength training

sashi kata (J) [Ken-jutsu, Iaido] the proper way to carry swords in one's belt or sash

sasip (K) [Common Usage] forty

sasipo do (K) [Common Usage] forty-five-degree angle

sasoi (J) [Common Usage] to lure, to draw someone or something closer to oneself

sat (C) [Common Usage] knee

sat (K) [Common Usage] groin

sataguni (K) [Common Usage] crotch

sataguni chigi (K) [Common Usage] groin strike

satba (K) [Ssi Rum] groin/waist wrap worn during matches

sat baaih (C) [Common Usage] *see* shi bai

satba jabneun bang beop (K) [Ssi Rum] sash-grasping method

satba maeneun bang beop (K) [Ssi Rum] sash-tying method

sat chung (C) [Common Usage] to disgrace

sat deureo chigi (K) [Ssi Rum] technique in which one's head is placed between an opponent's legs and he is then lifted and thrown backward

sat mihn ji (C) [Common Usage] to lose face, to be shamed

Sato (J) [Iaido] the second *kata* in the Muso Shinden-ryu Omori-ryu Shoden series, which is done from *seiza*

satori (J) [Zen] enlightenment; comprehension; understanding

satsui (J) [Common Usage] murderous intent

satsujin to (J) [Common Usage] (*lit.* Murderous Sword) to create and/or consciously take advantage of an opponent's opening to defeat him; the opposite of *katsujin no ken*

Satsuma (J) [Common Usage] a clan from southern Japan, best known for their role in the rebellion against the Meiji government in 1877

sat tauh go (C) [Common Usage] knee joint

sa tu (K) [Common Usage] death match

sau (C) [Common Usage] **1** hand **2** to approve, to accept **3** to receive, to take

sau bei maht (C) [Common Usage] to keep a secret

sau chi (C) [Common Usage] ashamed

sau faat (C) [Common Usage] *see* shou fa

sau geuk (C) [Common Usage] sweeping leg

sau goi (C) [Common Usage] to change, to correct

sauh (C) [Common Usage] to suffer; to accept, to receive

sauh seung (C) [Common Usage] to be injured or wounded

sauh yahn (C) [Common Usage] enemy

sau jaang (C) [Common Usage] elbow

sau ji (C) [Common Usage] finger

sau ji gaap (C) [Common Usage] fingernail

sau tahn toih (C) [Common Usage] (*lit.* Sweeping Broom Kick) a low spinning leg sweep used to off-balance an opponent

sau touh (C) [Common Usage] to accept a student

sau wun (C) [Common Usage] wrist

sa xing zhuang (M) [Common Usage] *see* saam sing jong

saya (J) [Weapon] scabbard of a sword

saya ate (J) [Iaido] hitting someone or something with the scabbard of the *katana;* it was considered a great offense and would usually result in weapons being drawn; often it was intentionally used to provoke a confrontation

Saya no Uchi (J) [Style] another name for ken-jutsu

sayu (J) [Common Usage] left and right

sayu tsuki (J) [Karate] double side punch, as in the *kata* Sochin

se (M) [Common Usage] color

sebon gyeorugi (K) [Taekwondo] three-step sparring

Sechin (O) [Karate] a *kata* practiced in Uechi-ryu

Segangata (O) [Karate] a *kata* practiced in Kojo-ryu

sege (K) [Common Usage] strongly

sege mil da (K) [Common Usage] to shove, to thrust

segye (K) [Common Usage] world

Segye Dang Su Do Hyeophoi (K) [Tang Soo Do] World Tang Soo Do Association

Segye Taekwondo Yeonmaeng (K) [Taekwondo] World Taekwondo Federation

seh (C) [Common Usage] snake, serpent

seh cheung (C) [Weapon] *see* seh mah cheung

seh mah cheung (C) [Weapon] (*lit.* Snake Spear) a spear with a S-shaped tip used in southern styles of Chinese martial arts

sei (C) [Common Usage] **1** four **2** death, to die

Seichin (O) [Karate] a *kata* practiced in Uechi-ryu

Seichuto (J) [Iaido] the ninth *kata* in the Muso Shinden-ryu Omori-ryu Shoden series, which is done from *seiza*

Sei Daaih Gam Gong Kyuhn (C) [Sai Chong Baahk Hok Kyuhn] (*lit.* Four Big Golden Strong Fist Form) a hand form

Seienchin (O) [Karate] a *kata* in Naha-te

seigan (J) [Kendo, Iaido] a ready position with the sword tip pointed at the eyes of the opponent

seigan no kamae (J) [Kendo] *see* seigan

Seigo-ryu (J) [Style] a school specializing in *kumiuchi* and iai-jutsu

Sei Gwai Kyuhn (C) [Style] *see* Si Ji Quan

seiho (J) [Common Usage] an exercise that help blood flow in the muscle tissue

seika tanden (J) [Acupressure] a vital point used for resuscitation, located about ten centimeters below the navel; considered to be the source for *ki* generation; a spot where the *ki* energy of the body is concentrated

seiken (J) [Karate] fist

seiken tsuki (J) [Karate] straight punch

Seikokai (J) [Style] a branch of Mabuni's Shito-ryu, founded by Suzuki Seiko, who was a student of Sakagami Ryusho

seikotsu (J) [Style] the art of bone-setting

sei mohng (C) [Common Usage] death; to die

Sei Muhn (C) [Baahk Hok] *see* Si Men

Sei Muhn Daan Sau (C) [Chyu Ga] (*lit.* Four Gate Single Hand) the second hand form

Sei Muhn Jin (C) [Gau Kyuhn] *see* Si Men Jian

Sei Muhn Kyuhn (C) [Choy Ga] (*lit.* Four Gate Fist) a form

seioi otoshi (J) [Judo] a throw done with one knee down as the opponent is thrown over the shoulders

Seipai (O) [Karate] a *kata* practiced in Goju-ryu

sei pihng daaih ma (C) [Huhng Ga] (*lit.* Four Level Big Horse) a horse stance entered from a standing position by moving the left and right legs in a circular motion

sei pihng ma (C) [Common Usage] square horse stance

Seiryoku Zenyo (J) [Judo] Maximum Efficient Use of Energy; a phrase coined by Kano Jigoro to describe the theory behind judo technique

Seiryu (O) [Karate] one of five empty-hand *kata* introduced to the Meibukan Goju-ryu system by Yagi Meitoku

seiryuto uchi (J) [Karate] ox-jaw strike; a strike using the edge of the hand near the wrist, most often used against the collarbone

Seisai (O) [Karate] a form practiced in Kushin-ryu

Seisan (O) [Karate] a *kata* practiced in Goju-ryu, Uechi-ryu, and Shonrinji-ryu

seishin (J) [Common Usage] spirit, soul

seishin no mono (J) [Common Usage] (*lit.* Thing of the Spirit) a concept used by Yamaguchi Gogen to help define his style of Goju-ryu

seishin tanren (J) [Common Usage] the formation of a person's spirit as represented in the forging of iron when making a sword, used to refer to the goal and the process of training in the martial arts

Seitei Gata (J) [Kendo, Iaido] standard *kata* created by the Zen Nihon Kendo Renmei and the Zen Nihon Iaido Renmei, the two major governing bodies of sword arts in Japan

Seitei Iai (J) [Style] *see* Zen Nihon Kendo Renmei Seitei Iai

Seiunchin (O) [Karate] a *kata* practiced in Goju-ryu

seiza (J) [Common Usage] a kneeling position used in almost every traditional Japanese art, including tea, music, and martial arts

Seiza no Bu (J) [Iaido, Kendo] a series of three *kata* done from *seiza* in the Zen Nihon Kendo Renmei Seitei Iai

Se Jong pumse (K) [Taekwondo] form named after King Sejong

Sekitori (J) [Sumo] a term used to denote all professional *rikishi* in the Juryo and Makunouchi divisions of sumo

Sekiwake (J) [Sumo] the third-highest rank in sumo

semeru (J) [Common Usage] to attack

semete (J) [Karate] the partner who acts as the attacker or assailant in a *kata* practice session

sempai (J) [Common Usage] one's senior; the opposite of a *kohai*

sempai ni rei (J) [Common Usage] "Bow to the senior"; a command by the *sensei* after class, instructing the students to bow and show respect to their *sempai*

sen (J) [Common Usage] initiative; to anticipate an attack

senaka (J) [Common Usage] back, spine

Sengaku-ji (J) [Common Usage] a temple in Tokyo where the graves of the Forty-Seven Ronin were placed

seng xie (M) [Weapon] metal shoes used as a training device to strengthen the legs or as weapons

senjo (J) [Common Usage] battlefield

senjo-jutsu (J) [Style] the art of battlefield command or tactics; leading troops on the battlefield

Sen no Rikyu (J) [Master] a sixteenth-century tea master who created the modern tea ceremony

sen no sen (J) [Common Usage] simultaneous initiative; to launch one's technique at the same time as one's opponent does; also referred to as *sen no saki*

senryaku (J) [Common Usage] strategy

sensei (J) [Common Usage] teacher, professor, or doctor of an art or discipline; this term can be loosely used for almost anyone holding a respected position within the community

sensei ni mawatte (J) [Common Usage] command to "Turn toward the instructor"

sensei ni rei (J) [Common Usage] command to "Bow to the instructor"

sensen no sen (J) [Common Usage] preemptive initiative; to perform a technique in the moment between when an opponent thinks of attacking and when he physically launches the attack; also referred to as *sensen no saki*

senzen (J) [Common Usage] prewar; a term used in reference to Japan in the period just before World War II

seogi (K) [Taekwondo] stance

Seo In-Hyuk (K) [Master] founder of Kuk Sool Won

Seon (K) [Common Usage] Zen sect of Buddhism

seonbae (K) [Common Usage] (*lit.* Studied Before) a senior classmate

seonhoi ha da (K) [Common Usage] to pivot

seon in (K) [Common Usage] hermit with supernatural powers

Seon Mu Do (K) [Style] (*lit.* Zen Martial Way) a Korean Buddhist martial art that includes extensive internal energy training

seon palgup (K) [Taekwondo] straight elbow strike

seonsugweon dae hoi (K) [Common Usage] championship

seoreun (K) [Common Usage] thirty

seou (J) [Common Usage] to carry on one's back

seoye (K) [Common Usage] calligraphy

seppa (J) [Weapon] copper washers used to help make a tighter fit between the blade, the guard, and the hilt of a *katana*

seppuku (J) [Common Usage] ritual suicide by self-disembowelment

Seryu (O) [Karate] a *kata* practiced in Uechi-ryu

Sesan (O) [Karate] a *kata* that is practiced in virtually all Okinawan styles

Se Sok O Gye (K) [Common Usage] (*lit.* Five Tenets of the Hwarang) a moral code derived from Buddhism and Confucianism that is said to have influenced the moral aspects of many modern Korean martial arts

Sesoko no Kon (O) [Kobudo] a staff *kata* practiced in Ryukyu Kobudo

set (K) [Common Usage] three

seuhn (C) [Kahm Na] *see* shun

seui (C) [Common Usage] water; one of the five elements of Chinese cosmology

seui bou (C) [Common Usage] water pot, kettle

seui dai laauh yuht (C) [Huhng Ga] (*lit.* Fishing for the Moon Under Water) a double-handed scooping motion across the body made by the arms that ends with the right arm on top of the left and both palms facing upward

seuih si (C) [Common Usage] (*lit.* Sleeping Lion) the starting position in lion dance

seuk juk lihn ji (C) [Huhng Ga] a downward chopping motion to the neck of an opponent

seulgaegol (K) [Common Usage] kneecap

seumul (K) [Common Usage] twenty

seun (C) [Common Usage] trust, to trust, to believe

seun faht (C) [Common Usage] Buddhist; to believe in the Buddhist religion

seung (C) [Common Usage] *see* shuang

seung (C) [Common Usage] wound, to wound

Seung Daan Yuhn Bin (C) [Huhng Ga] (*lit.* Double Single Soft Whip) a weapons form using two steel whips taught in this southern style

seung dou (C) [Weapon] double daggers

seung fu jaau (C) [Huhng Ga] double tiger claw

Seung Fung Chiu Mau Dan Kyuhn (C) [Baahk Hok] (*lit.* Double Phoenix Imperial Red Fist Form) a hand form

seung gim chit kiuh (C) [Huhng Ga] (*lit.* Double Swords Cutting the Bridge) a two-handed vertical chop downwards

seung gung fuhk fu (C) [Huhng Ga] (*lit.* Double Bow Subduing the Tiger) a two-handed attack to the front of an opponent's body with the palms

seung gung gaan fa (C) [Huhng Ga] (*lit.* Double Bow Flower) a movement consisting of a double open-handed block thrusting downwards

seung kyuhn (C) [Wihng Cheun] double punches

seung leuhng (C) [Common Usage] to discuss

seung lo (C) [Common Usage] *see* seung loh

seung loh (C) [Wihng Cheun] upper level; refers to the region of the body above the sternum

seung luhng cheut hoi (C) [Huhng Ga] (*lit.* Double Dragon Emerging from the Sea) a double forward thrusting finger strike with the palms facing downwards

seung luhng gim (C) [Weapon] (*lit.* Twin-Dragon Twin-Edged Swords) a pair of straight swords with dragon designs on the blades

seungni ja (K) [Common Usage] winner

seung saan (C) [Common Usage] (*lit.* Go Up a Mountain) the journey people make to Shaolin in order to learn martial arts

Seung Seui Kyuhn (C) [Ngh Jou Kyuhn] (*lit.* Double Peaceful Fist) a hand form

seung taih yaht yuht (C) [Huhng Ga] a double uppercut performed while in a horse stance

seu nim (K) [Common Usage] monk (honorific title)

seun pyeonson ggeut (K) [Taekwondo] straight spear-fingers

seun yahm (C) [Common Usage] to trust

seweo jireugi (K) [Taekwondo] vertical punch

seweo makgi (K) [Tae Kyon] circular downward hand block

seweo milgi (K) [Tae Kyon] L-shaped pushing strike

sha (M) [Common Usage] sand

sha (M) [Common Usage] *see* saat

shaho (J) [Kyudo] methods of releasing the arrow in kyudo

Shahp Tong Kyuhn (C) [Huhng Kyuhn] *see* Shi Tang Quan

shaken (J) [Nin-jutsu] a sharp star-shaped *shuriken;* also called *kurumaken*

shaku (J) [Common Usage] a traditional unit of measurement equivalent to thirty-three centimeters

shakujo (J) [Common Usage] a priest's staff, carried by Buddhist monks; used in Shorinji kempo as a weapon

shakumyaku (J) [Acupressure] a vital point on the wrist

shan (M) [Common Usage] **1** mountain **2** fan **3** to avoid; a key movement found in the Zhang He style

Shandong Hei Hu Pai (M) [Style] *see* Saandung Haak Fu Paai

shang (M) [Common Usage] wound; to wound

Shang Chao Dai (M) [Common Usage] Shang Imperial dynasty, which ruled China from the sixteenth century to the eleventh century B.C.

shang lian (M) [Common Usage] *see* seung leuhng

shan shen da (M) [Zhu Jia] (*lit.* Avoiding the Body Strike) a form that involves hand and foot movements to evade and strike an opponent

shao (M) [Common Usage] *see* siu

shao hai (M) [Acupressure] a point located on the inside of the arm at the bend of the elbow

Shao Lin gun (M) [Weapon] a staff that can come in various sizes depending on the application

Shaolin Quan (M) [Style] (*lit.* Young Forest Fist) a northern style originating at the Shaolin-zi

Shaolin-zi (M) [Common Usage, Style] (*lit.* Young Forest Monastery) A Chinese Buddhist monastery built in 495 A.D. during the Northern Wei dynasty by the Emperor Xiaowen on Mt. Songshan in China's Henan Province. Legends tell of an Indian monk named Bodhidharma (Da Mo) who came to this monastery in the early sixth century and introduced *Dhyana* (known in Chinese as *Chan* or in Japanese as Zen). He also introduced a set of exercises to the monks that came to be know as the Shiba Luohan Shou, or Eighteen Hands of Luohan. It is believed that the forerunner of the Shaolin martial arts were developed from these exercises. The martial arts practiced at Shaolin were divided into two methods, the internal *(neijia)* and external *(weijia)*. During the Sui dynasty, the Shaolin monks became well known for their armed and unarmed martial skills and were often called upon by emperors to help them.

shao zhu (M) [Common Usage] roast pig; an offering made to ancestors in ceremonies such as *Jou Sin Daan* and New Year's

sharei (J) [Kyudo] a ceremonial form of shooting in kyudo

shat geng sau (C) [Wihng Cheun] (*lit.* Throat-Cutting Hand) a chop to the opponent's throat

she (M) [Common Usage] snake, serpent

shen (M) [Common Usage] kidneys

sheng cai (M) [Common Usage] *see* saang choi

sheng huo (M) [Common Usage] life, lifestyle

Sheng Men Baguazhang (M) [Style] (*lit.* Breakable Gate Eight Trigram Palm) a style of baguazhang

sheng ming (M) [Common Usage] life

sheng qi (M) [Common Usage] angry

sheng zhe (M) [Common Usage] winner

she qiang (M) [Weapon] *see* seh cheung

sheung kuen (C) [Common Usage] *see* seung kyuhn

shi (J) [Common Usage] four

shi (M) [Common Usage] **1** ten **2** form or style **3** teacher or instructor **4** lion **5** poem, poetry **6** to implement

shiai (J) [Common Usage] tournament; competition

shiai geiko (J) [Common Usage] practices held before a tournament

shiaijo (J) [Common Usage] tournament area, the area where matches are held in a tournament

shiatsu (J) [Acupressure] pressure-point massage; an ancient method for curing many ailments that originated in China

shi bai (M) [Common Usage] to fail

Shiba Luohan Shou (M) [Luohan Quan] (*lit.* The Eighteen Arhat Hands) A series of postures said to have been developed by Da Mo as a way to help the monks at the Shaolin Temple stay awake during the marathon meditative sessions required in *Chan* (Zen) Buddhism. These exercises are said to have been the basis of the Shaolin fighting arts.

shi bo (M) [Common Usage] *see* si baak

shi bo gong (M) [Common Usage] *see* si baak gung

shibori (J) [Common Usage] to squeeze, wring (out), press

shicha (O) [Common Usage] lower, below

shichi (J) [Common Usage] seven

shichidan (J) [Common Usage] *see* nanadan

shi chong (M) [Common Usage] *see* chi yuhk

shidachi (J) [Common Usage] the person performing a technique in a *kata;* the person acting as the defender

shi di (M) [Common Usage] *see* si daih

Shi Er Duan Jin (M) [Qigong] *see* ba duan jin

shi er xing (M) [Xingyiquan] (*lit.* Twelve Shapes) a fighting technique incorporating movements from the twelve animals: dragon, tiger, snake, eagle, bear, monkey, horse, water lizards, chicken, harrier, Chinese ostrich, and swallow

Shi Er Xing Gun (M) [Xingyiquan] (*lit.* Twelve Shape Staff) a weapons form using the staff

shi fu (M) [Common Usage] *see* si fuh

shi gong (M) [Common Usage] *see* si gung

shihan (J) [Common Usage] master teacher

Shi He (M) [Style] (*lit.* Hungry Crane) One of the branches of the Bai He style. A system that emphasizes striking techniques with the hand that resemble the beak of a crane; sometimes referred to as Feeding Crane

Shiho Giri (J) [Iaido] **1** the third *kata* in the Muso Shinden-ryu Okuden Suwariwaza series, which is done from *tatehiza* **2** the fifth *kata* done from *iaihiza* in the Tachiai no Bu of the Zen Nihon Kendo Renmei Seitei Iai

shiho hai (J) [Aikido] four-directional bow; this ancient way of paying respect to the gods was interpreted by Ueshiba Morihei as bowing to nature, the universe, our parents, and our fellow beings

shiho nage (J) [Aikido] (*lit.* Four Direction Throw) a technique that is similar to a sword movement in that *tori* grasps the *uke's* hands and raises them over his head, stepping under and pivoting, then cutting down as though with a sword

shi jian (M) [Common Usage] time

shi jie (M) [Common Usage] *see* si je

shijuhatte (J) [Sumo] the classical Forty-Eight Techniques of sumo; now used to mean "a great many" or "all the tricks or techniques of (something)"

Shikihide (J) [Sumo] a sumo *beya* located in Ryugasaki City, Ibaraki Prefecture

shikiri (J) [Sumo] toeing the mark before the onset of a bout; warm-up movements performed by the sumo wrestlers before a sumo match begins

shikko (J) [Aikido] (*lit.* Knee Walking) moving across the floor on one's knees

shiko (J) [Sumo] the ceremonial stomping before a sumo match; also a basic exercise for improving lower-body strength and flexibility

shiko dachi (J) [Karate] square stance in which the legs are deeply bent and wide apart, the toes pointing out at a forty-five-degree angle

shikomi zue (J) [Weapon] *see* shinobi zue

shikoro (J) [Nin-jutsu] a pointed saw used by ninja to cut wood or metal

shi li (M) [Common Usage] to use power; to influence

Shimabuku Eizo (O) [Master] a master of Shorin-ryu karate and a student of Kyan Chotoku, Motobu Choki, Miyagi Chojun, and Taira Shinken

Shimabuku Tatsuo (O) [Master] the founder of Isshin-ryu karate, he began his training in 1916, studying under Kyan Chotoku, Motobu Choki, and Miyagi Chojun

shi mao (M) [Weapon] a spear with a long serpentine blade decorated with tassels; the opposite end of the shaft is tipped with a metal point

shime (J) [Judo, Ju-jutsu] choke, stranglehold

shimei (J) [Karate] an attack that, if uncontrolled, would have a lethal result

shi mei (M) [Common Usage] *see* si muih

shime nawa (J) [Shinto] a white straw rope or cord found in shrines and Shinto household altars; it marks where the profane world ends and where the sacred area of a shrine begins

shimeru (J) [Common Usage] to close or tie; also, to squeeze, to strangle

shime waza (J) [Common Usage] strangulation or choking techniques

shimoseki (J) [Common Usage] the lower part of a dojo; the rear area where the junior students sit or stand

shimoza (J) [Common Usage] the lower-ranked area of the dojo; on the opposite side from the shrine

shi mu (M) [Common Usage] *see* si mouh

shinai (J) [Kendo] a sword used for training and competition; it is a little more than ninety centimeters in length made from four pieces of split, polished bamboo with leather on the hilt and tip

shinai geiko (J) [Kendo] training with a *shinai*

Shinbu (J) [Iaido] the fifth *kata* in the Muso Shinden-ryu Okuden Tachiwaza series, which is done from a standing position

shin chin (M) [Acupressure] a point located on the forehead

shindo (J) [Common Usage] vibration

Shingi Ittai (J) [Common Usage] (*lit.* Mind and Technique are One) a slogan in martial arts that refers to the unity of intent and action or the identity of thought and technique, "the thought is the deed"

Shin Han-Seung (K) [Master] influential master of Tae Kyon who was named a Human Cultural Asset by the Korean government

Shinjinbukan (O) [Style] a school of Shorin-ryu (Kobayashi-ryu) karate founded by Onaga Yoshimitsu

shinji zumo (J) [Sumo] matches fought as a way of giving thanks to the gods during Shinto religious festivals

Shinkage-ryu (J) [Style] A school of ken-jutsu founded in the mid-sixteenth century. The Shinkage-ryu gave rise to many schools of swordsmanship. The most famous of these was the Yagyu Shinkage-ryu, which became the official style of the Tokugawa family of shoguns. The Yagyu lineage eventually split into the Edo Yagyu Shinkage-ryu and the Owari Yagyu Shinkage-ryu.

shinken shobu (J) [Common Usage] a fight to the death; to be very serious about something

Shinken Shobu no Kata (J) [Judo] techniques for self-defense rather than for sport competition, including techniques that are normally prohibited in judo training such as kicking, striking, and punching; an alternate name for Kime no Kata

shinko kata (J) [Karate] an advanced *kata*

Shin Muso Hayashizaki-ryu (J) [Style] a school of ken-jutsu and iai-jutsu that was the original form of the Muso Shinden-ryu

shinobi (J) [Common Usage] a spy, another term for ninja; a term for nin-jutsu

shinobi gatana (J) [Nin-jutsu] *see* ninja to

shinobi kai (J) [Nin-jutsu] a ninja weapon consisting of a bamboo staff with a weighted chain attached to it

shinobi shozoku (J) [Nin-jutsu] a ninja's uniform (usually colored for camouflage)

shinobi zue (J) [Nin-jutsu] a staff with a hidden blade or chain within it

shinpan (J) [Common Usage] referee

shinshin ichinyo (J) [Common Usage] (*lit.* Body and the Mind are Unified) a phrase from Zen Buddhism signifying that the mind and body are one and the same and that people cannot separate or ignore one or the other

shinshin to (J) [Weapon] (*lit.* New New Sword) a *katana* made between 1781 and 1876

Shinshin Toitsu Aikido (J) [Style] a style of aikido created by Tohei Koichi

Shinto (J) [Common Usage] (*lit.* The Way of the Gods) the religion native to the Japanese, although today Shinto and Buddhism are both prominent in Japan

shin to (J) [Weapon] (*lit.* New Sword) a *katana* made between 1596 and 1781

Shinto Itten-ryu (J) [Style] a school of aikido that focuses on self-defense techniques

Shinto Shizen-ryu (J) [Karate] a school of karate-jutsu founded in 1934 by Konishi Yasuhiro, a senior student of both Funakoshi Gichin and Motobu Choki; he was also a very skilled exponent of kendo

shi nu (M) [Common Usage] *see* si jaht neui

Shioda Gozo (J) [Master] A pre-war live-in student of Ueshiba Morihei and founder of the Yoshinkai Aikido Association. Yoshinkai technique tends to be harder in form than other styles of aikido, with more *atemi waza* than other aikido schools.

shi po (M) [Common Usage] *see* si poh

Shirai-ryu (J) [Style] a school of shuriken-jutsu

Shiranui (J) [Sumo] one of two styles of *dohyo iri* performed by the Yokozuna, the other one is called *Unryu*

shiroboshi (J) [Sumo] (*lit.* White Star) a white circle signifying a win

shirogashi (J) [Common Usage] white oak used for making *bokken*

shiro hansoku (J) [Competitive Budo] (*lit.* White Violation) a term used by the referee to indicate that the "white" fighter has committed a violation of the rules

shiroi (J) [Common Usage] white

shiro ippon (J) [Competitive Budo] one point for the "white" fighter

shiro kiken (J) [Competitive Budo] a term used by the referee to indicate that the "white" fighter has conceded the bout

shiro no kachi (J) [Competitive Budo] the "white" fighter is the winner

Shi San Tai Bao Gong (M) [Qigong] (*lit.* Thirteen Grand Preservers Work) An old system of Taoist breathing exercises incorporating the benefits of *qigong* internal martial arts practices. This once-secret method is part of a set of exercises referred to as the Thirteen Grand Preservers.

shishin ken (J) [Nin-jutsu] an attack to a vital point with the little finger

shisho (J) [Sumo] the head of a sumo *beya*

shi shu (M) [Common Usage] *see* si suk

shi shu bo (M) [Common Usage] *see* si suk baak

shi shu gong (M) [Common Usage] *see* si suk gung

shi shu po (M) [Common Usage] *see* si suk poh

Shisochin (O) [Karate] a *kata* practiced in Goju-ryu

Shisouchin (O) [Karate] *see* Shisochin

shi suo (M) [Common Usage] A rectangular-shaped stone with a handle on top, for use in training. Commonly used for developing and strengthening the limbs.

shita (J) [Common Usage] **1** bottom, lower part **2** tongue

shita ago (J) [Acupressure] a vital point located on the lower jaw

Shi Tang Quan (M) [Hong Quan] (*lit.* Ten Around Fist) a hand form

shitate dashi nage (J) [Sumo] a throw in which the opponent's belt is grabbed by reaching underneath his arm; similar to *uwate dashi nage*

shitate hineri (J) [Sumo] a throw similar to *uwate hineri,* except that the belt is held by reaching under the opponent's arm

shitate nage (J) [Sumo] a throwing technique like *uwate nage,* except that the opponent's belt is grabbed by reaching under the arm rather than around it

shitateru (J) [Common Usage] to discipline, to educate

shitate yagura nage (J) [Sumo] a throw similar to *uwate yagura nage,* except that the controlling belt grab is done by reaching underneath the opponent's arm

shita zuki (J) [Karate] a low punch, a strike to the lower abdomen

Shi Tenno (J) [Common Usage] (*lit.* The Four Emperors of the Sword) a title shared by Hikida Bungoro, Marume Kurando, Shingo Izu no Kami, and Yagyu Tajima no Kami

shito ken (J) [Nin-jutsu] a nin-jutsu technique of applying pressure with the thumbs on vital pressure points

Shito-ryu (J) [Style] a karate style created by Mabuni Kenwa; the name is made up of the alternate pronunciations of two characters, one from the name of each of Mabuni's instructor's (*shi* from Itosu and *to* from Higashionna)

shi tou (M) [Common Usage] *see* si tauh

shitsurei (J) [Common Usage] rude, rudeness

shi wei (M) [Common Usage] lion tail; usually refers to the tail of the lion costume worn during lion dance

shi wu (M) [Common Usage] food

shi xiang (M) [Common Usage] *see* si hing

shi xiang di (M) [Common Usage] *see* si hing dai

Shiyako (O) [Karate] one of five empty-hand *kata* introduced to the Meibukan Goju-ryu system by Yagi Meitoku

shizen (J) [Common Usage] natural, nature

shizen no kamae (J) [Common Usage] a ready position with the legs and feet in a comfortable, upright, relaxed stance

shizentai (J) [Karate, Judo] natural stance

shi zhi (M) [Common Usage] *see* si jaht

shi zi (M) [Common Usage] older sister; refers to a female student of higher rank than oneself

Shi Zi Hou (M) [Style] *see* Si Ji Haau

shi zi yao tou (M) [Yang Taijiquan] (*lit.* The Lion Shakes Its Head) a movement in the Taiji Sword form

shizoku (J) [Common Usage] a title given to the samurai classes that were recognized as gentry in Japan after 1868

shochu geiko (J) [Judo] annual summer training session held during the hottest time of the year

shodan (J) [Common Usage] first-degree black belt, 1st Dan

Shoden (J) [Iaido] a series of twelve *kata* in Muso Shinden-ryu that are done from *seiza*; also known as Omori-ryu

shodo (J) [Common Usage] (*lit.* The Way of Calligraphy) traditionally *shodo* was an important part of the education of the *bushi*

shogatsu (J) [Common Usage] New Year's

shogun (J) [Common Usage] generalissimo, a military ruler

Sho Hatto (J) [Iaido] the first *kata* in the Muso Shinden-ryu Omori-ryu Shoden series, which is done from *seiza*

shomen (J) [Common Usage] **1** the front wall of the school, the place of honor in a dojo; usually where a shrine, scroll, or picture is located **2** in kendo and naginata, a direct, straight hit to the head

shomen ni rei (J) [Common Usage] command to "Bow toward the front"

shomen uchi (J) [Kendo, Aikido] a straight forward strike with a *shinai, katana,* or edge of the hand

Shoreikan (O) [Style] a school of Goju-ryu karate founded by Toguchi Seikichi

Shorei-ryu (O) [Style] a branch of Okinawan Naha-te karate

Shorin-ji (J) [Style] the Japanese reading for the Chinese characters for the Shaolin Temple

Shorinji Kempo (J) [Style] A style developed by Nakano Michiomi. Its name is the Japanese pronunciation of the Chinese characters for Shaolin *Quanfa*. The style is heavily influenced by Zen philosophy and is now officially called Nippon Shorinji Kempo, as a result of a legal battle that banned it from making reference to its Chinese roots.

Shorinji-ryu (O) [Style] a style of Shuri-te karate

Shorinji-ryu Kenkokan (J) [Style] a style of karate-do and kobudo founded by Hisataka Masayoshi and currently led by his son Masayuki

Shorin Motobu-ha (O) [Style] a lineage of Shuri-te karate

Shorin-ryu (O) [Style] A name used by most of the karate styles that still train in the Shuri-te tradition. The name can been written three different ways in Japanese: Small Forest Style, Young Forest Style, and Pine Forest Style; all three are pronounced Shorin-ryu.

Shoshingata (O) [Karate] a *kata* practiced in Kojo-ryu

shoshinsha (J) [Common Usage] a novice, a beginner

shotei ate (J) [Karate] palm-heel strike

shotei oshi (J) [Karate] push with the palm of the hand

shotei shita uke (J) [Karate] a downward block with the palm of the hand

shotei sotogawa uke (J) [Karate] a block with the palm of the hand from the outside

shoto (J) [Weapon] knife or dagger; short sword

Shotokan (J) [Style] a karate school founded by Master Funakoshi Gichin in Tokyo in 1936; today it is one of the largest karate organizations in the world

Shotokan-ryu (J) [Style] a name adopted by many Shotokan karateka after Funakoshi Gichin's death

shou (M) [Common Usage] **1** hand **2** to accept, to take in

shou bi (M) [Common Usage] arm

shou fa (M) [Common Usage] hand technique or method

shou mi mi (M) [Common Usage] *see* sau bei maht

shou peng ya fu (M) [Yang Taijiquan] (*lit.* Holding a Tablet) a movement in the Taiji Sword form

shou shang (M) [Common Usage] to be wounded

shou tu (M) [Common Usage] *see* sau touh

shou wan (M) [Common Usage] wrist

shou xin (M) [Common Usage] hand, palm of hand

shou zhi (M) [Common Usage] finger

shou zhijia (M) [Common Usage] fingernail

Showa jidai (J) [Common Usage] an era of Japanese history from 1926 to 1989

Showa to (J) [Common Usage] a sword made in the Showa era (1926–89)

shu (M) [Common Usage] **1** book **2** rat

Shuai Jiao (M) [Style] A Chinese wrestling art that was developed from an ancient battle dance. The dance was known as "Butting with Horns" and it developed into a form of wrestling used as a training method by armies in eastern China. It later evolved into a competitive sport that now has international competitions.

shuang (M) [Common Usage] double, pair

shuang bo (M) [Weapon] solid crescent-shaped bladed weapons usually used in pairs shaped like an open fan with the handles on the dull flat side of the weapon

shuang feng zhang (M) [Baguazhang] *see* ba xian guo hai

shuang gong cha hua (M) [Hong Jia] *see* seung gung gaan fa

shuang gong fu hu (M) [Hong Jia] *see* seung gung fuhk fu

shuang huan chang (M) [Baguazhang] *see* shuang huan zhang

shuang huan zhang (M) [Baguazhang] double change palm

shuang huo fu (M) [Weapon] hand-held weapons usually used in pairs consisting of metal crescent-shaped axes with spear tips at the end of the handles

shuang jian qie qiao (M) [Hong Jia] *see* seung gim chit kiuh

shuang long chu hai (M) [Hong Jia] *see* seung luhng cheut hoi

shuang qiang (M) [Weapon] double-ended spears usually used in pairs

shuang shou chi (M) [Weapon] flat double-edged swords with crescent-shaped guards usually used in pairs

shuang shou gou (M) [Weapon] hook swords; commonly used in pairs, each weapon has a crescent-shaped blade at the handle and a hook at the end of the sword

shuang shou yue (M) [Weapon] a type of hook sword; commonly used in pairs, each weapon has a crescent-shaped blade at the handle, and an axe-shaped blade with a snake tongue spear at the tip

Shuang Sui Quan (M) [Wu Zu Quan] *see* Seung Seui Kyuhn

shuang ti ri yue (M) [Hong Jia] *see* seung taih yaht yuht

shuang xi (M) [Common Usage] double happiness, marriage

shuchu (J) [Common Usage] concentration

shu di huang (M) [Medicine] prepared rehmannia; a dark resinous root used to nourish the blood and to heal joint and tendon injuries

Shugendo (J) [Common Usage] Mountain Asceticism; a blend of Buddhist and Shito religious beliefs and practices

shugyo (J) [Common Usage] ascetic exercise; austere discipline

shu ha ri (J) [Common Usage] an expression referring to the three stages of training (from simple imitation to development of one's own style) and personal development in the martial arts

shui (M) [Common Usage] water; one of the five elements in Chinese cosmology

shui di lao yue (M) [Hong Jia] *see* seui dai laauh yuht

shui hu (M) [Common Usage] water pot, kettle

shui jiao (M) [Common Usage] sleep, slumber; to sleep

shuko (J) [Acupressure, Nin-jutsu] **1** a vital point located on the back of the hand at the base of the thumb **2** spiked bands worn by ninja on the hands, used for climbing as well as for fighting

Shukun Sho (J) [Sumo] Outstanding Performance Prize; given to a *rikishi* who has beaten the most Ozeki or Yokozuna in a tournament

shukyo (J) [Common Usage] religion

shumatsu undo (J) [Common Usage] cool-down exercises

Shum Leuhng (C) [Master] a prominent master of Ying Jaau

Shum Leung (C) [Master] *see* Shum Leuhng

shun (M) [Qin Na] smooth

shuo (M) [Common Usage] to tell, to speak

shu qi (M) [Medicine] a plant used in Chinese herbal medicine

Shuri (J) [Common Usage] a residential district of Naha City in Okinawa; it was the ancient capital that housed the Royal palace; the ancient capital of the Ryukyu kingdom, and the birthplace of the Shuri-te karate lineage (Shorin-ryu)

shuriken (J) [Common Usage] metal throwing stars and darts used by ninja and bushi

shuriken-jutsu (J) [Style] the art of *shuriken* throwing

Shuri-te (O) [Style] the empty-hand fighting style developed in the Shuri area, referred to as Sui Di in the Okinawan dialect; it is known today as Shorin-ryu

shushin ho (J) [Judo] one of three principles of judo according to Kano Jigoro; the mental training that follows a strict moral code

shushin ichinyo (J) [Zen] practice and training are the same thing

Shushi no Kon (O) [Kobudo] two *kata* using the staff that are practiced in Ryukyu Kobudo: Shushi no Kon Sho and Shushi no Kon Dai

shuto uchi (J) [Karate] knifehand or swordhand strike

shuto uke (J) [Karate] knifehand or swordhand block

shy er hsing (M) [Xingyiquan] *see* shi er xing

Shy Er Hsing Gunn (M) [Xingyiquan] *see* Shi Er Xing Gun

si (C) [Common Usage] **1** teacher; instructor **2** lion **3** poem

si (M) [Common Usage] **1** four **2** to die **3** temple, monastery **4** to resemble, to be like

sian jeok jojeol (K) [Common Usage] timing

si baak (C) [Common Usage] older uncle or aunt; used to address a senior student from the previous generation

si baak gung (C) [Common Usage] great uncle; used to refer to the older brothers of the *si gung*

sibeom (K) [Common Usage] demonstration

sibeom ha da (K) [Common Usage] to demonstrate

si daih (C) [Common Usage] younger brother; used to address a junior male student of the same generation

sieh ma (C) [Common Usage] defensive

si fu (C) [Common Usage] *see* si fuh

si fuh (C) [Common Usage] father or master; used to address the instructor or mentor

si gung (C) [Common Usage] grandfather or grandmaster; used to address the grandmaster, or the master of the master

sihap (K) [Common Usage] contest, bout, match

sihap gyuchik (K) [Taekwondo] contest rules

sihap jang (K) [Common Usage] contest area

sih gaan (C) [Common Usage] time

si hing (C) [Common Usage] older brother; used to address a senior male student of the same generation

si hing dai (C) [Common Usage] older and younger brothers; used to refer to male or female students of the same generation

sihk (C) [Common Usage] to eat

Sihk Hok (C) [Style] *see* Shi He

sihk maht (C) [Common Usage] food

sihk ngaan (C) [Common Usage] to eat lunch

sihng gung (C) [Common Usage] to succeed

Sihng Luhng Jong Lauh (C) [Master] a monk from Tibet who introduced the Si Ji Haau style to China in the early nineteenth century

sihn hok chou (C) [Medicine] the whole plant is used in Chinese medicine to strengthen tendons, stop bleeding, and resist bacteria

Sihn Sau Ban Kyuhn (C) [Chat Sing Tohng Lohng] (*lit.* Skillful Hand Running Fist) a hand form practiced in this northern style

si jaht (C) [Common Usage] nephew; used to refer to male students of the next generation

si jaht neui (C) [Common Usage] niece; used to refer to female students of the next generation

sijak ha da (K) [Common Usage] to begin

si je (C) [Common Usage] older sister; used to address a senior female student of the same generation

Si Ji Haau (C) [Style] (*lit.* Lion's Roar) A martial arts style originating in Tibet founded by Hoh Da Do. It consists of eight fighting methods that include: eight fists, eight kicks, eight palm strikes, eight elbow strikes, eight foot sweeps, eight stances, eight finger strikes, and eight gripping methods. This style later influenced the Lama Paai, Haap Ga, and Sai Chong Baahk Hok Kyuhn styles.

Si ji Quan (M) [Style] (*lit.* Four Seasons Fist) a northern style of Chinese martial arts

si jou (C) [Common Usage] great grandfather or great grandmaster; used to address the great grandmaster or the great grandmaster's spouse

sik (C) [Common Usage] color

sil gyeok (K) [Taekwondo] disqualification

si li (M) [Common Usage] personal, private

Silla sidae (K) [Common Usage] Silla dynasty period (57 B.C.–A.D. 668)

Silla wangjo (K) [Common Usage] Silla dynasty, a political entity that ruled the southeastern part of the Korean peninsula

si meih (C) [Common Usage] *see* shi wei

Si Men (M) [Fei He, Shi He] (*lit.* Four Gates) a hand form practiced in these southern styles

Si Men Jian (M) [Gou Quan] (*lit.* Four Gate Arrow) a hand form

simgong (K) [Common Usage] spiritual power

si mouh (C) [Common Usage] mother or master's wife; used to address the *sifu's* wife

simpan (K) [Common Usage] judge

simpan weon (K) [Common Usage] referee

simsa (K) [Common Usage] test, examination

simsa gwan (K) [Common Usage] tester, examiner

sim san da (C) [Jyu Ga] *see* shan shen da

si muih (C) [Common Usage] younger sister; the term a martial arts student uses to address a junior female student of same generation

sin (C) [Common Usage] **1** fan **2** leek; used as an offering during lion dances

Sin Chaih Meih (C) [Baahk Hok] (*lit.* Iron Even Eyebrow) a weapons form using an eyebrow-height staff

sinchuk seong (K) [Common Usage] flexibility

Sin Deng Pah (C) [Baahk Hok] (*lit.* Iron Nail Fork) a weapons form using a trident

sing chihng (C) [Common Usage] personality or temperament

sing gaak (C) [Common Usage] character, personality

sing je (C) [Common Usage] winner

sing mihng (C) [Common Usage] life; lives

sin gong (K) [Common Usage] mental powers linked to *ki*

sin seon (K) [Common Usage] mountain wizard, ascetic

sip (K) [Common Usage] ten

sipchil (K) [Common Usage] seventeen

sipgu (K) [Common Usage] nineteen

si ping da ma (M) [Hong Jia] *see* sei pihng daaih mah

sipja makgi (K) [Kuk Sool] four-directional block

sipjin pumse (K) [Taekwondo] fifth-degree form

sipo (K) [Common Usage] fifteen

si poh (C) [Common Usage] grandmother or grandmaster's
   wife; used to address the grand master's wife

sippal (K) [Common Usage] eighteen

Sip Pal Gi (K) [Style] *see* Sip Pal Ki

Sip Pal Ki (K) [Style] (*lit.* Eighteen Weapons) a common name
   for Korean *gong fu*

sipsa (K) [Common Usage] fourteen

sipyuk (K) [Common Usage] sixteen

siseon (K) [Common Usage] eye focus

Sissan hyeong (K) [Tang Soo Do] form named after a karate
   form composed of one hundred movements

si suk (C) [Common Usage] younger uncle or aunt; the term a
   martial arts student uses to address a junior student from the
   previous generation

si suk baak (C) [Common Usage] younger and older uncles
   or aunts; used to refer to students from the previous generation

si suk gung (C) [Common Usage] grand uncle or aunt; used to
   address a junior or senior student from two previous genera-
   tions before

si suk poh (C) [Common Usage] grand uncle's wife

si tauh (C) [Common Usage] lion head; usually refers to the
   head of the lion costume worn during lion dance

siu (C) [Common Usage] to roast, to burn

Siu Baat Gihk Kyuhn (C) [Baat Gihk Kyuhn] (*lit.* Small Eight
   Ultimate Fist) a hand form

Siu Fu Yin Kyuhn (C) [Chat Sing Tohng Lohng] (*lit.* Small Tiger Swallow Fist) a hand form

Siu Hahng Kyuhn (C) [Ying Jaau] (*lit.* Small Walking Fist) a hand form

siu jyu (C) [Common Usage] *see* shao zhu

Siu Lahm (C) [Common Usage] *see* Shaolin

Siu Lahm Gam Gong Kyuhn (C) [Faht Ga] (*lit.* Golden Strong Fist) a hand form

Siu Lahm Ji (C) [Common Usage] *see* Shaolin zi

Siu Lahm Loh Hon Kyuhn (C) [Choy Leih Faht] (*lit.* Shaolin Buddha Fist) a hand form

Siu Mihn Jeung (C) [Ying Jaau] (*lit.* Small Cotton Palm) a hand form

Siu Nihm Tau (C) [Wihng Cheun] (*lit.* Little Idea Form) the first hand form, it is used to develop strength and sensitivity and to teach all the fundamental techniques

Siu Nim Tau (C) [Wihng Cheun] *see* Siu Nihm Tau

siu sam (C) [Common Usage] to be careful, cautious

siu teui (C) [Common Usage] calf, lower part of the leg

Siu Yihng (C) [Master] a prominent female master of Huhng Ga

Siu Ying (C) [Master] *see* Siu Yihng

si wang (M) [Common Usage] death; to die

siwi (K) [Kung Do] bow string

si yahn (C) [Common Usage] personal, private

si zhi cheng tian (M) [Hong Jia] *see* wu luhng hei seui

skiko dachi (J) [Karate] a deep wide stance, with the feet pointing out at a forty-five-degree angle

so (C) [Kahm Na] *see* suo

soa (K) [Common Usage] child

Sochin (O) [Karate] a *kata* practiced in many major Okinawan lineages

sode (J) [Common Usage] sleeve

Sode Surigaeshi (J) [Iaido] the seventh *kata* in the Muso Shinden-ryu Okuden Tachiwaza series, which is done from a standing position

sode tsurikomi goshi (J) [Judo] a variation of *tsurikomi oshi* done while gripping both the opponent's sleeves

Sodome (J) [Iaido] the fourth *kata* in the Muso Shinden-ryu Okuden Tachiwaza series, which is done from a standing position

So Doshin (J) [Master] a name adopted by Nakano Michiomi, the founder of Nippon Shorinji Kempo

Soeishi no Kon (O) [Kobudo] a staff *kata* practiced in Ryukyu Kobudo

sohei (J) [Common Usage] a warrior monk

soh muhk (C) [Medicine] the body or stem of this plant is commonly used in Chinese medicine to reduce blood clots and bruising

soi noi (K) [Kung Do] crossbow

soi sal (K) [Common Usage] dart

sojang geup (K) [Ssi Rum] under 75-kilogram adult weight class of amateur competition

so-jutsu (J) [Style] (*lit.* Art of the Spear) the art of the *yari,* or spearmanship

sokdo (K) [Common Usage] speed

Soken (J) [Iaido] the third *kata* in the Muso Shinden-ryu Okuden Tachiwaza series, which is done from a standing position

Soken Hohan (O) [Master] A student of Shuri-te karate under his uncle Matsumura Nabe, Soken spent most of his adult life in Argentina. Upon his return to Okinawa he taught Kuda Yuichi, Aragaki Seiki, and Kise Fuse, among others

sokumen awase uke (J) [Karate] augmented block with the palm of the hand

sokutei mawashi uke (J) [Karate] crescent-kick block with the sole of the foot

sokuto (J) [Common Usage] **1** the edge of the foot **2** immediate response or answer

son (K) [Common Usage] hand

son badak (K) [Common Usage] palm

son badak gisul (K) [Common Usage] palm technique

son badak mit (K) [Common Usage] palm heel

son boho janggap (K) [Common Usage] protective gloves, hand pads

son deung (K) [Common Usage] back of the hand

songarak (K) [Common Usage] finger

songarak ggeut (K) [Common Usage] fingertip

songarak gwanjeol (K) [Common Usage] knuckle, finger joint

songarak jireugi (K) [Taekwondo] finger jab

Song Chao (M) [Common Usage] Song Imperial dynasty, which consists of the Northern and Southern Song, ruled China from 960 to 1279 A.D.

Song Duk-Ki (K) [Master] influential Tae Kyon master who was named a Human Cultural Asset by the Korean government

son gisul (K) [Common Usage] hand technique

song niao shang lin (M) [Yang Taijiquan] (*lit.* Sending the Birds to the Woods) a movement in the Taiji Sword form

song zi (M) [Medicine] the seeds of a pine tree used in Chinese herbal medicine for treating arthritis

son jabi (K) [Kum Do] handle

son jangsim (K) [Tae Kyon] palm

sonjil (K) [Tae Kyon] collective term for hand techniques

son jipge (K) [Taekwondo] pincer hand

son jipigi (K) [Ssi Rum] hand-grasping technique

sonmok (K) [Common Usage] wrist

sonmok bbaegi (K) [Kuk Sool] wrist escape

sonmok biteulgi (K) [Common Usage] twisting wristlock

sonmok deonjigi (K) [Hapkido] wrist-throwing technique

sonmok deung (K) [Taekwondo] bow wrist

sonmok dolligi (K) [Common Usage] wrist turning

sonmok hoijeon (K) [Common Usage] wrist rotation

sonmok su (K) [Kuk Sool] wrist technique

son moseori (K) [Tae Kyon] blade of the hand

sonnal (K) [Taekwondo] blade of the hand, knifehand

sonnal arae makgi (K) [Taekwondo] low knifehand block

sonnal dallyeon (K) [Taekwondo] knifehand training

sonnal deung (K) [Taekwondo] reverse knifehand, ridgehand

sonnal eotgeoreo arae makgi (K) [Taekwondo] cross knife-hand low block

sonnal makgi (K) [Taekwondo] knifehand block

sonnal mok chigi (K) [Taekwondo] knifehand strike to neck

sonomama (J) [Common Usage] (*lit.* As Is) an order given by the referee to a competitor not to move, to remain still, to remain as is

sontop (K) [Common Usage] fingernail

Soo Bahk (K) [Style] (*lit.* Hand Striking) Korean martial art that legends claim was developed by the Hwa Rang warriors in the fifth century

Soo Bahk Do (K) [Style] (*lit.* Hand Striking Way) a modern martial art created in 1960 by Hwang Kee

sori (K) [Common Usage] sound

sori jireu da (K) [Common Usage] to shout

Sorim Sa (K) [Common Usage] Shaolin Temple

Soshin (O) [Karate] a form practiced in Honshin-ryu

sotai renshu (J) [Common Usage] training with a partner

sotgu chigi (K) [Tae Kyon] evasive jumping technique

soto (J) [Common Usage] exterior, outside, external

soto gake (J) [Judo] outside hook

soto gedan barai (J) [Karate] outside downward sweeping block

soto kaiten nage (J) [Aikido] outside spinning throw

soto muso (J) [Sumo] a take-down done by pulling down on one arm while pushing against the outside of the leg with the other

soto ude uke (J) [Karate] outside forearm block

soto uke (O) [Karate] Block toward the outside; sometimes in mainland Japan, the terminology for this block and the *uchi uke* are reversed. In Okinawa this block's name refers to the direction in which it moves (toward the outside) while in mainland Japan the same block is referred to by the blocking surface used. *Uchi ude uke* (inner forearm block) is often shortened to *uchi uke,* which is in fact the reverse movement in Okinawan karate vocabulary.

sou ba (C) [Weapon] broom

sou cheuih (C) [Common Usage] roundhouse knockout punch

Sou Ging Tihn (C) [Master] *see* Su Jing Tian

sou mook (C) [Medicine] *see* soh muhk

ssang (K) [Common Usage] double

ssangbal chagi (K) [Taekwondo] double kick

ssanggeom sul (K) [Kuk Sool] double-knife technique

ssanggon sul (K) [Kuk Sool] double-stick technique

ssang gwansu jireugi (K) [Hapkido] double-spearhand thrust

ssang gweon (K) [Common Usage] double punch

ssangjeol bong (K) [Common Usage] two-sectional staff, *nun-chaku;* also called *ssangjeol gon*

ssang mejumeok (K) [Taekwondo] double hammerfist

ssang palmok makgi (K) [Taekwondo] double wrist block

ssang pyeong su (K) [Kuk Sool] double palm strike

ssangsudo makgi (K) [Common Usage] double knifehand block

ssangsu makgi (K) [Common Usage] double hand block

Ssi Reum (K) [Style] *see* Ssi Rum

Ssi Rum (K) [Style] a traditional Korean form of wrestling

su (K) [Common Usage] hand

Su Bak (K) [Style] *see* Soo Bahk

Su Bak Do (K) [Style] *see* Soo Bahk Do

Su Bak Hi (K) [Style] alternate historical name for Su Bak

Su Byeok Ta (K) [Style] ancient fighting art often translated as "Open Hand Striking"

Suchin (O) [Karate] a *kata* practiced in the Bugeikan style

sudo (K) [Common Usage] chop with the hand, knifehand

sudo batang (K) [Taekwondo] knifehand base

sudo daebi makgi (K) [Taekwondo] knifehand guarding block

sudo gonggyeok (K) [Tang Soo Do] knifehand attack

sudo ha da (K) [Common Usage] to chop with the hand

sudo makgi (K) [Taekwondo] knifehand block

sudo naeryeo chigi (K) [Hapkido] downward knifehand strike

sudo yeop ddaerigi (K) [Taekwondo] side knifehand strike

su du (M) [Common Usage] speed

sugi (K) [Taekwondo] hand technique

Su He (M) [Style] *see* Zhan He

Suhp Luhk Duhng Kyuhn (C) [Luhng Yihng Kyuhn] a hand form

suiba-jutsu (J) [Style] the art of horsemanship in water

Sui Chao Dai (M) [Common Usage] Sui Imperial dynasty, which ruled China from A.D. 581 to 618

suiei-jutsu (J) [Style] the art of swimming and combat in water, including grappling, swordsmanship, and use of matchlock firearms

sui fu (C) [Common Usage] water pot, kettle

suigetsu (J) [Common Usage] the pit of the stomach

suih (C) [Common Usage] to sleep

suijohoko-jutsu (J) [Style] (*lit.* The Art of Water Crossing) it involves techniques ranging from bridge-building to boat construction

Suikagata (O) [Karate] a *kata* practiced in Kojo-ryu

suiken no kamae (J) [Karate] drunken fighting posture

suiren (J) [Nin-jutsu] ninja water training; it involves everything from swimming and fighting in water, to making and carrying boats and rafts

suiton no jutsu (J) [Nin-jutsu] camouflage methods involving the use of water

suji (J) [Kendo, Naginata] the direction of an attack

sujik jumeok (K) [Taekwondo] vertical fist

Su Jing Tian (M) [Master] a prominent master of baguazhang and a third-generation disciple

sukejo (J) [Common Usage] a title given to a sword smith by the emperor

Suk Hok (C) [Style] *see* Zhan He

sukiya (J) [Common Usage] an arbor for tea ceremony

suk se (C) [Common Usage] dormitory, place of residence

sukui nage (J) [Judo] scooping throw; almost always used as a counter to an attacker's grab from behind

sukui uke (J) [Karate] scooping block

sumi (J) [Common Usage] **1** corner, angle **2** ink

sumo (J) [Style] the traditional style of Japanese wrestling, it combines aspects of Shinto religious ritual with belt-wrestling; it is considered Japan's national sport

sumotori (J) [Common Usage] a sumo wrestler; the preferred term is *rikishi*

sumswi da (K) [Common Usage] to breathe

sumswigi (K) [Common Usage] breathing

sumswigi undong (K) [Ssi Rum] breathing exercise

sumtong (K) [Common Usage] windpipe

Sunadomari Kanshu (J) [Master] founder of Manseikan Aikido and a student of Ueshiba Morihei

Sun Bao An (M) [Master] a prominent master of Sun taijiquan

Sunegakoi (J) [Iaido] the second *kata* in the Muso Shinden-ryu Okuden Suwariwaza series, which is done from *tatehiza*

sun gun cho (C) [Medicine] *see* san gun chouh

Sun Jian Yun (M) [Master] a prominent master of Sun taijiquan

Sun Lu Tang (M) [Master] a prominent master of xingyiquan, Hao taijiquan, and a second-generation disciple of baguazhang, as well as founder of Sun taijiquan

sun shang (M) [Common Usage] wound, injury

Sunsu (O) [Karate] a *kata* practiced in Isshin-ryu

Sun taijiquan (M) [Style] This is an internal style that was developed by Sun Lu Tang and influenced by xingyi, bagua, and Hao taijiquan. It is characterized by agile footwork and open- and closed-hand methods.

Sun Tzu Ping Fa (M) [Common Usage] *The Art of War;* a classical treatise on military tactics and philosophy written by Sun Tzu

suo (M) [Qin Na] to lock

Suparinpe (O) [Karate] *see* Suparinpei

Suparinpei (O) [Karate] a *kata* practiced in Goju-ryu; also called Peichurin

supyeong jireugi (K) [Taekwondo] horizontal punch; also called *supyeong jumeok*

sureru (J) [Common Usage] to rub, chafe

suri ashi (J) [Common Usage] sliding the feet along the ground; sliding step

Surichin Nicho Kama (O) [Kobudo] a *kama kata* practiced in Ryukyu Kobudo

suruchin (O) [Weapon] a long piece of rope or chain weighted at both ends

surujin (O) [Kobudo] *see* suruchin

surushin (O) [Kobudo] *see* suruchin

suryeon dobok (K) [Tang Soo Do] training uniform

suryeon jido beop (K) [Taekwondo] exercise-leading method

su sul (K) [Taekwondo] an ancient kicking-oriented style

sutegeiko (J) [Judo] training in which one person allows himself to be thrown without resistance, allowing his partner to develop his timing and execution of technique

sutemi waza (J) [Judo] a throwing techniques in which one's own balance is sacrificed in order to complete the technique

sutiku (O) [Weapon] a stick approximately one meter in length

suwari waza (J) [Aikido, Iaido] seated technique; techniques performed while sitting in *seiza*

suwaru (J) [Common Usage] to sit

swaegol (K) [Common Usage] collarbone

swi da (K) [Common Usage] to rest

swieo (K) [Common Usage] a command to "rest"

syu (C) [Common Usage] **1** book **2** to forgive, to pardon, to excuse (usually a person of a lower rank or ability) **3** to lose

syuhn (C) [Common Usage] boat

syuhn fung toih (C) [Huhng Ga] (*lit.* Tornado Kick) a jumping spinning crescent kick

Syu Jjin (K) [Tang Soo Do] advanced form named after a karate *kata*

syun (C) [Common Usage] to choose

syun bou (C) [Common Usage] *see* bao gao

syun jaahk (C) [Common Usage] to choose between alternatives

Syun Luhk Tohng (C) [Master] *see* Sun Lu Tang

syun seung (C) [Common Usage] injury, wound

Syun Taai Gihk Kyuhn (C) [Style] *see* Sun taijiquan

— T —

ta (M) [Common Usage] *see* daahp

taai douh (C) [Common Usage] attitude

taai gihk kyuhn (C) [Style] *see* taijiquan

Taai Ji Gam Kyuhn (C) [Mouh Ga Kyuhn] *see* Tai Zi Jin Quan

Taai Jou Kyuhn (C) [Style] *see* Tai Zi Quan

taam waan (C) [Common Usage] to be playful

tabi (J) [Common Usage] traditional Japanese split-toed socks

tachi (J) [Common Usage] **1** a long sword, worn slung from the belt or sash with the cutting edge downward **2** stance, position

tachiai (J) [Sumo] the initial clash between two *rikishi* at the onset of a bout

Tachiai no Bu (J) [Iaido, Kendo] a series of six *kata* done from a standing position in the Zen Nihon Kendo Renmei Seitei Iai

tachi dori (J) [Ken-jutsu, Aikido] (*lit.* Sword Taking) unarmed defense against a sword

tachi kata (J) [Common Usage] methods of standing

tachi mochi (J) [Sumo] a *rikishi* who carries the sword onto the *dohyo* during the *dohyo iri* for a Yokozuna

Tachi uchi (J) [Style] an ancient name for ken-jutsu

tachi waza (J) [Iaido, Judo, Aikido] techniques performed while standing

tae (K) [Taekwondo] kick, smash with the foot

Tae Baek pumse (K) [Taekwondo] third-degree form named after Tae Baek mountain

Taegeukgweon hyeong (K) [Tang Soo Do] Grand Ultimate Fist form

Taegeuk pumse (K) [Taekwondo] (*lit.* Great Eternity Form) a set of eight modern forms

Taegweondo (K) [Style] *see* Taekwondo

Taek Kyon (K) [Style] *see* Tae Kyon

Taekwondo (K) [Style] (*lit.* Foot Fist Way) the most popular

Korean martial art and martial sport, includes extensive kicking techniques

Taekwondo in (K) [Taekwondo] Taekwondo practitioner

Tae Kyon (K) [Style] (*lit.* Push Shoulder) a traditional martial art composed mainly of kicking techniques

taeng hwa (K) [Common Usage] Buddhist wall painting

taesan milgi (K) [Taekwondo] push-mountain movement

Tae Soo Do (K) [Style] (*lit.* Foot Hand Way) modern martial art very similar to Taekwondo

Tae Su Do (K) [Style] *see* Tae Soo Do

taeyangsin gyeongchong (K) [Common Usage] solar plexus

Tahm Saam (C) [Master] a disciple of Jeung Yihm and founder of the Bak Sihng Choy Leih Faht style

tai (M) [Common Usage] sage

Tai Chi Chuan (M) [Style] *see* taijiquan

tai chong (M) [Acupressure] a point located between the first toe and the big toe

tai du (M) [Common Usage] attitude

taih (C) [Common Usage] to lift

Taih Lauh Dou (C) [Baat Gihk Kyuhn] (*lit.* Withdrawing the Willow Saber) a weapons form using a broadsword

Taiho (J) [Sumo, Weapon] **1** a sumo *beya* located in Koto Ward, Tokyo **2** cannon

taiho-jutsu (J) [Style] (*lit.* Arresting Art) methods of arrest and personal defense used by the Japanese police; a synthesis of several arts including weaponless *(toshu)* techniques and the use of the baton *(keibo)* and riot baton *(keijo)*

Taiho-jutsu Kihon Kozo (J) [Taiho-jutsu] an official police manual on the fundamentals of taiho-jutsu

taih sau (C) [Wihng Cheun] lifting arms

taijiquan (M) [Style] (*lit.* Great Ultimate Fist) a style of internal *gong fu* that legends claim was founded by Zhang San Feng during the Song dynasty and emphasizes the cultivation of *qi*

tai-jutsu (J) [Style] the art of unarmed combat; another name for ju-jutsu

taikai (J) [Common Usage] tournament

taiko (J) [Common Usage] a drum used for festivals in Japan

taikyokuken (J) [style] the Japanese name for taijiquan

tai otoshi (J) [Judo] body drop; a technique often used in competition

Taira Shinken (O) [Master] Considered by many to be the most renowned master of Okinawan kobudo in the postwar era, he was a student of both Funakoshi Gichin and Mabuni Kenwa and heir to Yabiku Moden's lineage of kobudo. Among his most famous students were Higa Seiichiro, Akamine Eisuke, Sakagami Ryusho, and Inoue Motokatsu.

tai sabaki (J) [Common Usage] (*lit.* Body Movement) methods of entering, turning, and shifting the body while performing techniques

tai seung (C) [Common Usage] the study of facial features; used in fortune telling

taiso (J) [Common Usage] physical exercise

taito (J) [Iaido, Kendo] (*lit.* Belted Sword) the sword inserted through the sash or being held at hip level as though being worn/carried on the hip

tai yang (M) [Acupressure] a point located on the left side of the head on the temple region

tai ying (M) [Acupressure] a point located on the right side of the head on the temple region

Tai Zi Jin Quan (M) [Wu Jia Quan] (*lit.* Prince's Gold Fist) a hand form practiced in this southern system

Tai Zu Quan (M) [Style] a Chinese system founded by Song Tai Zu during the Song dynasty

Takadagawa (J) [Sumo] a sumo *beya* located in Edogawa Ward, Tokyo

Takasago (J) [Sumo] a sumo *beya* located in Taito Ward, Tokyo

Takashima (J) [Sumo] a sumo *beya* located in Edogawa Ward, Tokyo

take (J) [Common Usage] bamboo

Takeda Sokaku (J) [Master] a prominent master of Daito-ryu aiki-jutsu and teacher of Ueshiba Morihei, Sagawa Yukiyoshi, Hisa Takuma, and Horikawa Taiso and Kodo

take maki (J) [Karate] a training device used to strengthen the forearms, made of thin bamboo strips and twisted along its length

Takenouchi-ryu (J) [Style] a school founded in the middle of the sixteenth century especially noted for its grappling techniques *(koshi no mawari,* ju-jutsu, *kogusoku, torite),* bo-jutsu, ken-jutsu, and iai-jutsu

take taba (O) [Kobudo] a bundle of bamboo rods used for striking the feet and arms

taki (O) [Common Usage] spleen

Taki Otoshi (J) [Iaido] the ninth *kata* in the Muso Shinden-ryu Hasegawa Eishin-ryu Chuden series, which is done from *tatehiza*

Tak Kyon (K) [Style] old name for the martial art of Tae Kyon

Tamanoi (J) [Sumo] a sumo *beya* located in Adachi Ward, Tokyo

tamashii (J) [Common Usage] soul; spirit

tambo (J) [Weapon] *(lit.* Short Staff) a short staff, about a meter in length, that is used in much the same way as the longer weapon; also called *hanbo*

tameshi (J) [Common Usage] experimenting, testing

tameshi giri (J) [Iaido, Iai-jutsu] *(lit.* Test Cutting) practice cutting with a real, or live blade, usually by cutting bamboo and rolled-up straw

tameshi wari (J) [Karate] *(lit.* Test Breaking) practice breaking wooden boards, bricks, concrete blocks, or fruit to find out whether or not one is developing proper power in one's technique

tampo (J) [Naginata, So-jutsu] a cloth, leather, or rubber guard covering the tips of training weapons used in *yari* and *naginata* practice; this is done for safety

Tanashita (J) [Iaido] the sixth *kata* in the Muso Shinden-ryu Okuden Suwariwaza series, which is done from *tatehiza*

tanbo (O) [Kobudo] a pair of short stubby sticks

tanden (J) [Common Usage] the lower abdomen; the center of the body's *ki,* or vital energy

tandoku renshu (J) [Common Usage] solo training

Tang Chao (M) [Common Usage] the Tang Imperial dynasty, which ruled China from A.D. 618 to 907

Tang Lang Quan (M) [Style] (*lit.* Praying Mantis Fist) A northern Chinese style that imitates the fighting movements of a praying mantis. This system was created by Wang Lang who learned the martial arts at the Shaolin Temple.

Tang Soo Do (K) [Style] (*lit.* Tang (dynasty) Hand Way) traditional martial art composed of hand and foot techniques more oriented to self-defense than sport

Tan Gun (K) [Common Usage] legendary founder of Korea

Tan Gun hyung (K) [Taekwondo] a form named after Tan Gun, the legendary founder of Korea

tan huan chang (M) [Baguazhang] *see* dan huan zhang

tanken-jutsu (J) [Style] (*lit.* Short Sword Art) use of the short sword; it is a subset of ken-jutsu; also called tanto-jutsu

tankon (O) [Weapon] a stick approximately sixty centimeters in length for one-handed use

tanren (J) [Common Usage] discipline, strict training or drilling

tanryeok (K) [Common Usage] elasticity

tan sau (C) [Wihng Cheun] palm-up arm; a block using the outer edge of the arm with the palm facing oneself

tanto (J) [Weapon] a dagger-like short sword; it was always worn by warriors, even in situations when long swords were not permitted to be worn, such as inside a castle, house, or shop

tanto-jutsu (J) [Style] *see* tanken-jutsu

tanuki gakure-jutsu (J) [Nin-jutsu] the art of tree-climbing for concealment

tao (M) [Qin Na] to cover

taolu (M) [Common Usage] forms, routines

tao lun (M) [Common Usage] *see* tou leuhn

Tao Te Ching (M) [Common Usage] *see* Dao De Jing

taruikada mizugumo (J) [Nin-jutsu] a water-walking device used by ninja

taryu jiai (J) [Common Usage] Tokugawa-period challenge matches between different martial arts schools; these were eventually banned by the *bakufu* on the grounds that they led to brawling and unnecessary injuries or deaths of participants

tatami (J) [Common Usage] Japanese mats made of rice straw; used as floor covering in traditional home decor

tate (J) [Common Usage] **1** standing, vertical **2** length

tate empi uchi (J) [Karate] vertical elbow strike

tate gyoji (J) [Sumo] head referee

tatehiza (J) [Iaido] a sitting position in which one sits on the one leg and ankle while the other foot is flat on the ground with the knee raised

tate shuto uke (J) [Karate] vertical knifehand block

tate tsuki (J) [Karate] vertical punch

tate uke (J) [Karate] vertical block

tati (O) [Common Usage] length

tatsu (J) [Common Usage] to stand up, to get on one's feet

Tatsunami (J) [Sumo] a sumo *beya* located in Sumida Ward, Tokyo

Tatsutagawa (J) [Sumo] a sumo *beya* located in Katsushika Ward, Tokyo

tau (C) [Common Usage] to steal

tau bi (M) [Common Usage] *see* bei mihn

tau gwat cho (C) [Medicine] *see* tou gwat chou

tauh (C) [Common Usage] head

tauh faat (C) [Common Usage] hair

tauh wahn (C) [Common Usage] dizzy

tau ma (C) [Common Usage] (*lit.* Stealing Horse) a retreating stance in which one foot is positioned behind the other

tau sau (C) [Jyu Ga] *see* tou shou

tau yan (C) [Common Usage] *see* tou yanh

tawara (J) [Common Usage] a bale of rice straw

te (J) [Common Usage] hand

Te (O) [Karate] (*lit.* Hand) pronounced "di" in the Okinawan dialect; Te is a generic term used for empty-hand fighting arts native to the Ryukyu archipelago

Techigata (O) [Karate] a *kata* practiced in Kojo-ryu

techu (O) [Weapon] a ten-centimeter metal or wooden rod

tapered at both ends, with a swivel ring at the midpoint of the rod

tegatana (J) [Aikido, Ju-jutsu, Karate] swordhand, knifehand; also called *shuto*

tegatana juji uke (J) [Karate] open-handed X-block

tegatana uchi (J) [Karate] a knifehand strike

tegatana uke (J) [Karate] a knifehand block

teiji dachi (J) [Karate] T-stance; the front foot points forward while the back foot is pointed sideways

teisho (J) [Karate] heel of the hand; palm heel

teisho tsuki (J) [Karate] palm heel thrust

teisho uchi (J) [Karate] palm heel strike

teisho uke (J) [Karate] palm heel block

tek (C) [Common Usage] to kick

teki (J) [Common Usage] enemy

Tekki (J) [Karate] *see* Naifanchi

tekko (O) [Weapon] metal knuckle-dusters, usually used in pairs

tekubi (J) [Common Usage] wrist

tekubi junan undo (J) [Aikido] exercises used to strengthen and loosen the wrists

tekubi kake uke (J) [Karate] wrist-hook block

ten (J) [Common Usage] heaven

tenchi (J) [Common Usage] heaven and earth; the universe; nature

tenchin (O) [Karate] body movement

tenchinage (J) [Aikido] (*lit.* Heaven and Earth Throw) A basic aikido technique in which *tori's* hands are grasped by the *uke. Tori* then separates both of his hands, one pointing up and over, then down the *uke's* back and the other hand being directed down and to the rear diagonal of the *uke. Tori* then moves through *uke's* centerline and effects the throw.

Tenchingata (O) [Karate] a *kata* practiced in Kojo-ryu

Tendai-shu (J) [Common Usage] a sect of esoteric Buddhism, the head temple of which is on Mt. Hiei overlooking Kyoto

teng (C) [Common Usage] to listen

teng gin (C) [Common Usage] to hear

tenkan (J) [Aikido] a pivoting movement used to evade an attack

Tenno Hai (J) [Sumo] the Emperor's Cup; one of the many prizes given to the winner of a sumo tourney

Ten no Kata (O) [Karate] a *kata* practiced in Kojo-ryu

tenran zumo (J) [Sumo] a sumo match in the presence of the emperor

Tenshi (O) [Karate] one of five empty-hand *kata* introduced to the Meibukan Goju-ryu system by Yagi Meitoku

tenshin sho (J) [Shinto] the divine power or truth credited for the inspiration given to the founders of classical martial arts schools or traditions *(ryuha)*

Tenshin Shoden Katori Shinto-ryu (J) [Style] a comprehensive school of martial arts that is thought to be the oldest surviving bu-jutsu *ryuha*

Tensho (O) [Karate] a *kata* taught in Goju-ryu

tento (J) [Acupressure] vital point at the top of the skull

teok (K) [Common Usage] chin

teol (K) [Common Usage] body hair

teppo (J) [Common Usage] gun; firearms

tera (J) [Common Usage] *see* o-tera

tessen (J) [Weapon] iron fan used as a weapon; it is either a solid iron truncheon or a real fan with metal ribs

tessen-jutsu (J) [Style] (*lit.* Iron Fan Art) use of the iron fan as a club or truncheon; this was a secondary system or art in a number of bu-jutsu *ryuha*

tetsubishi (J) [Weapon] *see* igadama

tetsubo (J) [Weapon] a solid metal staff or a wooden staff studded with iron

tetsubo-jutsu (J) [Style] (*lit.* Iron Staff Art) use of the iron staff as a weapon; this was always an idiosyncratic art and does not appear to have been taught on a systematic basis by any bu-jutsu *ryuha*

tetsu geta (J) [Karate] iron clogs used to strengthen the legs

tetsuko (J) [Weapon] *see* tekko

tettsui (J) [Karate] hammerfist; a strike with the bottom of the closed fist

tettsui uchi (J) [Karate] bottom fist or hammerfist strike

tettsui uke (J) [Karate] bottom fist or hammerfist block

teui (C) [Common Usage] thigh

teui fa (C) [Common Usage] to degrade

teui jeung (C) [Common Usage] two-handed palm thrust

te waza (J) [Karate, Judo] hand technique

ti (M) [Common Usage] **1** to kick **2** to lift

ti (O) [Common Usage] hand

tian (C, M) [Common Usage] sky, heaven

tian bao yao (M) [Common Usage] *see* tin bou yauh

Tian Di Ren Jian Quan (M) [Wu Zu Quan] *see* Tin Deih Yan Gaan Kyuhn

tian gang pi shui (M) [Weapon] a fan designed for use as a weapon; it consists of a rod with a leaf-shaped surface tipped with animal hair

tian rong (M) [Acupressure] a point located behind the ear

Tian Zi Liu Zhou (M) [Wu Jia Quan] (*lit.* Six Circuits over the Character Tian) a hand form

tiao (M) [Common Usage] to jump, to hop

Tiao Ka (M) [Wu Zu Quan] *see* Tiu Kaat

tiao yue (M) [Common Usage] aerial techniques

tiao zhan (M) [Common Usage] to challenge

tie (M) [Qin Na] to stick

tie bu shan (M) [Common Usage] (*lit.* Iron Shirt) a Chinese training method that toughens the body internally and externally to make it invulnerable

tie da fen (M) [Medicine] *see* tit da fan

tie da jiu (M) [Medicine] *see* tit da jau

tie da wan (M) [Medicine] *see* tit da yun

tie di (M) [Weapon] a flute

tie fu (M) [Weapon] an axe

tie gao (M) [Weapon] a pickaxe with a metal blade and wooden handle

tie pu gong fan (M) [Common Usage] falling, stunts, and turning

Tie Qiao San (M) [Common Usage] *see* Tit Kiuh Saam

tie sao zhou (M) [Weapon] a broom made from straw

tie sau (C) [Wihng Cheun] *see* taih sau

tie shan zi (M) [Weapon] a collapsible metal fan

tie suo (M) [Common Usage] a rectangular-shaped iron training weight with a handle on its top part; used for developing and strengthening the limbs

Tie Xian Quan (M) [Hong Jia] *see* Tit Sin Kyuhn

tie yan dai (M) [Weapon] a long smoking pipe

tie zhao zi (M) [Weapon] claw-shaped metal gloves usually used in pairs

tihn chyut (C) [Medicine] a root commonly used in Chinese medicine to reduce swelling and pain

Tihn Gong Kyuhn (C) [Sai Chong Baahk Hok Kyuhn] (*lit.* Heaven Strong Fist) a hand form

Tihn Jih Luhk Jaau (C) [Mouh Ga Kyuhn] *see* Tian Zi Liu Zhou

tiko (J) [Weapon] *see* tekko

tin (C, O) [Common Usage] heaven

tinbe (O) [Weapon] a shield, traditionally made of a tortoise shell or wicker

tin bou yauh (C) [Common Usage] heaven's protection or blessings

tin chut (C) [Medicine] *see* tihn chyut

Tin Deih Yan Gaan Kyuhn (C) [Ngh Jou Kyuhn] (*lit.* Heaven Places Man Between Fist) a hand form

ting (M) [Common Usage] **1** hall **2** to listen, to hear

ting jian (M) [Common Usage] to hear

tip (C) [Kahm Na] *see* tie

tit (C) [Common Usage] steel

tit bou saam (C) [Common Usage] *see* tie bu shan

Tit Chi Kyuhn (C) [Chat Sing Tohng Lohng] (*lit.* Iron Teeth Fist) a hand form

tit da (C) [Common Usage] Chinese chiropractic techniques

tit da fan (C) [Medicine] (*lit.* Iron Hitting Powder) Chinese herbs that are ground up into a powder and used in making herbal plasters

tit da jau (C) [Medicine] (*lit.* Iron Hitting Wine) a Chinese liniment used to promote circulation and dissipate blood clots and bruises

tit da yun (C) [Medicine] (*lit.* Iron Hitting Pill) herbs that have been ground into a fine powder and mixed with various binders, such as honey, water, and bee's wax

Tit Kiuh Saam (C) [Master] a prominent master of Huhng Ga and one of the Guangdong Sahp Fu

tit lin (C) [Weapon] chain whip

tit sin (C) [Weapon] steel fan

Tit Sin Kyuhn (C) [Huhng Ga] (*lit.* Iron Thread Fist) An internal strength form that is the last form taught in the Huhng Ga style. It is designed to increase the flow of *hei* throughout the body and to build strength and power.

tiu (C) [Common Usage] to jump, to hop

tiu jin (C) [Common Usage] to challenge

Tiu Kaat (C) [Ngh Jou Kyuhn] (*lit.* Carrying Block) a form

tobi (J) [Common Usage] jump

Toda-ha Buko-ryu (J) [Style] a classical martial arts school that now specializes in *naginata;* it is best known for its use of the *ai naginata* (naginata against naginata), *naginata kusari-gama awase* (*naginata* against chain-and-sickle), and the *kagetsuki naginata* (a glaive with a crossbar that is used to trap or block an opponent's weapon)

tode (O) [Common Usage] (*lit.* Chinese Hand) One of the ancient names for the Okinawan art of karate, usually pronounced either *toudi* or *karate*. The Chinese characters used to write *tode* make reference to the Chinese Tang dynasty. As a result of anti-Chinese sentiment in Japan during the 1920s the Okinawan masters changed this name to the current one, using the characters for "empty hand."

tode-jutsu (J) [Style] *see* tode

Tode Sakugawa (O) [Master] *see* Sakugawa Kanga

togi (J) [Weapon] sword polishing

Toguchi Seikichi (O) [Master] a master of Goju-ryu who studied under Miyagi Chojun and Higa Seiko; head of the Shorei-kan organization

Tohei Koichi (J) [Master] founder of the Shinshin Toitsu Aikido system, former head instructor at the Aikikai Hombu Dojo and a student of Ueshiba Morihei

Tohng Lohng Cheut Duhng (C) [Chyu Ga] (*lit.* Praying Mantis Comes Out of its Cave) the third hand form in this southern style

Tohng Lohng Cheut Duhng Kyuhn (C) [Chat Sing Tohng Lohng] (*lit.* Praying Mantis Comes Out of the Cave) a form

Tohng Lohng Mah (C) [Chyu Ga] (*lit.* Praying Mantis Horse Stance) The primary stance used in the Chyu Ga style. The feet are placed shoulder width apart, and the knees slightly bent. The front foot is turned slightly inward and the back foot is pointed forward. The weight is evenly distributed between the legs.

toho (J) [Style] an alternate name for ken-jutsu

toigol (K) [Common Usage] femur

Toi Gye hyung (K) [Taekwondo] form named after the pen name of Yi Hwang

toih (C) [Common Usage] stage

to-jutsu (J) [Style] an alternate name for ken-jutsu

Tokashiki Iken (O) [Master] founder of the Gohakukai karate school, he studied Goju-ryu under Fukuchi Seiko and Tomari-te under Nakasone Seiyu

toki (J) [Nin-jutsu] ninja climbing gear

Tokitsukaze (J) [Sumo] a sumo *beya* located in Sumida Ward, Tokyo

tok sau (C) [Wihng Cheun] elbow lifting hands

Tokugawa (J) [Common Usage] a family of shoguns that ruled Japan from 1600 to 1868

tokushu keibo (J) [Weapon] a collapsible baton used by the Japanese police

Tomari (O) [Common Usage] a port city in Okinawa where the Tomari-te karate lineage was developed

Tomari-te (O) [Style] one of the original styles of Okinawan karate; it has virtually disappeared except for what has been incorporated by hybrid lineages in Okinawa

tomeru (J) [Common Usage] to stop

Tomiki Kenji (J) [Master] founder of Tomiki-style Aikido; a student of Ueshiba Morihei and Kano Jigoro

Tomiki-ryu (J) [Style] a style of aikido founded by Tomiki Kenji, a student of Ueshiba Morihei and Kano Jigoro; it differs from other forms of aikido in that it has competition in which an unarmed person defends against a knife attack

Tomozuna (J) [Sumo] a sumo *beya* located in Koto Ward, Tokyo

tonfa (O) [Weapon] a wooden weapon consisting of a short shaft with a protruding grip; derived from handles used to turn a mill for hulling grain

tong (M) [Common Usage] *see* tung

Tong Bei Quan (M) [Style] (*lit.* Back Wisdom Fist) a style founded by Bai Yuan Dao Ren (White Ape Taoist) that mimics the motions of an ape's long arms; also referred to as Tong Bi Quan (The Arm's Wisdom Fist)

Tong Bi Quan (M) [Style] *see* Tong Bei Quan

tong chui (M) [Weapon] a ball hammer

tonghap (K) [Common Usage] unification, integration

tongil (K) [Common Usage] unity, unification

tongje (K) [Common Usage] control

tong lu (M) [Medicine] copper rust; used in Chinese herbal medicine

tong men (M) [Common Usage] *see* tuhng muhn

tong milgi (K) [Taekwondo] push-barrel movement

tong zhi (M) [Common Usage] to inform, to notify

tong zi bai fo (M) [Hong Jia] *see* tuhng ji baai faht

Torabashiri (J) [Iaido] the eighth *kata* in the Muso Shinden-ryu Okuden Suwariwaza series, which is done from *tatehiza*

Tora Issoku (J) [Iaido] the second *kata* in the Muso Shinden-ryu Hasegawa Eishin-ryu Chuden series, which is done from *tatehiza*

tori (J) [Aikido, Judo, Ju-jutsu] the person performing the technique in a *kata*

torii (J) [Shinto] a gateway that marks the entrance to the sacred precincts of a shrine

torikumi (J) [Sumo] a sumo match

torinoko (J) [Nin-jutsu] a loud firecracker used by ninja to confuse their enemies

Torite (O) [Karate] a *kata* practiced in Motobu-ryu

Toritekaeshi (O) [Karate] a *kata* practiced in Motobu-ryu

To San hyung (K) [Taekwondo] form named after the alias of patriot An Chang-Ho

tou (C) [Common Usage] **1** earth, ground **2** form **3** rabbit **4** in Kahm Na, to cover

tou (M) [Common Usage] head

toudi (O) [Style] *see* tode

tou fa (M) [Common Usage] hair

tou gwat chou (C) [Medicine] the body of this plant is used in Chinese medicine to reduce pain and strengthen the bones

touh (C) [Common Usage] **1** belly, abdomen **2** student, pupil, apprentice

touh beih (C) [Common Usage] to escape

touh dai (C) [Common Usage] student; the term a master uses to refer to a student

tou leuhn (C) [Common Usage] to explore, to think about

tou shou (M) [Zhu Jia] (*lit.* Stealing the Hand) a hand strike used in this southern style

tou yahn (C) [Common Usage] a seed

tou you (M) [Common Usage] dizzy

Towaki (J) [Iaido] the fifth *kata* in the Muso Shinden-ryu Okuden Suwariwaza series, which is done from *tatehiza*

Tozume (J) [Iaido] the fourth *kata* in the Muso Shinden-ryu Okuden Suwariwaza series, which is done from *tatehiza*

Tsing Wu (M) [School] *see* Jing Wu

tsuba (J) [Weapon] the sword guard on a Japanese sword

tsuba giri (J) [Nin-jutsu] a fork-shaped ninja tool used to open doors and cut locks

tsue (O) [Weapon] a stick approximately one meter in length

tsuka (J) [Weapon] the hilt of a *katana* or *shinai*

Tsuka Ate (J) [Iaido] a *kata* done from *iaihiza* in the Iaihiza no Bu of the Zen Nihon Kendo Renmei Seitei Iai

tsuka ito (J) [Weapon] the cord wrapping found on the hilt of Japanese swords

Tsuken Shitahaku no Jo (O) [Kobudo] a *jo kata* practiced in Ryukyu Kobudo

Tsuken Sunakake no Kon (O) [Kobudo] a staff *kata* practiced in Ryukyu Kobudo

tsuki (J) [Common Usage] punch, thrust

tsuki age (J) [Judo] uppercut

tsuki kata (J) [Karate] punching/thrusting

tsukioshi waza (J) [Sumo] pushing and thrusting techniques

tsuki waza (J) [Karate] punching or thrusting techniques

tsukuri (J) [Judo] placing oneself in the proper position to execute a throw

tsumasaki (J) [Common Usage] tips of the toes

tsuna (J) [Sumo] a hawser-like rope worn by a Yokozuna as a symbol of his rank during his *dohyo iri*

tsuppari (J) [Sumo] slapping techniques directed to the chest and shoulders; called *harite* when directed to the face

Tsure Dachi (J) [Iaido] the second *kata* in the Muso Shinden-ryu Okuden Tachiwaza series, which is done from a standing position

tsuri goshi (J) [Judo] lifting hip throw

tsuri komi (J) [Judo] lifting-pulling action used in a number of throwing techniques

tsuri komi ashi harai (J) [Judo] sweeping drawing ankle throw; used as the opponent is moving backwards

tsuri komi goshi (J) [Judo] lifting-pulling hip throw; this technique is often used by smaller men in competition

tsuru ashi dachi (J) [Karate] crane stance

tsurugi (J) [Weapon] alternate pronunciation of *ken;* a straight sword, usually with two cutting edges

Tsuruoka Masami (J) [Master] a master of Chito-ryu karate and direct student of Chitose Tsuyoshi

tsuyoi (J) [Common Usage] strong

tu (M) [Common Usage] earth; ground; one of the five elements of Chinese cosmology

tuan jie (M) [Common Usage] to unite; united

tu chung (M) [Medicine] eucommia; bark containing a rubbery resin used for strengthening tendons and bones, and to reduce high blood pressure

tu di (M) [Common Usage] student; pupil; apprentice

tu di (M) [Common Usage] *see* touh dai

tugi beop (K) [Common Usage] throwing method

tugi sul (K) [Kuk Sool] throwing technique

tuhng hyun (C) [Common Usage] brass rings

tuhng ji baai faht (C) [Huhng Ga] (*lit.* The Virgin Prays to Buddha) a strike with fingertips while the palms are clasped together while in a bow and arrow stance

tuhng muhn (C) [Common Usage] fellow student; used in reference to members of the same martial arts school

tuhng yahn jong (C) [Common Usage] copper man dummy; a device used for training in Chinese martial arts

tui (M) [Common Usage] leg

tui hua (M) [Common Usage] to degrade

tui shou (M) [Common Usage] push-hands

tunfa (O) [Kobudo] *see* tonfa

tung (C) [Common Usage] hurt, pain; to ache, to be sore

Tung Hai Chuan (M) [Master] *see* Dong Hai Chuan

tung ji (C) [Common Usage] to inform, to notify

tung moon (C) [Common Usage] *see* tuhng muhn

tuo tian cha (M) [Weapon] A trident that has the outer prongs curved outwards and tassels at the base of the trident blade. The trident is mounted on a wooden shaft and has a spear tip on the opposite end.

Tu Seok Sul (K) [Style] (*lit.* Stone-throwing Skill) an ancient martial art

tu zi (M) [Common Usage] rabbit, hare

tyuhn git (C) [Common Usage] to unite; united

tyun gwat (C) [Common Usage] broken bones, fracture

— U —

u (K) [Common Usage] right

uchi (J) [Common Usage] inner, interior

uchidachi (J) [Bu-jutsu] attacker; the person acting as the attacker in a *kata*

uchideshi (J) [Common Usage] a disciple or student who is living in the dojo or home of a teacher

uchi gake (J) [Sumo] inner leg trip, one of the seventy winning techniques in sumo

uchi hachi no ji dachi (J) [Karate] (*lit*. Inward Figure Eight Stance) a stance in which the toes of the feet point inward, as in the Chinese character for the number eight

uchi kaeshi (J) [Kendo] repetitive striking practice used to develop stamina and fighting spirit by rapidly striking to the right and left sides of the head

uchiko (J) [Weapon] finely powdered polishing stone, like talcum powder, that is used for cleaning the blade of *katana*

uchi komi (J) [Judo, Ju-jutsu] training drills for throwing techniques in which the throw is never fully executed, although the movements are done repeatedly at full speed

uchi komi ningyo (J) [Ken-jutsu, Kendo] training dummy used as a target for striking practice with a *shinai* or *bokuto*

uchi mata (J) [Judo] inner thigh reaping throw; a very common technique in contest, especially with bigger men

uchi muso (J) [Sumo] a throw in which the inside of the opponent's leg is brushed or clipped, causing him to fall down

Uchinan (O) [Common Usage] Okinawa

Uchinanchu (O) [Common Usage] an Okinawan person

Uchinanguchi (O) [Common Usage] the Okinawan language

uchine (J) [Weapon, Kyudo] **1** heavy hand-thrown dart **2** in kyudo, the technique of throwing this weapon by hand

uchi okoshi (J) [Kyudo] the act of raising and pulling the arrow back before releasing it

uchi otoshi waza (J) [Kendo, Naginata] an attack from above hitting an opponent's weapon from above to knock it down and then attacking

uchi ude uke (J) [Karate] inner forearm block; the same block as the Okinawan *soto uke*

uchi uke (O) [Karate] mid-section block toward the centerline of the body; not to be confused with *uchi ude uke*

ude (J) [Common Usage] arm

ude garami (J) [Judo, Ju-jutsu] (*lit.* Entwined Arm-lock) a joint-lock that applies pressure on the elbow of the opponent's bent arm

ude gatame (J) [Judo] (*lit.* Arm-lock) a joint-lock that uses the forearm to apply pressure directly against the opponent's elbow

ude hishigi (J) [Aikido, Judo] (*lit.* Elbow Crush) a joint-lock in which the opponent's arm is placed in one's armpit and pressure is applied to his elbow

ude hishigi hiza gatame (J) [Judo] (*lit.* Knee Arm-lock) a joint-lock in which one controls the opponent's straightened arm by applying pressure to his elbow with one's knee

ude hishigi juji gatame (J) [Judo] cross arm-lock; a joint-lock against the elbow when the opponent's arm is held in a straight, stretched-out position

ude kimenage (J) [Aikido] a throw in which the opponent's arm is twisted and pushed, thereby throwing him

ude kubi (J) [Common Usage] wrist

ude uke (J) [Karate] forearm block

udi (O) [Common Usage] arm

ue (J) [Common Usage] up, upper, above

Uechi Kambun (O) [Master] Founder of the Uechi-ryu karate. He studied the Chinese martial arts in Fuzhou City, in Fujian Province, China, in the 1890s and began teaching his system in Wakayama City in mainland Japan in 1932. He later returned to Okinawa and established the Uechi-ryu Hombu Dojo in 1946.

Uechi Kanei (O) [Master] the son of Uechi Kambun, the founder of Uechi-ryu, he added five *kata* to his father's system (he developed Kanshiwa, Kanchin, and Seryu himself, Kanshu was developed by Uehara Saburo, and Sechin, was developed by one of Uechi Kanei's other students)

Uechi Kanmei (O) [Master] master and second-generation heir of the Uechi-ryu style

Uechi-ryu (O) [Style] A style of Okinawan karate brought from southern China believed to be related in origin to Goju-

ryu. Like Goju-ryu, it generates power through hard breathing and body-building exercises and it employs many open-
handed circular blocking techniques.

ue ni (J) [Common Usage] upward; in an upward direction

Ueshiba Morihei (J) [Master] The founder and spiritual fig-
urehead of aikido, Ueshiba was a student of a number of bu-
jutsu and a deeply religious man. When he developed aikido,
he synthesized several classical styles of grappling, swordsmanship, and use of the spear and bayonet. Today, he is felt
by many people to be one of the greatest masters of the
martial arts of the modern era. He was honored by the Japanese emperor for his achievements and is usually referred to
by the honorific title of O-Sensei. Ueshiba Kisshomaru, his
son, has succeeded him as the head of the Aikikai and the
style of aikido that Morihei headed until his death.

ui (O) [Common Usage] upper, above

u jase (K) [Hapkido] right posture

uke (J) [Aikido, Judo, Ju-jutsu] the person receiving the technique being applied by the *tori*

ukedachi (J) [Bu-jutsu] attacker; the person acting as the attacker in a *kata;* sometimes used instead of *uchidachi*

uke dachi (J) [Karate] blocking stance

uke kaeshi (J) [Karate, Kendo] to block and counter

uke kata (J) [Kendo, Karate] methods or forms of blocking

uke kotae (J) [Kendo] counterattack

ukemi (J) [Aikido, Judo, Ju-jutsu] breakfalls; methods of falling or receiving techniques safely

Uke Nagashi (J) [Iaido] **1** the third *kata* done from *tatehiza* in
the Seiza no Bu of the Zen Nihon Kendo Renmei Seitei Iai **2**
the tenth *kata* in the Muso Shinden-ryu Okuden Tachiwaza
series, which is done from a standing position

uki ashi dachi (J) [Karate] (*lit.* Floating Leg Stance) a blocking stance resembling a large *neko ashi dachi*

uki goshi (J) [Judo] floating hip throw; a basic judo technique
that is seldom used in competition

Uki Gumo (J) [Iaido] the fourth *kata* in the Muso Shinden-ryu Hasegawa Eishin-ryu Chuden series, which is done from *tatehiza*

uko (J) [Common Usage] the nerve that runs along the side of the neck

Ul Ji hyung (K) [Taekwondo] form named after a Koguryo-dynasty general

umjikim (K) [Common Usage] movement

umuti (O) [Common Usage] surface

undo (J) [Common Usage] exercise; movement

undong (K) [Common Usage] exercise

undong ha da (K) [Common Usage] to exercise

ungkeuri da (K) [Common Usage] to crouch

Unryu (J) [Sumo] one of two styles of *dohyo iri* performed by the Yokozuna, the other one is called the *Shiranui*

Unryugata (O) [Karate] a *kata* practiced in Kojo-ryu

Unsu (O) [Karate] a *kata* practiced in most major Okinawan lineages

Unsu hyeong (K) [Tang Soo Do] advanced form named after a karate form

unsui (J) [Zen] an itinerant Buddhist monk or priest

ura (J) [Common Usage] **1** opposite, reverse; the opposite of *omote* **2** in aikido, rear-entry technique; a technique that is performed by making a turning movement **3** the side of a sword blade that faces inside or toward the bearer when the sword is worn in the scabbard at the person's side; when held in the normal fashion, this would be the right side of the blade

uraken (J) [Karate] backfist

uraken shomen zuki (J) [Karate] straight backfist thrust to the face or body

uraken uchi (J) [Karate] backfist strike

ura mawashi geri (J) [Karate] reverse roundhouse or hook kick

ura nage (J) [Judo] (*lit.* Back Throw) a rear sacrifice technique taught in the Nage no Kata

Urasoe no Kon (O) [Kobudo] a staff *kata* practiced in Ryukyu Kobudo

ura tsuki (J) [Karate] inverted fist punch

Uroko Gaeshi (J) [Iaido] the seventh *kata* in the Muso Shinden-ryu Hasegawa Eishin-ryu Chuden series, which is done from *tatehiza*

Useishi (O) [Karate] an advanced *kata* in Shuri-te

Useshi (O) [Karate] *see* Useishi

Ushiro (J) [Common Usage] **1** from behind, back **2** the second iaido *kata* done from *seiza* in the Seiza no Bu of the Zen Nihon Kendo Renmei Seitei Iai

ushiro empi uchi (J) [Karate] backward elbow strike

ushiro geri (J) [Karate] backward kick

ushiro geri keage (J) [Karate] backward snap kick

ushiro geri kekomi (J) [Karate] backward thrust kick

ushiro goshi (J) [Judo] rear hip throw

ushiro jime (J) [Aikido, Judo] stranglehold or choke from behind

ushiro katate dori kubi jime (J) [Aikido] choke hold performed with one hand while the other holds the opponent's wrist

ushiro katate eri dori (J) [Aikido] immobilizing attack from behind performed by holding the opponent by one of the lapels of his jacket and one of the opponent's hands

ushiro kesagatame (J) [Judo] pinning technique performed by holding the opponent's upper body and an arm from behind his head

ushiro kiri otoshi (J) [Aikido] rear pull-down technique; it is performed by moving behind the opponent and then dropping both one's arms on his shoulders and cutting down as though with a sword

ushiro mawashi geri (J) [Karate] back roundhouse kick

ushiro ryo hiji dori (J) [Aikido] immobilizing the opponent from behind by grasping both of his elbows

ushiro ryo sode dori (J) [Aikido] immobilizing the opponent from behind by grasping both of his sleeves

ushiro ryo tekubi dori (J) [Aikido] immobilizing the opponent from behind by grasping both of his wrists

ushiro tekubi dori (J) [Aikido] grasping one of the opponent's wrists from behind

ushiro ukemi (J) [Aikido, Judo] backwards breakfall or roll

Uto (J) [Iaido, Acupressure] **1** the third *kata* in the Muso Shinden-ryu Omori-ryu Shoden series, which is done from *seiza* **2** the pressure point at the root of the nose, between the eyes

utsu (J) [Common Usage] to hit someone/something

utsuri goshi (J) [Judo] hip shift; a technique used to counter an attacker's hip throw

uwate dashi nage (J) [Sumo] the opponent is thrown with full force while still being held by the belt with the left hand

uwate yagura nage (J) [Sumo] a throw in which the opponent is pushed over by applying pressure on the thigh while holding on to his belt

— W —

wa (C) [Common Usage] picture, painting

wa (J) [Common Usage] love, harmony, peace

wa (M) [Qin Na] to scoop

waaih yih (C) [Common Usage] suspicion; to be suspicious

waat (C) [Kahm Na] to scoop

Wado-ryu (J) [Style] a style of karate founded by Otsuka Hironori in 1939 and based on a synthesis of Shotokan karate and Shinto Yoshin-ryu ju-jutsu

wagi (K) [Kuk Sool] lying-down technique

Wah Kyuhn (C) [Style] *see* Hua Quan

wahn (C) [Common Usage] dizzy

wahn geuk (C) [Common Usage] a side kick

wahng sau cheuih (C) [Common Usage] horizontal *sau cheuih* aimed at the opponent's kidneys

wahn gung (C) [Common Usage] to practice *hei gung;* to centralize internal energy

wai dan (M) [Qigong] a training method that cultivates *qi* in the body's extremities in order to transfer it to the rest of the body

wai gong (M) [Common Usage] (*lit.* External Work) a style or practice that relies on the use of external methods, such as muscle power and strength

waih (C) [Common Usage] stomach

waih bui (C) [Common Usage] disobedient; to disobey

wai hip (C) [Common Usage] to threaten, to intimidate

waih jyuh (C) [Common Usage] to surround, to encompass

waih yahn (C) [Common Usage] personality

wai jarn (C) [Wihng Cheun] *see* gwai jaan

wai men (M) [Common Usage] *see* ngoih muhn

wai suk (C) [Common Usage] *see* wei xie

wa-jutsu (J) [Style] (*lit.* Soft Art) a close-combat art derived from *yoroi kumiuchi;* another name for ju-jutsu

wakaishu (J) [Sumo] an apprentice *rikishi;* an unsalaried sumo wrestler in any of the lower divisions below Juryo

Wakamatsu (J) [Sumo] a sumo *beya* located in Sumida Ward, Tokyo

wakarimasen (J) [Common Usage] "I do not understand"

wakarimasu (J) [Common Usage] "I understand"

wakarimasu ka (J) [Common Usage] "Do you understand?"

wakaru (J) [Common Usage] to know, to understand

wakeru (J) [Common Usage] to divide, to separate

waki (J) [Common Usage] side

waki no kamae (J) [Kendo] a position in which the sword is held at the side with the tip to one's rear so it is not very easily seen by the opponent; also, referred to as *waki gamae*

wakizashi (J) [Common Usage] a short sword worn singly or together with a long sword as part of a set *(daisho)*

wan (M) [Common Usage] wrist

wang (K) [Common Usage] king

Wang Hsiang (M) [Master] *see* Wang Xiang

wangjo (K) [Common Usage] dynasty

Wang Shu Chin (M) [Master] *see* Wang Shu Jin

Wang Shu Jin (M) [Master] a prominent master of xingyi and baguazhang

Wangsyu hyeong (K) [Tang Soo Do] form named after a karate form composed of seventy-eight movements

Wang Xiang (M) [Master] a prominent master and potential founder of baguazhang

Wang Yin Lin (M) [Master] *see* Wohng Yan Lahm

wan ji (M) [Common Usage] to forget

Wankan (O) [Karate] a *kata* from Tomari-te

wan mai (M) [Acupressure] a point located on the base of the thumb near the wrist

Wanshu (O) [Karate] a *kata* from Tomari-te

Wansu (O) [Karate] *see* Wanshu

washi (O) [Common Usage] toward the rear

wa shou (M) [Taijiquan] tile hand; an open-handed technique typically used in the practice of taijiquan

wa sou (M) [Taijiquan] *see* wa shou

wata (O) [Common Usage] belly, abdomen

waza (J) [Common Usage] technique

waza ari (J) [Competitive Budo] half point

waza wo korosu (J) [Competitive Budo] to attack the opponent's incoming attack, rather than the opponent himself

wei (M) [Common Usage] **1** stomach **2** tail **3** dedicated, committed

wei bei (M) [Common Usage] disobedient, to disobey

wei long (M) [Acupressure] a point located on the tailbone

wei suo (M) [Common Usage] *see* wei xie

wei xie (M) [Common Usage] to threaten or intimidate

wei zhong (M) [Acupressure] a point located on the leg at the base of the hamstring

wei zhu (M) [Common Usage] to surround, to encompass

wen (M) [Common Usage] to ask

wen ti (M) [Common Usage] question, problem

wen wu (M) [Common Usage] humanities and the martial arts

Weon Hyo hyeong (K) [Taekwondo] *see* Won Hyo hyung

weonsungi (K) [Common Usage] monkey

weon yeoksudo (K) [Taekwondo] inner-circle hand strike, arc hand

wi (K) [Common Usage] stomach

wiheom (K) [Common Usage] danger

wiheom ha da (K) [Common Usage] to be dangerous

Wihng Cheun (C) [Style] (*lit.* Eternal Springtime) A southern style said to have been founded by a Buddhist nun by the name of Ngh Mui. This short-range system is known for its fast simultaneous attacks and defense movements, its unique way of trapping an opponent's limbs, and its wooden man dummy techniques; also referred to as Wing Chun, Wing Shun, and Wing Tsun.

Wihng Hohng Yihp (C) [Master] a prominent master of Luhng Yihng Kyuhn

wimakgi (K) [Taekwondo] rising block, high block

Wing Chun (C) [Style] *see* Wihng Cheun

Wing Hong Yip (C) [Master] *see* Wihng Hohng Yihp

Wing Shun (C) [Style] *see* Wihng Cheun

Wing Tsun (C) [Style] *see* Wihng Cheun

wo (M) [Qin Na] to grasp or hold

woh gaai (C) [Common Usage] to reconcile

woh hou (C) [Common Usage] to reconcile

wohng (C) [Common Usage] yellow

Wohng Fei Huhng (C) [Master] A master of Huhng Ga and a Chinese herbalist who was known for his virtues. He was taught by his father Wohng Kai Ying. Born in 1847 in the province of Guangdong, he was famous for his lion dance and for his shadowless kick, as well as for refining and developing the Fu Hohk Seung Yihng Kyuhn form.

Wohng Gau Chuhn (C) [Master] a fifth-generation disciple of Huhng Ga

Wohng Gong (C) [Master] a prominent master of Choy Leih Faht

Wohng Ha (C) [Master] a prominent master of Choy Leih Faht

Wohng Kai Ying (C) [Master] A master of Huhng Ga and a Chinese herbalist who was known for his martial virtues as well as for being one of the Guangdong Sahp Fu. He was taught by his father Wohng Taai, as well as his father's teacher, Luhk Ah Choi, who was a direct student of Huhng Hei Gun.

Wohng Li (C) [Master] a prominent master of Huhng Ga

Wohng Lohng (C) [Master] the founder of the northern Praying Mantis style of *Gong fu*

Wohng Luhm Hoi (C) [Master] a student of the monk Sihng Luhng Jong Lauh, and founder of Lama Paai

Wohng Luhm Hoi Kyuhn Gihng (C) [Lama Paai] a book written by Wohng Luhm Hoi, which contains the theory, philosophy, and fighting applications of the Lama Paai style

Wohng Luhng Chyun Sam Gwan (C) [Luhng Yihng Kyuhn] (*lit.* King Dragon Pierces the Heart Staff) a weapons form using the staff

Wohng Ngang Ga (C) [Huhng Kyuhn] *see* Huang Ying Jia

wohng sik (C) [Common Usage] *see* huang se

Wohng Taai (C) [Master] a prominent master of Huhng Ga who was taught by Luhk Ah Choi

wohng ting (C) [Common Usage] (*lit.* Yellow Hall) a place for meditation; a spot in the abdomen where the generation of an embryo is possible

Wohng Wah Bo (C) [Master] a prominent master of Wihng Cheun

Wohng Yan Lahm (C) [Master] a third-generation disciple of Huhng Ga

Wohng Yihm Luhm (C) [Master] one of the Guangdong Sahp Fu and founder of Haap Ga, he studied under the monk Sihng Luhng Jong Lauh

Wohng Yihng Sahm (C) [Master] a prominent master of Choy Leih Faht

Wohng Yuhng Sahng (C) [Master] a student of Leih Saam Jihn, and a fourth-generation disciple of the Praying Mantis style

Woh Sou Toi (C) [Common Usage] a Buddhist temple in Guangdong Province were the Dragon style originated

Wong Fei Hung (C) [Master] *see* Wohng Fei Huhng

Wong Ha (C) [Master] *see* Wohng Ha

Won Hyo hyung (K) [Taekwondo] form named after Buddhist monk Won Hyo

wu (C) [Common Usage] kettle

wu (M) [Common Usage] **1** five **2** responsibility, duty

Wu Chao Dai (M) [Common Usage] Five Dynasties, consisting of the Later Liang, Tang, Jin, Han, and Zhou, which collectively ruled China from A.D. 907 to 960

wu chi (M) [Common Usage] shameless

wu chia pi (M) [Medicine] acanthopanax; a grayish yellow root that is used in medicine to regulate external harmful influences

Wu Dang (M) [Common Usage] Wu Dang Mountain; located in the Hubei Province, where a variety of Chinese styles have originated

Wu Dang baguazhang (M) [Style] a style of baguazhang developed near the Wu Dang mountain

Wu Dang taijiquan (M) [Style] a style of taijiquan developed near the Wu Dang mountain

wu de (M) [Common Usage] martial virtue; martial arts morality or ethics

Wu Dip Dou (C) [Weapon] **1** (*lit.* Butterfly Swords) A single-edged broadsword with a protective hand guard usually used in pairs. It is commonly found in southern styles of Chinese martial arts and can be used to lock an opponent's weapons. **2** a weapons form using the butterfly swords in Huhng Ga sometimes referred to as "Son Mother Swords"

Wu Dip Kyuhn (C) [Huhng Ga] (*lit.* Butterfly Palm Fist) a hand form

Wu Dip Seung Fei Kyuhn (C) [Baahk Hok] (*lit.* Butterfly Double Flying Fist) a hand form

wu gong (M) [Medicine] the body of a dried centipede; used in Chinese herbal medicine

wu he zhang (M) [Weapon] hand-held weapons usually used in pairs consisting of long rods with hand-shaped ends

wuh sau (C) [Wihng Cheun] protective arm

Wu Hsing Dau (M) [Xingyiquan] *see* Wu Xing Dao

Wu Hsing Jen (M) [Xingyiquan] *see* Wu Xing Jian

Wu Hsing Lien Hwan (M) [Xingyiquan] *see* Wu Xing Lien Huan Quan

Wu Hu Zhan Quan (M) [Wu Zu Quan] *see* Ngh Jou Kyuhn

wuih daap (C) [Common Usage] to respond, to answer

Wuih Sei Suk (C) [Master] *see* Hui Si Shu

Wu Jia Dan Dao (M) [Wu Jia Quan] (*lit.* Wizard Family Single Sword) a weapons form using a broadsword

Wu Jia Liu He Pa (M) [Wu Jia Quan] (*lit.* Wizard Family Six Combination Fork) a weapons form using a trident

Wu Jia Quan (M) [Style] (*lit.* Wizard Family Fist) a southern style originating in Fujian Province

wu long xi shui (M) [Hong Jia] *see* wu luhng hei seui

wu lonh tu zhu (M) [Hong Jia] *see* wu luhng tou jyu

wu luhng baai meih (C) [Huhng Ga] (*lit.* Black Dragon Swings Tail) a blocking technique used to defend against low punches and kicks

wu luhng hei seui (C) [Huhng Ga] (*lit.* Black Dragon Plays in Water) a finger thrust with the palm facing the ground

wu luhng hei seui sei ji chaang tin (C) [Huhng Ga] (*lit.* Four Fingers Supporting Heaven) a blocking movement using the base of the hand

wu luhng tou jyu (C) [Huhng Ga] (*lit.* Black Dragon Spitting Pearl) a straight punch using the left hand

wun (C) [Common Usage] *see* wan

wu nga leuhng yihk (C) [Huhng Ga] (*lit.* Black Crow Double Wings) a double elbow technique in which one elbow strikes to the right of the body, and the other to the left

wu ru (M) [Common Usage] to insult; an insult

wu sau (C) [Wihng Cheun] *see* wuh sau

wushu (M) [Common Usage] martial arts; martial technique; the standard term used in the People's Republic of China for the Chinese fighting traditions

Wu taijiquan (M) [Style] a style of taijiquan that was strongly influenced by the theories of the Yang style developed by Wu Quan You

wut hei (C) [Common Usage] energy of a living creature

Wu Xing Dao (M) [Xingyiquan] (*lit.* Five Elements Saber) a weapons form using a broadsword

Wu Xing Jian (M) [Xingyiquan] (*lit.* Five Elements Sword) a weapons form using the sword

Wu Xing Lian Huan Quan (M) [Xingyiquan] (*lit.* Five Elements Continuing Fist Set) a hand form

Wu Xing Quan (M) [Hong Jia] *see* Ngh Yihng Kyuhn

wu ya liang yi (M) [Hong Jia] *see* wu nga leuhng yihk

Wu Zu Quan (M) [Style] *see* Ngh Jou Kyuhn

— X —

xi (M) [Common Usage] **1** knee **2** west

xia (M) [Common Usage] to scare, to frighten

Xia Chao Dai (M) [Common Usage] Xia dynasty, which ruled China from the twenty-first to sixteenth century B.C.

xian (M) [Common Usage] **1** immortal, deity **2** to betray

Xian Ding Pa (M) [Bai He] *see* Sin Deng Pah

xiang (M) [Common Usage] **1** elephant **2** incense, used during ceremonies and for paying respects to ancestors, spirits, and gods

xiang pi (M) [Medicine] elephant skin as used in Chinese herbal medicine

xian jing (M) [Common Usage] trap

Xian Qi Mei (M) [Bai He] *see* Sin Chaih Meih

xian ren zhi lu (M) [Yang Taijiquan] (*lit.* Fairy Shows the Way) a movement in the Yang taijiquan form

xiao guai xing (M) [Yang Taijiquan] (*lit.* The Yellow Bee Enters the Hole) a movement in the Taiji Sword form

xiao tui (M) [Common Usage] calf of the leg

xiao xin (M) [Common Usage] careful

xiao yao (M) [Acupressure] a point located on the lower back near the spine

xia tian (M) [Common Usage] summer season

Xi Cang Bei Hei Quan (M) [Style] *see* Sai Chong Baahk Hok Kyuhn

xie (M) [Common Usage] **1** ribs **2** shoes

xie feng bai liu (M) [Hong Jia] *see* cheh fung baai lauh

xin (M) [Common Usage] **1** heart or mind **2** to trust; trust

xing (M) [Common Usage] to walk

Xing Quan (M) [Hong Quan] (*lit.* Walking Fist) a hand form

xingyiquan (M) [Style] (*lit.* Shape and Mind Fist) A northern Chinese style created by Yue Fei during the Song dynasty. This internal style contains short simple forms and is based on the five elements of Chinese cosmology.

xi niu wang yue (M) [Yang Taijiquan] (*lit.* Rhinoceros Looking at the Moon) a movement in the Taiji Sword form

xin kan (M) [Acupressure] a point located at the solar plexus

xin yong (M) [Common Usage] trust; a virtue taught to those who study martial arts

xiong (M) [Common Usage] **1** older brother **2** bear

Xi Sui Jing (M) [Style] (*lit.* Washing Marrow Classic) An internal training method that concentrates *qi* in the marrow of the body. It is believed that this type of training is the key to longevity.

xiu chi (M) [Common Usage] shame

xiu li cang hua (M) [Hong Jia] *see* jauh leuih chohng fa

xiu qi (M) [Qigong] a Buddhist training method that is used to nurture the *qi*

xiu xi (M) [Common Usage] to relax, to rest

Xi Yu Hua Quan (M) [Style] *see* Hua Quan

xuan (M) [Common Usage] to choose

xuan bu (M) [Common Usage] *see* bao gao

xuan ze (M) [Common Usage] to choose; a choice

xu bu (M) [Common Usage] Cat stance; a stance or posture used in traditional Chinese martial arts. The back leg is bent and firmly planted, while the front foot is slightly forward, resting lightly on the tip of the toe.

xue (M) [Common Usage] **1** blood **2** pressure points

xue zhu lian zhi (M) [Hong Jia] *see* seuk juk lihn ji

— Y —

ya (J) [Common Usage] arrow

ya (M) [Qin Na] to crush

Yabiku Moden (O) [Master] a master of Ryukyu Kobudo and teacher of Taira Shinken

Yabu Kentsu (O) [Master] A student and assistant instructor under Itosu Yasutsune, he is credited with being one of the first teachers of martial arts in the Okinawan school system. He was the first person to instruct in the United States when he taught at a YMCA in Hawaii in 1927.

yabusame (J) [Style] mounted archery; demonstrations are held at important Shinto shrines throughout the year as a form of offering to the deities

yadome-jutsu (J) [Style] (*lit.* Arrow-Stopping Art) a technique for knocking down an arrow in mid-flight with a sword or a *naginata*

Yagi Meitoku (O) [Master] A student of Miyagi Chojun and the founder of the Meibukan school of Goju-ryu karate. Considered by some to be the heir to the Naha-te tradition, he is one of the most influential masters in Okinawa in the postwar period.

Yagyu Shinkage-ryu (J) [Style] a ken-jutsu style that was derived from the Shinkage-ryu; it became the official style of the Tokugawa shogunate

yahn (C) [Common Usage] person, man

yaht chi chung kuen (C) [Wihng Cheun] *see* yaht chi chung kyuhn

yaht chi chung kyuhn (C) [Wihng Cheun] thrusting punch; a vertical thrusting punch

yaht chi kuen (C) [Wihng Cheun] *see* yaht chi kyuhn

yaht chi kyuhn (C) [Wihng Cheun] (*lit.* Sun Character Fist) a vertical fist strike

Yaht Louh Kyuhn (C) [Choy Ga] a hand form

Yaht Tiu Dihn Kyuhn (C) [Baahk Hok] a hand form

Yaka no Jo (O) [Kobudo] a *jo kata* practiced in Ryukyu Kobudo

yakhan gonggyeok (K) [Common Usage] weak attack, controlled attack

yakiba (J) [Weapon] the temper line on the blade of a Japanese weapon

yakjeom (K) [Common Usage] weak point, vulnerable point

yakjeomeul jilli da (K) [Common Usage] to be struck at a vulnerable point

yakji (K) [Common Usage] ring finger

yaksok daeryeon (K) [Taekwondo] pre-arranged sparring

yakusoku (J) [Common Usage] pre-arranged; agreement

yakusoku kumite (J) [Karate] pre-arranged two-man practice forms

yam (C) [Common Usage] **1** a philosophical term used to describe the feminine, dark and soft and/or negative forces in the universe **2** to drink

yamabushi (J) [Common Usage] practitioners of esoteric asceticism affiliated with mountain deities; also, warrior monks or priests who lived in the mountains; they are sometimes credited with being the first ninja

Yamaguchi Gogen (J) [Master] a master of Goju-ryu karate; one of the heirs of Miyagi Chojun's style, he was one of the people who popularized it in mainland Japan; nicknamed the "Cat"

Yamani-ryu (O) [Style] a style of bo-jutsu founded by Chinen Masami, a student of Sakugawa Kanga

Yamato (J) [Common Usage] the ancient name for Japan and the Japanese people

Yamato damashii (J) [Common Usage] the Japanese soul

Yamato gokoro (J) [Common Usage] the Japanese spirit

Yamato-ryu (J) [Style] a school of kyu-jutsu founded in the seventeenth century

yama tsuki (J) [Karate] U-punch

yam chaap (C) [Common Usage] corkscrew punch

yam chah (C) [Common Usage] to drink tea

yame (J) [Competitive Budo] stop; a command given to fighters by the referee to stop an action

ya men (M) [Acupressure] a point located on the right side of the back of the neck

yam sihk (C) [Common Usage] food and drink

yam si jih (C) [Common Usage] (*lit.* Hell Notes) paper money that is burnt as an offering to the spirits

yan (C) [Common Usage] **1** favor, benevolence **2** to be patient, to tolerate

yang (M) [Common Usage] **1** a philosophical term that describes the light, masculine, hard, and positive forces in the universe **2** sheep

Yang Cheng Fu (M) [Master] a prominent master of Yang taijiquan

yang dari ga supyeong doige andda (K) [Common Usage] to do a split

yang dari gonggyeok (K) [Common Usage] a double-leg tackle

yang gu (M) [Acupressure] a point located on the hand below the little finger

yang jagan eui gyeoltu (K) [Common Usage] duel

Yang Lu Chan (M) [Master] a prominent master and founder of the Yang taijiquan style

yangson daegeom (K) [Kum Do] double-handed great sword

yangson japgi (K) [Kuk Sool] double hand-grab escape technique

Yang taijiquan (M) [Style] a style of taijiquan that was developed by Yang Lu Chan who learned the Chen family taijiquan style from Chen Chen Xing

yan jeuhng (C) [Wihng Cheun] stamping palm

yan jing (M) [Common Usage] eye

yan muhn (C) [Common Usage] to hide; to keep in secrecy

yan sau (C) [Wihng Cheun] stamping hand

yan xi (M) [Common Usage] banquet, feast

Yan Xing Pi Gua Quan (M) [Pi Gua Quan] *see* Yin Yihng Pek Gwa Kyuhn

Yan Zi Quan (M) [Style] (*lit* Sparrow Fist) a northern style of Chinese martial arts

yan zi shen ni (M) [Yang Taijiquan] (*lit.* The Sparrow Picks Up Mud with Its Beak) a movement in the Yang taijiquan form

yan zi zhao shui (M) [Yang Taijiquan] (*lit.* The Sparrow Looks For Water) a movement from the Yang Taiji Sword form

yao (M) [Common Usage] waist or loins

yaocho (J) [Competitive Budo] fixed match

yao dai (M) [Common Usage] waist belt

yao qing (M) [Common Usage] to invite

yari (J) [Weapon] spear

ya sai (M) [Acupressure] a point located on the side of the jaw

yasumu (J) [Common Usage] to rest

yasurime (J) [Weapon] file marks on the blade of a sword

yat (C) [Common Usage] one

Yat Lihng Baat Sau Sou (C) [Ying Jaau] (*lit.* One Hundred and Eight Locking Hands) a form used to introduce locking techniques

yau (C) [Common Usage] to worry

yauh (C) [Common Usage] right, right side

yauh diu geuk ma (C) [Common Usage] (*lit.* Hanging Leg Horse) right cat stance

yauh sau po paaih (C) [Huhng Ga] (*lit.* Right Hand Breaking Ribs) a grasping and striking movement that traps the opponent's arm with one hand while striking the ribcage with the other

yauh sei pihng ma (C) [Common Usage] right square horse stance

yauh wahn yauh kiuh (C) [Huhng Ga] (*lit.* Right Delivering the Soft Bridge) A blocking movement that originates with both arms extended in front of the body and the hands in the *kiuh sau* position. This technique is completed with both hands blocking the right side of the body. This movement can also be used to redirect an opponent's force.

yau lai maauh (C) [Common Usage] to have manners, to be polite

yau sauh (C) [Common Usage] to worry

yau sik (C) [Common Usage] to rest, to relax

yawara (J) [Style] an alternate name for ju-jutsu

yawarakai (J) [Common Usage] soft, pliant, flexible

ya zhi cao (M) [Medicine] this plant is used in Chinese herbal medicine

yebeop (K) [Common Usage] etiquette

yee chi kim yeung ma (C) [Wihng Cheun] *see* yih chi kihm yeung mah

yee heung (C) [Medicine] *see* yih heung

ye eui (K) [Common Usage] etiquette

Yee Yung Tong (C) [Common Usage] *see* Yih Yuhng Tohng

yeh ma tiao jen (M) [Yang Taijiquan] *see* ye ma tiao ren

yehng (C) [Common Usage] to win

Yeh Sei Sik (C) [Huhng Kyuhn] *see* Nian Si Shi

ye ma tiao ren (M) [Yang Taijiquan] (*lit.* Wild Horse Jumps the Stream) a movement in the Taiji Sword form

yen tzu chao shui (M) [Yang Taijiquan] *see* yan zi zhao shui

yen tzu shen ni (M) [Yang Taijiquan] *see* yan zi shen ni

yeodeol (K) [Common Usage] eight

yeoja (K) [Common Usage] woman

yeoja hosin sul (K) [Common Usage] women's self-defense

yeok do (K) [Common Usage] weight lifting

Yeokgeom hyeong (K) [Kuk Sool] inverted sword form, reverse sword form

yeokgeom sul (K) [Kuk Sool] inverted sword skill, reverse sword skill

Yeok Geun Gyeong (K) [Common Usage] *see* Yi Ji Jing

yeok jireugi (K) [Taekwondo] reverse punch

yeoksa (K) [Common Usage] history

yeok sa geup (K) [Ssi Rum] 85.1-kilogram to 90-kilogram adult weight class of amateur competition

yeoksudo (K) [Kuk Sool, Taekwondo, Tang Soo Do] ridgehand, reverse knifehand

yeoksudo dollyeo chigi (K) [Common Usage] spinning reverse knifehand

yeol (K) [Common Usage] ten

yeolahop (K) [Common Usage] nineteen

yeoldaseot (K) [Common Usage] fifteen

yeoldul (K) [Common Usage] twelve

yeolhana (K) [Common Usage] eleven

yeolilgop (K) [Common Usage] seventeen

yeolnet (K) [Common Usage] fourteen

yeolset (K) [Common Usage] thirteen

yeolyeodeol (K) [Common Usage] eighteen

yeolyeoseot (K) [Common Usage] sixteen

yeonghon (K) [Common Usage] spirit

yeongu ha da (K) [Common Usage] to research

yeonhaeng sul (K) [Common Usage] come-along technique, arresting technique

yeonjang geori (K) [Ssi Rum] intertwined-leg technique

yeonjang ha da (K) [Common Usage] to extend

yeonmaeng (K) [Common Usage] federation

yeonmuseon (K) [Common Usage] line and direction of movement

yeonseup (K) [Common Usage] practice

yeonseup ha da (K) [Common Usage] to practice

yeonseup sangdae (K) [Common Usage] training partner

yeonsok chagi (K) [Taekwondo] continuous kick

yeonsok gisul (K) [Common Usage] sequence of techniques

yeonsok gonggyeok (K) [Common Usage] continuous attack

yeonsok gonggyeok ha da (K) [Common Usage] to attack continuously

yeop (K) [Common Usage] side

yeop baljil (K) [Tae Kyon] side kick

yeop bbeodeo chagi (K) [Taekwondo, Tang Soo Do] side extension kick

yeop chaegi (K) [Ssi Rum] knee-grasping side-throwing technique

yeop chagi (K) [Common Usage] side kick

yeop cha jireugi (K) [Taekwondo] side thrust kick

yeop cha naerigi (K) [Hapkido] downward side kick

yeop cha olligi (K) [Taekwondo] side rising kick

yeop chigi (K) [Common Usage] side strike

ycop ddaerigi (K) [Taekwondo] side strike

yeopeuro mil da (K) [Common Usage] to push to the side

yeop georeum (K) [Common Usage] sidestep

yeop huryeo chagi (K) [Taekwondo] side whip kick, hook kick

yeop makgi (K) [Common Usage] side block

yeop mureup chigi (K) [Common Usage] side knee thrust

yeop mureup chigi (K) [Ssi Rum] side-knee-striking technique

yeop nakbeop (K) [Common Usage] side falling technique

yeop palgup chigi (K) [Taekwondo, Tang Soo Do] side elbow strike

yeoseot (K) [Common Usage] six

yesul (K) [Common Usage] art

yet beop (K) [Tae Kyon] hammerfist

Yeuh Fei (M) [Common Usage] *see* Yue Fei

yeuhk (C) [Common Usage] weak

yeuhng (C) [Common Usage] a philosophical term used to the describe light, masculine, hard and/or positive forces in the universe

yeuhng (C) [Common Usage] sheep

Yeuhng Taai Gihk Kyuhn (C) [Style] *see* Yang taijiquan

yeuk sai (C) [Common Usage] (*lit.* Soaking Medicine) a heated liquid herbal preparation used to promote the healing of bruises, sprains, and tendon injuries

yeung chaap (C) [Common Usage] straight punch

yeung kiuh (C) [Common Usage] mirror hand

Yeun Haih (C) [Master] a prominent master of Choy Leih Faht

ye xing fei biao (M) [Qigong] (*lit.* A Knife or Dart in Flight at Night) a breathing exercise in Shi San Tai Bao Gong

yi (C) [Common Usage] to heal, to cure, to treat

yi (M) [Common Usage] **1** one **2** mind

yi fu (M) [Common Usage] shirts and pants; apparel

Yi Fu (M) [Master] a student of Dong Hai Chuan and founder of the Yi Shi baguazhang style

Yi Fuhk (C) [Common Usage] *see* Yi Fu

Yi Gin Ching (M) [Style] *see* Yi Ji Jing

yi ging (C) [Common Usage] *Book of Changes* or *Book of Divinations; Bagua yin-yang* theory originated in this work

yih (C) [Common Usage] two

yih chi kihm yeung mah (C) [Wihng Cheun] Pigeon-toed stance; a basic stance or posture commonly used in Wihng

Cheun. The feet are slightly turned toward each other with the knees bent, and the body is slanted.

yih fu chohng jung (C) [Huhng Ga] (*lit.* Two Tigers Returning to a Cave) a stance or posture with the practitioner standing upright as the hands form tight fists at waist level

yih heung (C) [Medicine] a sap or resin used in Chinese medicine to stop bleeding, heal cuts, speed healing, and reduce pain

yih jai (C) [Common Usage] ear

yihk (C) [Kahm Na] to oppose

yihk gan ging (C) [Common Usage] *see* Yi Ji Jing

Yihn Chihng Dou (C) [Chat Sing Tohng Lohng] (*lit.* Green Swallow Saber) a weapons form using the saber

Yihngyi Kyuhn (C) [Style] *see* xingyiquan

yi hohk bok sih (C) [Common Usage] a doctor of medicine

Yihp Mahn (C) [Master] A prominent master of Wihng Cheun who was born in Guangdong Province. He studied under Chahn Wah Shuhn and is credited for introducing and popularizing the Wihng Cheun style in Hong Kong.

yih sam (C) [Common Usage] *see* huai yi

yiht douh (C) [Common Usage] eye socket

Yih Yuhng Tohng (C) [Huhng Ga] (*lit.* Chivalrous/Righteous Brave Hall) a traditional Chinese martial arts school that was founded in the early twentieth century by Huhng Ga master Dang Fong in Guangdong Province

Yi Ji Jing (M) [Style] *Changing Muscle Tendon Classic;* a book describing an internal style of *qigong* supposedly written by Bodhidharma (Da Mo)

Yi Jing (M) [Common Usage] the *I-Ching* or *Book of Changes;* an ancient text on divination and fortune-telling that contains a compilation of philosophical writings compiled over many centuries

Yijo (K) [Common Usage] Yi dynasty, also called the Joseon (Chosun) dynasty, a political entity that ruled all of the Korean peninsula (all of modern North and South Korea, but none of modern China)

Yijo sidae (K) [Common Usage] Yi dynasty period (1392–1910)

Yik Ha Chun Jim Fa Seung Gok Kyuhn (C) [Baahk Hok] a hand form

yi li (M) [Common Usage] perseverance; a virtue taught to those who study martial arts

Yi Loh Muih Fa Cheuhng (C) [Chat Sing Tohng Lohng] (*lit.* Second Route Plum Flower Spear) a weapons form using the spear

yin (M) [Common Usage] **1** a philosophical term to describe the dark, feminine, soft, and negative forces in the universe **2** silver; money **3** to swallow **4** to lead

yin cha (M) [Common Usage] to drink tea

Yin Ching Daan Dou (C) [Chat Sing Tohng Lohng] (*lit.* Green Swallow Single Sword) a weapons form using a broadsword

ying (C) [Common Usage] eagle

ying (M) [Common Usage] to win

ying gong (M) [Common Usage] (*lit.* Hard Gong Fu) a Chinese practice or style that employs powerful muscular training

Ying Jaau (C) [Style] (*lit.* Eagle Claw) a northern Chinese martial art that mimics the fighting style of an eagle, utilizing attacking methods that concentrate on hitting and grasping vital points of the body

Ying Jaau Nighm Kiuh (C) [Baahk Meih] a hand form

yi ngoih (C) [Common Usage] accident

ying shua (M) [Weapon] hand-held weapons usually used in pairs consisting of long-handled brooms that are used in some Shaolin-based styles

ying sihng (C) [Common Usage] to make a promise

Ying Zhao (M) [Style] *see* Ying Jaau

Yin Hahng Kyuhn (C) [Ying Jaau] a hand form

yin shi (M) [Common Usage] *see* sihk maht

yin-yang (M) [Common Usage] the philosophical concept of the universe being composed of two primary polar opposing forces that must be in balance for harmony

Yin Yang baguazhang (M) [Style] (*lit.* Yin-Yang Eight Trigram Palm) a style of Baguazhang

yin yang jian (M) [Weapon] a handle connected to a flat, rectangular metal blade by five chain links

Yin Yihng Pek Gwa Kyuhn (C) [Pek Gwa Kyuhn] (*lit.* Swallow Form Chopping Hanging Fist) a hand form

Yip Man (C) [Master] *see* Yihp Mahn

yi qi (M) [Common Usage] to be loyal to one's friends

Yi Sahp Baat Suk (C) [Mihng Hok Kyuhn] *see* Er Shi Ba Su

Yi Sahp Sei Jiu Faat (C) [Jung Hok Kyuhn] *see* Er Shi Zhao Fa

Yi Sahp Sei Kyuhn (C) [Ngh Jou Kyuhn] (*lit.* Twenty-Four Fist) a hand form

yi sang (C) [Common Usage] Chinese doctor

yi seuhng (C) [Common Usage] shirts and pants; apparel

yi shang (M) [Common Usage] *see* yi seuhng

yi sheng (M) [Common Usage] doctor

Yi Shi Baguazhang (M) [Style] (*lit.* Yi Style Eight Trigram Palm) a style of baguazhang developed by Yi Fu

yiu (C) [Common Usage] waist

yiu (C) [Kahm Na] *see* rao

yiu ching (C) [Common Usage] to invite

yiu daai (C) [Common Usage] waist belt

yiuh (C) [Common Usage] *see* gwan

yiuh luhng gwai duhng (C) [Huhng Ga] (*lit.* Swaying Dragon Returns Home) a retraction of the fist to the chest with the arm horizontal to the ground

yiuh syu (C) [Common Usage] to forgive, to pardon, to excuse

yi wai (M) [Common Usage] accident

yi xin (M) [Common Usage] suspicion; to be suspicious

Yi Yong Tang (M) [Common Usage] *see* Yih Yuhng Tohng

Yi Yu Zhang (M) [Master] a prominent master of the Yi Shi baguazhang style

yi zhi (M) [Common Usage] persistence; a virtue taught to those who study martial arts

yobidashi (J) [Sumo] the announcer at a sumo tournament

yogolbu (K) [Hapkido] inside-forearm area, when used as a striking surface

yoi (J) [Common Usage] Command to "Prepare" or "Assume a ready position"

yoko (J) [Common Usage] **1** sideways, to the side **2** width

yoko aruki (J) [Nin-jutsu] a method of walking sideways; used to pass through narrow passages and to confuse the enemy as it is difficult to determine the direction the ninja is traveling due to the sideward placement of footprints

yoko empi uchi (J) [Karate] sideward elbow strike

yoko gake (J) [Judo] side body drop; the attacker off-balances the opponent toward his front corner, sweeping his ankle and dropping himself in front of the opponent; this checks his movement and throws him

yoko geri (J) [Karate] side kick

yoko geri keage (J) [Karate] side snap kick

yoko geri kekomi (J) [Karate] side thrust kick

Yokogumo (J) [Iaido] the first *kata* in the Muso Shinden-ryu Hasegawa Eishin-ryu Chuden series, which is done from *tatehiza*

yoko guruma (J) [Judo] side wheel; a sacrifice technique used to stop counterattacks

yokomen uchi (J) [Aikido] an attack to the side of the head

yoko otoshi (J) [Judo] side drop; a sacrifice technique done while the opponent is moving to the side

yoko shiho gatame (J) [Judo] sideways four-corner hold

yoko tobi geri (J) [Karate] jumping side kick

Yokozuna (J) [Sumo] Grand Champion; the highest rank in sumo

yoku (O) [Common Usage] width

yon (J) [Common Usage] four

yondan (J) [Common Usage] fourth grade; fourth-degree black belt

yong (K) [Common Usage] dragon

yong (M) [Common Usage] courageous, enthusiastic

Yong Chun (M) [Style] *see* Wihng Cheun

Yong Chun Bai He (M) [Style] (*lit.* Yong Chun White Crane) the White Crane tradition that was fostered in and around Yongchun Village in Fujian Province

yong gan (M) [Common Usage] bravery; a virtue taught to those who study martial arts

Yong Jia Quan (M) [Style] (*lit.* Yong Family Fist) a northern style of Chinese martial arts

yong quan (M) [Acupressure] a point located on the bottom of the foot

yongsa geup (K) [Ssi Rum] 80.1-kilogram to 85-kilogram adult weight class of amateur competition

yonkyo (J) [Aikido] (*lit.* Fourth Principle) a technique to pin the wrist by applying pressure to a nerve along the forearm; also called *yonkajo* and *tekubi osae*

Yool Sool (K) [Style] a martial art that uses soft, flexible response to redirect an attack; similar to Hapkido and Kuk Sool in its modern incarnation

Yoo Moo Kwan (K) [Style] a Taekwondo school founded by Sup Chung Sang in 1946

Yoo Sool (K) [Style] (*lit.* Soft Skill) the Korean pronunciation of the characters for ju-jutsu

yorikiri (J) [Sumo] (*lit.* Force Out) the most common technique in sumo, in which the attacker grabs the belt of his opponent and forces him backward out of the *dohyo*

yoroi doshi (J) [Weapon] a dagger used to pierce an enemy's armor

yoroi kumiuchi (J) [Style] grappling or hand-to-hand combat art while dressed in armor; exponents were trained to use daggers or other weapons to overcome an opponent

Yoshinkai (J) [Aikido] a school of aikido founded by Shioda Gozo, a senior student of Ueshiba Morihei

Yoshinkan (J) [Aikido] the Hombu dojo of the Yoshinkai association

you shou po pai (M) [Hong Jia] *see* yauh sau po paaih

you yun rou qiao (M) [Hong Jia] *see* yauh wahn yauh kiuh

yowaki (J) [Common Usage] weakness of character; lack of inner strength

yu (J) [Common Usage] bravery

yu (M) [Common Usage] fool

yu (M) [Common Usage] *see* yuhk

yuan (M) [Common Usage] to grumble, complain

Yuan Chao Dai (M) [Common Usage] Yuan Imperial dynasty, which ruled China from A.D. 1271 to 1368

yuan hen (M) [Common Usage] *see* fennu

yuan shou tong bi (M) [Qigong] (*lit.* A Monkey's Hand Pokes its Arm) a breathing exercise in Shi San Tai Bao Gong

yuan yin (M) [Common Usage] reason, cause

yu bei (M) [Common Usage] get ready

yu bei hao (M) [Common Usage] *see* yuh beih hou

yubi (J) [Common Usage] finger

yudanja (K) [Common Usage] person with a black belt

Yudo (K) [Style] (*lit.* Soft Way) Korean way of pronouncing judo

yudong dongjak (K) [Common Usage] fluid movement

yudu (K) [Common Usage] nipple

Yue Fei (M) [Common Usage] a Chinese general who lived during the Song dynasty and is credited with creating the Xingyiquan, Ba Duan Jin, and Ying Zhao styles

Yueh Fei (M) [Master] *see* Yue Fei

Yue Shan Bajiquan (M) [Style] *see* Bajiquan

yue ya chan (M) [Weapon] A monk spade consisting of a long wooden shaft with a crescent-shaped blade at one end, and two rings on each side of the blade. On the other end of the shaft, there is a flat bell-shaped blade also containing two rings on each side of it.

yu faai (C) [Common Usage] joyous

yugamae (J) [Kyudo] the correct body position from which to release an arrow

yugeupja (K) [Common Usage] person ranked below black belt

yu gweon (K) [Taekwondo, Tang Soo Do] **1** bottom of the fist, hammerfist in Taekwondo **2** in Tang Soo Do, a fist that utilizes the second knuckles of the first two fingers

Yu Gweon Sul (K) [Style] (*lit.* Soft Fist Skill) an old name for Hapkido

Yugyo (K) [Common Usage] Confucianism

yuh (C) [Common Usage] **1** bruise **2** fool

yuh beih (C) [Common Usage] to prepare

yuh beih hou (C) [Common Usage] to be ready, to be prepared

yuhk (C) [Common Usage] jade; a precious stone believed by the Chinese to have powers of protection and healing, also known as a wisdom stone

yuhn (C) [Common Usage] soft

yuhng (C) [Common Usage] *see* yong

yuhng yih (C) [Common Usage] easy, not difficult

yuhn yan (C) [Common Usage] reason, cause

yuht bing (C) [Common Usage] parade; usually done on anniversaries or special events and often involving martial arts performances and lion dances

Yu Jia Quan (M) [Style] Yu Family Fist

yuk (K) [Common Usage] six

yukata (J) [Common Usage] a lightweight summer kimono or robe

yukdan (K) [Common Usage] sixth-degree black belt

yuken (J) [Kendo] opponents' *shinai* are in contact; the opposite of *muken*

yuk geup (K) [Common Usage] sixth rank under black belt

Yuki Chigai (J) [Iaido] the sixth *kata* in the Muso Shinden-ryu Okuden Tachiwaza series, which is done from a standing position

Yuki Tsure (J) [Iaido] the first *kata* in the Muso Shinden-ryu Okuden Tachiwaza series, which is done from a standing position

yuko datotsu bui (J) [Kendo; Naginata] valid targets that are allowed in kendo or naginata matches

yuksip (K) [Common Usage] sixty

yu kuai (M) [Common Usage] *see* yu faai

Yul Gok hyeong (K) [Taekwondo] *see* Yul Kok hyung

Yul Kok hyung (K) [Taekwondo] a form named after the pseudonym of a great scholar called Yi I

Yu Men Quan (M) [Style] Fish Fist

yumi (J) [Kyudo] the Japanese bow used in kyudo

yumitori shiki (J) [Sumo] the bow twirling ceremony performed after each day of tournament competition

yun (C) [Common Usage] to grumble, to complain

yun (M) [Common Usage] dizzy

yung (C) [Common Usage] *see* yong

Yung Yi Kyuhn (C) [Style] *see* xingyiquan

yun hahn (C) [Common Usage] *see* fennu

Yun Lihng (C) [Master] a prominent master of Huhng Ga

Yu Sin hyung (K) [Taekwondo] form named after General Kim Yu-Sin

Yu Sul (K) [Style] *see* Yoo Sool

yu tiao long men (M) [Yang Taijiquan] (*lit.* Fish Jumping into the Dragon's Gate) a movement in the Taiji Sword form

yu tiao long mun (M) [Yang Taijiquan] *see* yu tiao long men

yuyeonseong (K) [Common Usage] flexibility

— Z —

zabuton (J) [Common Usage] a small pillow used as a seat cushion

zafu (J) [Zen] a cushion on which one sits during meditation

zai shuo (M) [Common Usage] *see* zai zuo

zai zuo (M) [Common Usage] to repeat

zanshin (J) [Common Usage] a state of alertness or attentiveness that is stressed during sparring or while doing *kata;* the maintenance of awareness of one's opponent after having completed a technique

zarei (J) [Common Usage] bow performed while kneeling or sitting in Japanese fashion

zashiki (J) [Common Usage] a Japanese-style room; a room furnished with tatami

zazen (J) [Zen] seated Zen meditation

zempo kaiten ukemi (J) [Aikido, Judo] forward roll or break-fall

Zen (J) [Common Usage] a philosophy and religious practice brought from China to Japan in the twelfth century by a monk named Eisai; *Chan* in Chinese

zendo (J) [Zen] a Japanese Zen monastery or temple

zengo (J) [Common Usage] forward and backward

Zeng Qing Huang (M) [Master] a prominent master of Nan Quan from Guangdong Province

zenkutsu (J) [Karate] bending forward

zenkutsu dachi (J) [Karate] front stance

Zen Nihon Kendo Renmei (J) [Kendo] the All Japan Kendo Federation

Zen Nihon Kendo Renmei Seitei Iai (J) [Iaido, Kendo] a series of ten *kata* used as the official standard for testing purposes by the All Japan Kendo Federation; they were developed to give kendo exponents some experience in handling a real sword

zenshin (J) [Common Usage] to be a good person, to have a good heart

zensho yusho (J) [Sumo] a tournament championship with a perfect record

zenwan (J) [Common Usage] forearm

zhai (M) [Bai He] to pluck; a key movement found in the Zhang He style

zhan (M) [Common Usage] **1** to exhibit **2** shaking; a key movement found in the Zhang He style

zhang (M) [Common Usage] puffy, swollen

zhang cheng (M) [Common Usage] regulations

Zhang He (M) [Style] (*lit.* Ancestor Crane) a branch of the Bai He style; also referred to as Zhang He (Trembling Crane) or Su He (Sleeping Crane)

zhang men (M) [Acupressure] a point located on the side of the waist near the kidneys

zhang pi hua shan (M) [Qigong] (*lit.* Palm Dividing a Flower Mound) a breathing exercise in Shi San Tai Bao Gong

Zhang San Feng (M) [Master] the legendary founder of taiji-quan, who is said to have lived during the Song dynasty

Zhan He (M) [Style] (*lit.* Trembling Crane) a branch of the Bai He style; also referred to as Zhang He (Ancestor Crane) and Su He (Sleeping Crane)

zhao (M) [Common Usage] claw

zhen cha (M) [Common Usage] *see* jam chah

zheng lun (M) [Common Usage] dispute

zheng qi (M) [Common Usage] neat, tidy

zheng que (M) [Common Usage] correct, accurate

zheng yi (M) [Common Usage] righteousness; a virtue taught to those who study martial arts

zhi (M) [Common Usage] *see* ji

zhi bu bei li (M) [Bai Mei] *see* ji bouh bui liah

zhi ding zhong yuan (M) [Hong Jia] *see* ji dihng jung yuhn

zhi jue (M) [Common Usage] intuition

zhi wei cheng tian (M) [Hong Jia] *see* ji meih chaang tin

zhong (M) [Common Usage] **1** middle, center **2** swelling; swollen **3** bell

zhong cheng (M) [Common Usage] loyalty; a virtue emphasized in the martial arts

Zhong Guan Quan (M) [Wu Zu Quan] *see* Jung Gwun Kyuhn

zhong ju (M) [Common Usage] middle range; the minimum distance from your opponent at which either oneself or one's opponent can connect with kicks but not with punches

Zhong Kuang (M) [Ming He Quan] (*lit.* Middle Frame) a hand form practiced in this southern style

zhong long ci pa (M) [Bai Mei] *see* jung laahn chi pah

zhong shun (M) [Common Usage] loyal, obedient

zhong xin (M) [Yong Chun] *see* jung sam

zhong yi (M) [Common Usage] Chinese doctor, herbalist

zhou (M) [Common Usage] **1** elbow **2** to grasp, to hold **3** a movement in taijiquan that is used to attack with the elbow or to unbalance an opponent

Zhou Dai (M) [Common Usage] Zhou dynasty, which ruled China from 1030 to 221 B.C.

zhou fu bei qian (M) [Qigong] (*lit.* Boatman Carrying a Towline) a breathing exercise in Shi San Tai Bao Gong

zhu (M) [Common Usage] **1** bamboo **2** pig

zhua (M) [Common Usage] to catch, seize

zhuan (M) [Common Usage] to turn

zhuan tang guai (M) [Weapon] a pair of crutches used in various Shaolin styles

Zhu Jia (M) [Style] A southern Chinese style originating in Fujian Province, China. This style is known for its short-range arm techniques, which include: the tiger paw, dragon claw, spear hand, palm hand, and phoenix eye fist. The phoenix eye fist is the primary attack method used in Zhu Jia.

zhu kuai zi (M) [Weapon] a set of chopsticks that vary in size

zhun bei (M) [Common Usage] ready; a stance used prior to executing a technique or movement

zhuo (M) [Common Usage] *see* jeuk

zi mu yuan yang jian (M) [Weapon] a pair of swords

zi mu yuan yang yao (M) [Weapon] knives usually used in pairs consisting of two overlapping sharp crescent-shaped blades, with one of the arcs used as a handle

zi ran dong (M) [Medicine] pyrite; used as a herbal medicine for broken bones and controlling pain

zi se (M) [Common Usage] purple

zi wu ding (M) [Weapon] Hand-held weapons usually used in pairs that have three sharp points. One point protrudes from each side of the hand, and the third protrudes from between the third and fourth digits of the hand.

zi wu zhu qiao (M) [Hong Jia] *see* ji ngh jyu kiuh

Zong He (M) [Bai He] *see* Zhan He

zori (J) [Common Usage] straw sandals; Japanese sandals

zou (M) [Common Usage] to walk

zu (M) [Qin Na] to obstruct

zu bing (M) [Acupressure] a point located at the base of the calf muscle

zubon (J) [Common Usage] trousers

zui (M) [Common Usage] **1** lips **2** guilt

Zui Ba Xian Quan (M) [Style] Drunken Eight Immortal Fist

i Quan (M) [Style] (*lit.* Drunken Fist) a style whose unorthodox movements make the practitioner appear intoxicated

Zui Quan (M) [Zui Quan] (*lit.* Drunken Spear) a weapons form using a spear

zun gui (M) [Common Usage] honorable

zun jing (M) [Common Usage] respect; a martial virtue

zun zhong ren (M) [Common Usage] *see* jyun jung yahn

zuo ma dan qio (M) [Hong Jia] *see* joh mah daan kiuh

zuo shou po pai (M) [Hong Jia] *see* jo sau po paaih

zuo yun rou qiao (M) [Hung Jia] *see* jo wahn yauh kiuh

Zuo Zhan Quan (M) [Wu Zu Quan] *see* Jo Jin Kyuhn

ABOUT THE AUTHORS

Sun-Jin Kim began studying martial arts at age fifteen at the Geung Nak Temple in her native South Korea. Her first instructor, a Buddhist monk, taught her a Korean form of Shaolin *gung fu*. She later studied Kuk Sool Won, Japanese karate, and Filipino Kali. She is a graduate of Radford University and is a consultant to *The Korean Martial Arts Resource,* a newsletter concerning Korean martial arts culture and history.

Daniel Kogan, a longtime student of Okinawan and Japanese karate, started his studies at the age of nine in Vancouver, Canada. He has lived in Japan and Okinawa where he studied and researched the Japanese language, culture, and martial arts. He is currently a student of Onaga Yoshimitsu *Shihan,* the current Shorin-ryu chairman and president of the Zen Okinawa Karate-do Renmei. As the North American representative of the Onaga Karate Dojo, he is the head instructor for the Shinjinbukan Shorin-ryu (Kobayashi) of Canada.

Nikolaos Kontogiannis started his study of Huhng Ga at age eight in Vancouver, Canada. He is a longtime student of Gwaan Fei Gong *Sifu* and has traveled throughout mainland China researching Chinese culture and the histories of various *gung fu* styles. His close ties to the Fujian Wushu Association have allowed him to meet and train with several of China's top masters. He is the head instructor of the Yee Yung Tong Siu Lum Hung Gar and the Simon Fraser University Gung Fu School.

Hali Wong started her study of Choy Leih Faht in Vancouver's Chinatown under Peter Wong, the president of the Canadian Choy Leih Faht Federation. She is currently a student of Wong Ha *Sifu,* the "Father of Canadian Choy Leih Faht." She has also studied Yang-style taijiquan. As well as being a student and instructor of Choy Leih Faht, she also leads a traditional Chinese lion dance team.